WHY VOICE MATTERS

CULTURE AND POLITICS AFTER NEOLIBERALISM

NICK COULDRY

Los Angeles | London | New Delhi
Singapore | Washington DC

First published 2010
Reprinted 2011

SAGE Publications Ltd
1 Oliver's Yard
55 City Road
London EC1Y 1SP

SAGE Publications Inc.
2455 Teller Road
Thousand Oaks, California 91320

SAGE Publications India Pvt Ltd
B 1/I 1 Mohan Cooperative Industrial Area
Mathura Road
New Delhi 110 044

SAGE Publications Asia-Pacific Pte Ltd
33 Pekin Street #02-01
Far East Square
Singapore 048763

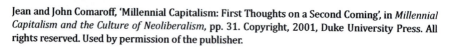

Library of Congress Control Number: 2009940424

British Library Cataloguing in Publication data

A catalogue record for this book is available from the British Library

ISBN 978-1-84860-661-6
ISBN 978-1-84860-662-3 (pbk)

Typeset by C&M Digitals (P) Ltd, Chennai, India
Printed in the UK by the MPG Books Group
Printed on paper from sustainable resources

In memory of my mother, Lilian Couldry (1921–2006)

'The thing to avoid, I don't know why, is the spirit of system.'
Samuel Beckett[1]

'We can hope for something better than the humanization of the inevitable.'
Roberto Mangabeira Unger[2]

'Only a crisis – actual or perceived – produces real change. When this crisis occurs, the actions that are taken depend on the ideas that are lying around. That, I believe, is our basic function: to develop alternatives to existing policies, to keep them alive and available until the politically impossible becomes politically inevitable.'

Milton Friedman[3]

Contents

Preface and Acknowledgements

As Milton Friedman acknowledged more than 25 years ago, major crises can precipitate major shifts in thinking.[4] In autumn 2008 the world faced a deep financial crisis, the long-term economic, social and political consequences of which are, and will continue to be, most serious. The causes of that financial crisis derive directly from the implementation and normalization of the neoliberal doctrines with which Friedman was so closely associated. While reports of the death of neoliberalism are surely exaggerated, we can at least ask whether a new shift in thinking will now occur. Only, following Friedman's insight, if the ideas that articulate those shifts are 'lying around'. This book aims to make a modest contribution to that pool of ideas.

The basis of that contribution lies in affirming the value of voice in response to the parallel crisis of voice that is inseparable from the long ascendancy of neoliberal discourse. Voice as a process – giving an account of oneself and what affects one's life – is an irreducible part of what it means to be human; effective voice (the effective opportunity to have one's voice heard and taken into account) is a human good. 'Voice' might therefore appear unquestionable as a value. But across various domains – economic, political, cultural – we are governed in ways that deny the value of voice and insist instead on the primacy of market functioning. Part of this crisis of voice is our own hesitancy in invoking the value of voice to challenge, even identify, such rules as voice-denying. Identifying this crisis and reviewing the resources that might help us think beyond it are the aims of this book.

The resulting story gains some general interest, I hope, from neoliberal discourse's own pretence to normative universality. However, the story told here could be told in radically different ways, depending on what position in global power hierarchies provides its context, for example from China whose millennia-long centralization of power in the state now meets the more recent rise of a huge Chinese working class,[5] or from countries where neoliberal discourse was violently imposed as a condition of multilateral external finance, whether in Latin America[6] or (with the added burden of a racist colonial history) in Africa.[7]

Instead I am writing this book from Britain. In spite of the obvious limitations, there are some good reasons for telling this story from here. Britain was not only one of the sites where neoliberal doctrine found an enthusiastic home in the late 1970s; it is also one of the developed countries most shaken by the current economic crisis. My reading and writing for this book began in early 2007 but the surrounding context has changed rapidly: a global financial crisis, the emergence of Barack Obama as a credible challenger to the neoconservative regime of George W. Bush, Tony Blair's accelerated resignation as UK Prime Minister in mid 2007. The particular clarity in Britain of neoliberal democracy's contradictions still offers a salutary tale of what is wrong with neoliberalism.

* * *

Thanks to my colleagues in Goldsmiths' Department of Media and Communications and Centre for the Study of Global Media and Democracy for providing a congenial home in which to write this book. Thanks to three institutions that hosted me during periods of working on this book: the Institut d'Etudes Politiques de Toulouse, University of Toulouse; the Department of Communication, Business and Information Technologies, Roskilde University, Denmark; and above all Barbie Zelizer and the Scholars Program in Culture and Communication at the Annenberg School for Communication, University of Pennsylvania, my hosts during the fall semester of 2008. Thanks also to two networks from which I have derived regular inspiration: the NYLON doctoral research network led by Richard Sennett and Craig Calhoun, and the Mediatized Stories network funded by the Research Council of Norway and led by Knut Lundby of University of Oslo.

I am very grateful to Mila Steele, my commissioning editor at Sage, for her enthusiasm and support for the book's project since summer 2007. Among the friends who have given me needed encouragement in the conceiving and writing of this book, I want to single out Henry Giroux, Jeremy Gilbert, Dave Hesmondhalgh, Jo Littler and Clemencia Rodriguez, for support and inspiration over many years; Jeremy Gilbert specifically for a trenchant and timely criticism of an earlier version of Chapter Five; Robin Mansell for inspiring the engagement with economics, and particularly the work of Amartya Sen, that led eventually to Chapter Two; and Sarah Banet-Weiser for the inspiration (even after my manuscript was submitted) of a talk on her latest work on 'self-branding'. Stephen Coleman, James Curran, Melissa Gregg, Kate Nash, Angela McRobbie and Bruce Williams all generously gave their time to comment on chapter drafts. Thanks to audiences at ANZCA 2009 (held at QUT, Brisbane, Australia), McMaster University, Hamilton, Canada, and Nottingham University, UK, for their responses to earlier versions of my argument. Thanks to colleagues in Australia (Bob Lingard, Jo Tacchi, Tanja Dreher) for alerting me to important references that I might have missed. The responsibility for any remaining errors and confusions is mine alone.

Chapter Four reproduces material originally published as part of 'Reality TV, or the Secret Theatre of Neoliberalism' in *The Review of Education, Pedogogy and Cultural Studies* (2008) 30(1): 1–13; thanks to Taylor & Francis for permitting this republication. Thanks also to Duke University Press, Grove/Atlantic, Inc., Hart Publishing, Verso, and Faber and Faber for permission to quote copyright material in the book's and its chapters' epigraphs.

My deepest thanks as ever to my wife Louise Edwards for her love and support, without which this book could never have been written.

* * *

This is a book not only about voice, but also about what happens when voice is missing or obstructed: the hope of voice can never be separated from the threat of silence. I dedicate this book to the dear memory of my mother, Lilian Couldry who, through her deafness later in life, endured much silence.

NICK COULDRY, LONDON, SEPTEMBER 2009

Notes

1   Beckett (1975: 8).
2   Unger (1998: 28).
3   Friedman (1982: ix).
4   See note 3. Naomi Klein (2007: 6) uses this quote too.
5   Qiu (2009).
6   Unger (1998).
7   Mbembe (2001: 73-77).

Chapter 1

Voice as Value

Human beings can give an account of themselves and of their place in the world: 'we have no idea', writes Paul Ricoeur, 'what a culture would be where no one any longer knew what it meant to narrate things'.[1] Treating people as if they lack that capacity *is* to treat them as if they were not human; the past century provides many shameful examples of just this. Voice is one word for that capacity, but having a voice is never enough. I need to know that my voice matters; indeed, the offer of effective voice is crucial to the legitimacy of modern democracies, while across economic and cultural life voice is offered in various ways. Yet we have grown used to ways of organizing things that ignore voice, that assume voice does not matter. We are experiencing a contemporary *crisis* of voice, across political, economic and cultural domains, that has been growing for at least three decades.

Telling the story of this crisis is important, since one of its aspects is a loss of the connecting narratives that would help us to grasp many specific breakdowns as dimensions of the same problem. In countries such as the UK and the USA, we can easily miss the wider pattern: offers of voice are increasingly unsustainable; voice is persistently offered, but in important respects denied or rendered illusory; and at the root of these contradictions is a doctrine (neoliberalism) that denies voice matters. My aim in this book is to name that crisis and identify some resources for thinking beyond it.

That involves using the word 'voice' in a particular way. Two senses of the word 'voice' are familiar. First, we can mean the sound of a person speaking: yet while the sonic aspect of voice generates important insights (discussed in Chapter Five), this usage does not capture the range of ways, not necessarily involving sound, in which I can give an account of myself. Second, we have in the sphere of politics become accustomed to equating 'voice' with the expression of opinion or, more broadly, the expression of a distinctive perspective on the world that needs to be acknowledged. This political use of the word 'voice' continues to be useful, especially in contexts where long-entrenched inequalities of representation need to be addressed; it has been applied, for example, to media's role in development settings.[2] But in other circumstances it is in danger of becoming banal – we all have 'voice', we all celebrate 'voice' – so how far can using the term in this sense take us?

I would like, however, to use the term 'voice' differently, in a way that distinguishes between two levels: voice as a *process* (already relatively familiar) and voice as a *value*. First, we need to get clearer on voice as a value. This dimension is particularly important at times when a whole way of thinking about social political and cultural organization (neoliberalism) operates on the basis that for certain crucial purposes voice as a process does *not* matter. By voice as a value, I shall refer to the act of valuing, and choosing to value, those frameworks for organizing human life and resources that *themselves* value voice (as a process). Treating voice as a value means discriminating *in favour* of ways of organizing human life and resources that, through their choices, put the value of voice into practice, by respecting the multiple interlinked processes of voice and sustaining them, not undermining or denying them. Treating voice as a value means discriminating *against* frameworks of social economic and political organization that deny or undermine voice, such as neoliberalism. Valuing voice then involves particular attention to the conditions under which voice as a process is effective, and how broader forms of organization may subtly undermine or devalue voice as a process. This reflexive concern with the conditions for voice as a process, including those that involve its *devaluing*, means that 'voice', as used here, is a value *about* values or what philosophers sometimes call a 'second order' value.

Why should this distinction be important? What can the term 'voice', used in this special way, add to other terms, such as democracy or justice, in helping us think about political change? The reason lies in a historically specific situation. A particular discourse, neoliberalism, has come to dominate the contemporary world (formally, practically, culturally and imaginatively). That discourse operates with a view of economic life that does not value voice and imposes that view of economic life on to politics, via a reductive view of politics as the implementing of market functioning. In the process of imposing itself on politics and society, neoliberal discourse evacuates entirely the place of the social in politics and politics' regulation of economics. These moves have been implemented in various ways in different countries, whether or not they are formal democracies and to greater or lesser degrees using the disguise of democracy. The result is the crisis of voice under neoliberalism.

I offer 'voice' here as a *connecting* term that interrupts neoliberalism's view of economics and economic life, challenges neoliberalism's claim that its view of politics as market functioning trumps all others, enables us to build an alternative view of politics that is at least partly oriented to valuing processes of voice, and includes within that view of politics a recognition of people's capacities for social cooperation based on voice. I use one word – voice – to capture both the value that can enable these connections and the process which is that value's key reference-point. The term 'voice', as used here, does not derive from a particular view of economic processes (consumer 'voice') or even mechanisms of political representation (political 'voice'), but from a broader account of how human beings are. The value of voice articulates some basic aspects of human life that are relevant *whatever* our views on democracy or justice, so establishing common ground between contemporary frameworks for evaluating economic, social and political organization (for example, the varied work of philosophers Paul Ricoeur and Judith Butler, development economist Amartya Sen, social theorist Axel Honneth and political theorist Nancy Fraser); and it links our account of today's crisis of voice to a variety of sociological analyses (from diagnoses of the contemporary workplace to accounts of particular groups' long-term exclusion from effective voice). All are resources for addressing the contemporary crisis of voice and thinking beyond the neoliberal framework that did so much to cause it.

This book, then, attempts to work on multiple levels, each interacting with the others: first, there is the primary process of voice, the act of giving an account of oneself, and the immediate conditions and qualities of that process (more on this shortly); then there is the 'second order' value of voice (the commitment to *voice that matters*) which is defended throughout; third, there is the work of connecting the value of voice to other normative frameworks and uncovering their implicit appeal to a notion of voice (see Chapter Five); and finally, there is the work of uncovering the processes which obstruct voice, what Judith Butler calls the 'materialization' which allows some types of voice to emerge as possible and others not (see Chapters Six and Seven), and reflecting on how those processes might be resisted.

It is also worth commenting on the relation between 'voice', as I use the term here, and politics. The concept of 'voice' operates both within and beyond politics. It starts from an account of the process of voice which is not necessarily political at all. This is important if 'voice' is to be a broad enough value to connect with diverse normative frameworks and be applied in multiple contexts beyond formal politics: whether in the economic/political sphere (Amartya Sen's work on development and freedom, discussed in Chapter Two) or in the social/political sphere (Axel Honneth's work on recognition discussed in Chapter Three). The price of making these multiple connections is, inevitably, to shake each loose of the detailed philosophical traditions from which it emerged, but the benefit is to reveal a broader consensus around voice that can mount a combined challenge against the discourse of neoliberalism, and on terms that go beyond the exclusive domain of representative politics. The book's argument remains, however, oriented all along to politics in a broader sense as the space where struggle and debate over 'the authoritative allocation of goods, services and values'[3] takes place. It argues for a rejection of neoliberalism's reductive view of democratic politics and its replacement by a view of politics as broad mechanisms for social cooperation that can be traced back to the early twentieth-century US political theorist John Dewey. Free of the straitjacket of neoliberal thinking, we can even identify a broader consensus here, going beyond Dewey, Sen and Honneth, to include recent work on social production and social media (for example, Yochai Benkler's work on networks and Hardt and Negri's work on 'the common').

Admittedly, my use of the term 'voice' cuts across Aristotle's well-known discussion in the *Politics*[4] where he distinguishes *mere* 'voice' (*phoné*) from 'speech' (*logos*); for Aristotle only the latter is the medium of political deliberation and action, the former being the capacity that humans share with most animals of communicating basic sensations of pain and the like. But there is a reason for my emphasis on the word 'voice'. The modern integration of lifeworld and system, intensified practically in the work regimes of the digital media age and ideologically by neoliberal doctrine, disrupts the basic space of voice/expression which Aristotle felt could safely be assumed 'beneath' political speech. Workers' rights are not relatively, but absolutely, excluded by fundamentalist market logics; migrant workers are not relatively, but absolutely, excluded from membership of most territorially-based citizenships.[5] The nature of social and political organization under neoliberalism requires us to focus on how the *bare preconditions* of speech are being challenged (a parallel with Giorgio Agamben's work on 'bare life'),[6] and to reaffirm the need to meet those basic conditions of possibility. So this book is about the value not just of speech, but of something more basic and more fundamental: voice.

The neoliberal context

What type of object do we understand neoliberalism to be? The economic policies with which neoliberalism is associated are well known and are easily listed, for example in the form of the orthodoxy which emerged as the conditions imposed in Latin America and elsewhere in return for multilateral finance in the 1980s and 1990s. These came to be known in economist John Williamson's phrase as 'the Washington consensus': strong fiscal discipline, reductions in public expenditure, tax reform to encourage market investors, interest rates determined by markets and not the state, competitive exchange rates, trade liberalization, the encouragement of foreign direct investment, privatization of public services and assets, deregulation of financial and other markets, and the securing of private property rights.[7] But neoliberalism has also been a policy framework adopted voluntarily by many rich countries such as the USA and the UK. Neoliberalism, then, is not just the Washington Consensus but more broadly the range of policies that evolved internationally from the early 1980s to make market functioning (and the openness of national economies to global market forces) the *overwhelming* priority for social organization. Neoliberalism did not start as a theory about politics, but as a new economic 'policy regime' in Richard Peet's phrase.[8] Neoliberalism took root as the rationale behind a particular interpretation of the 1970s global economic crisis and policy responses to it. By reading that crisis as the result of the failure of a preceding economic policy regime (Keynesianism), neoliberalism authorized a quite different approach to politics *and* economics which saw *market competition* as their common practical and normative reference-point, with state intervention in the economy now the aberration.[9]

The elites and adviser circles involved in developing this new 'rationality' of economic and political management were more than technical consultants; they were, in Peet's words, 'centres of the creation of meaning'.[10]

We need, however, to distinguish different levels on which neoliberalism works as the creation of meaning. First, there are the market fundamentalist principles of Ludwig von Mises, Friedrich von Hayek, Milton Friedman, and other thinkers which explicitly install market functioning as the dominant reference-point of economics and, bizarrely as it might once have seemed, political and social order as well. Let's call this *neoliberalism proper*. Second, there is a wider set of metaphors, languages, techniques and organizational principles that have served to implement neoliberalism proper as the working doctrine of many contemporary democracies. Let's call this *neoliberal doctrine*. One form of this doctrine was the Washington Consensus; another was the shift towards marketization as an active principle of government in countries such as the UK from the mid 1980s onwards (whose particular consequences are discussed in Chapter Three). Compared with Keynesianism, a consequence of neoliberal doctrine was the increasingly unequal distribution of the benefits of economic growth: greater inequality between countries and within countries.[11]

At this point, however, you might ask: does neoliberalism still *need* to be opposed a decade into the twenty-first century? Weren't the follies and hollowness of 'market populism', particularly in the USA but also in the UK and elsewhere, fully exposed by Thomas Frank almost a decade ago?[12] Weren't the unimaginativeness and contradictions of the 'Washington consensus' also exposed by a range of thinkers from the Brazilian social and legal theorist Roberto Unger to figures much closer to economic policy-making such as Joseph Stiglitz, former Chief Economist at the World Bank, and multi-billionaire investor George Soros?[13] Didn't a decade of spectacular protests since the Seattle World Trade Organisation meeting in 1999 help provoke such a realization? And didn't the President of the World Bank James Wolfensohn himself announce in 2002 that 'the Washington consensus is dead'?[14] Going even further back, the development economist Albert Hirschman pointed out his fellow economists' inattention to 'voice' as a crucial dynamic in economic life in a book that, in academic circles, had considerable impact as early as 1969.[15]

Yet none of this stopped neoliberal doctrine from operating as a dominant working principle in the Bush and Blair/Brown governments of the 2000s and working through to many levels far below explicit government policy during the same period. So when we now try to think beyond the horizon of neoliberalism, it is at the end of an extended history of neoliberalism's *normalization*, the *embedding* of neoliberalism as rationality in everyday social organization and imagination: this is the third level of neoliberalism as meaning, to which we must pay attention. It is a level which may have been challenged by aspects of the recent financial crisis, but has certainly not been abolished by it. Note also that my concern is with neoliberalism, not with the particular brand of religion-fuelled utopianism ('neoconservatism') that developed alongside neoliberalism under the particular leaderships of Tony Blair and George W. Bush, important though that may be from other perspectives.[16] The embedding of neoliberalism provides already a broad enough focus.

What must be opposed, then, is not just neoliberalism proper but a whole way of life for which neoliberal discourse provides the organizing metaphors, a 'culture' of neoliberalism if you like. This task is particularly important in those countries I will call 'neoliberal democracies' (such as the USA and the UK) where neoliberalism proper and neoliberal doctrine have become deeply embedded in political culture and in the processes of government. Neoliberalism, though it can serve specific ideological ends, is much more than an ideology as traditionally understood (a set of false or illusory beliefs). It is better understood as 'hegemony', Antonio Gramsci's word for the broader horizon of thought that sustains, as acceptable, unequal distributions of resources and power by foregrounding some things and excluding others entirely from view.[17] Although French sociologists Boltanski and Chiapello retain the term 'ideology', they capture better than anyone how hegemony works: the 'schemas' of thought and performance on which the 'strong as well as the weak ... rely ... to represent to themselves the operation, benefits and constraints of the order in which they find themselves immersed'.[18] Neoliberalism, in short, is a 'hegemonic rationality'[19] and like all rationalities it reduces the complexities of what it describes. The fundamental term in neoliberalism's reduction of the world is '*market*': neoliberalism presents the social world as made up of markets, and spaces of potential competition that need to be organized *as* markets, blocking other narratives from view.

Given neoliberalism's strategy of simplification, it is no objection to this book's argument to say that neoliberal doctrine's *actual* implementation in policy practice is much more complicated than the term 'neoliberalism' allows. Of course it is! But the point of hegemonic terms is to convince us to treat, as similar, things that are very different; that is why such strategies must be opposed, by name, in a reverse strategy of simplification (which is not to deny, of course, the importance or interest of the complex variations which a neoliberal framework may undergo under particular political circumstances).[20] Resisting the hegemony of 'neoliberalism' means identifying it as a *bounded* discourse, a 'term' – in the double sense of word and limit[21] – whose limitations we can think and live beyond.

By suggesting that neoliberalism is the type of object that can and should be opposed on the level of *meaning*, I will seem to some to be starting in the wrong place. Some see neoliberalism as part of a broader intensification of global economic pressures that evacuate entirely the site of conventional politics, requiring a complete rebuilding of social, economic and political life from the bottom up. To represent this position, here is Pau from the Movement for Global Resistance, quoted by anthropologist Jeffrey Juris: 'when the economic system is globalized, a government can't do much to change things in a single place. ... [G]overnments no longer have the credibility to promote real change. They have created a system in which transformation can no longer come through the state'.[22] While I don't intend to argue that a post-neoliberal politics can be built *without* major adjustments to the practice of politics (see Chapter Seven), I think we need to notice the caution of Juris himself in his important account of the 'anti-corporate globalization movements' where he notes that what the transformation activists such as Pau insist upon is very much a 'long-term process' that 'is likely to produce few immediate results'.[23] We need, however, to address the crisis of voice, and the vacuum of effective politics, in formal democracies such as the UK that results. It is because of that immediate challenge that I focus here not on possibilities for entirely new forms of social organization (important though visions of utopian change certainly are), but on resources already available, if only we would use them, for contesting the rationality of neoliberalism as it continues to work in the body politic.

Voice as a process

Let me now run through some principles which capture what is distinctive about voice as a process. Some details of this approach will have to be deferred until Chapter Five, but I will try to explain enough to help us grasp why such a process might be worth valuing.

By voice as a process, I shall mean, as already suggested, the process of giving an account of one's life and its conditions: what philosopher Judith Butler calls 'giving an account of oneself'.[24] To give such an account means telling a story, providing a narrative. It is not often, perhaps, that any of us sits down to tell a story with a formal beginning and end. But at another more general level, *narrative* is a basic feature of human action: 'a narrative history of a certain kind turns out to be a basic and essential genre for the characterization of human actions'.[25] This is because, as Charles Taylor put it, man is 'a self-interpreting animal'.[26] What we do – beyond a basic description of how our limbs move in space – already comes embedded in narrative, our own and that of others. This is why to deny value to another's capacity for narrative – to deny her potential for voice – is to deny a basic dimension of human life. A form of life that systematically denied voice would not only be intolerable, it would, as Paul Ricoeur noted in the quote at the start of this chapter, barely be a culture at all. Recognizing this is common to a wide range of philosophy from the Anglo-American tradition (Alisdair MacIntyre, Charles Taylor) to the continental tradition (Paul Ricoeur) to post-structuralism (Judith Butler, Adriana Cavarero).

The aspect of voice which matters most then for voice as a value is people's practice of giving an account, implicitly or explicitly, of the world within which they act. It is worth noting that this approach to voice is some way from the more abstract formulation given by Albert Hirschman in his pioneering early work in economics, which defined voice as 'any attempt at all to change, rather than escape from, an objectionable state of affairs'.[27] This abstracts somewhat from the content that is distinctive of voice – the practice of giving an account – concentrating instead on the effects of voice's exercise in market systems. If, by contrast, we define voice at one level as the capacity to make, and be recognized as making, narratives about one's life, some further general principles follow.

Voice is socially grounded. Voice is not the practice of individuals in isolation.[28] This is for two reasons. First, voice depends on many prior conditions, above all the shared resources of material life, and the specifically social resources (including but not limited to language) that enable and sustain practices of narrative. Having a voice requires resources: both practical resources (language) and the (seemingly purely symbolic) status necessary if one is to be recognized by others as having a voice. Both are part of the materiality of voice, the 'matter' without which voice is impossible; like most matter, they are unevenly distributed. A non-social (or purely individual) account of voice would therefore miss a vital dimension. We touch here on a wider point about human experience as productive beings that geographer David Harvey notes, quoting Marx: 'production by an individual ... outside society ... is as much an absurdity as is the language without individuals living together and talking to each other'.[29] Second, and more fundamentally, narrative as a process is unimaginable except as part of an ongoing *exchange* of narratives with others. As MacIntyre put it, 'the narrative of anyone's life is part of an interlocking set of narratives';[30] Cavarero is even more eloquent when she writes of 'an identity which, from beginning to end, is intertwined with other lives – with reciprocal exposures and innumerable gazes – and needs the other's tale'.[31]

Voice is a form of reflexive agency. The exchangeable narratives that constitute our voices are not random babblings that emerge, unaccountably, from our mouths, hands and gestures. Voice is a form of agency, and the act of voice involves taking responsibility for the stories one tells, just as our actions more generally, as Hannah Arendt argues, 'disclose' us 'as subjects'.[32] Voice therefore is always more than discourse, and its intrinsic links with the wider field of our actions, emphasized by John Dewey,[33] will become important when in Chapter Seven we link the value of voice to Dewey's reinterpretation of democracy as social cooperation, rather than (as in approaches influenced by Jürgen Habermas) deliberation or speech.[34] Such a view of voice does not, however, commit us to a naïve view of agency, only to the view that we cannot understand voice except by linking it, as Harvey notes once more, to what '"individuals", "persons", or social movements might want or be able *to do* in the world'.[35] A key part of that agency is *reflexivity*. Since taking responsibility for one's voice involves telling an additional story – of oneself as the person who *did* say this or do that – voice necessarily involves us in an ongoing process of reflection, exchanging narratives back and forth between our past and present selves, and between us and others. This process is not accidental, but necessary: humans have a *desire* to narrate, as Cavarero puts it, a desire to make sense of their lives.[36]

Voice is an embodied process. The voice of each of us, our history of reflection and self-interpretation, is part of our embodied history: this results from the relation between voice and action. It follows that voice is irreducibly plural. Even if the resources on which each voice draws are inherently social, the *trajectory* of each voice is distinct. Since voice involves the reflexive narrative trajectory of each individual, it cannot be read off at a distance, like purchase data, from the details of that trajectory. For voice is the process of articulating the world *from a distinctive embodied position*.[37] Failing to respect the inherent differences between voices means, once again, failing to recognize voice at all. Yet voice does not involve a claim to a unique interiority, but only a claim that the way we are each exposed to the world is unique: to quote Cavarero, 'uniqueness is an embodied uniqueness – this and not another, all his life, until who is born dies'.[38] But this implies that an effective process of voice *always* means more than just being able to speak. Voice as a social process involves, from the start, both speaking *and listening*,[39] that is, an act of attention that registers the uniqueness of the other's narrative.

This necessary plurality encompasses not just external differences between voices, but also the *internal diversity* within a particular voice. It would be absurd to imagine that a life comprised just one story, or just one continuous sequence of action. The inherent internal plurality of each voice encompasses the processes whereby we reflect from one narrative stream on to another, and think about what one strand of our lives mean for other strands. This is especially important in modernity where almost all of us are embedded in multiple narrative settings (family, work, leisure, public display).[40] Of course, none of us is able continuously to reflect, let alone tell a satisfying story, about all the potential connections between the many aspects of our lives. But to block someone's capacity to bring one part of their lives to bear on another part – for example, by discounting the relevance of their work experience to their trajectory as a citizen – is, again, to deny a dimension of voice itself. It follows that the potential *injuries* to voice may easily, perhaps particularly, work across more than one domain (see Chapter Six).

Voice requires a material form which may be individual, collective or distributed. Voice does not simply emerge from us without support. We saw earlier that voice requires social resources, but more than that it also requires a form: both are aspects of the materiality of voice. Since voice is a process, so too is the sustaining of voice's material form. But the material form of voice need not be under the exclusive control of the individual; often I recognize myself in a collectively produced voice: this, incidentally, is to use the term 'recognition' in a general sense, not yet the specific sense in which Honneth uses it.[41] Sometimes we can recognize ourselves in the outcome of a production where specific individual and collective inputs cannot easily be separated from a broader flow. This form of voice is not individual or collective but 'distributed'. Under conditions we discuss in detail in Chapter Five, it can count too as voice and is a feature today of all networks, and much online production, as many commentators have noted.

The material form of voice cannot, in any case, be exclusively individual: we do not generate the means by which we narrate, we emerge as subjects into a narrative form.[42] So 'voice' as a value does not involve individualism (for example, liberal individualism), or disregarding the importance of collective forms of action. Defending voice as a value simply means defending the potential of voices anywhere to matter.

If, through an unequal distribution of narrative resources, the materials from which some people must build their account of themselves are *not* theirs to adapt or control, then this represents a deep denial of voice, a deep form of oppression. This is the oppression W. B. Dubois described as 'double consciousness', a 'sense of always looking at oneself through the eyes of others';[43] Chapter Six will draw on what we have learned from histories of racism and class, feminism and sexuality to develop this point. Voice is a continuing process of reflecting back and forth between actions, experiences and thought, an open-ended process of giving an account in which each person is engaged. If the material form of voice obstructs such reflexivity for one reason or another, then the form of voice also *fails to fit* the conditions of experience; as a result, once more, there is no effective voice.

We may take for granted the fit between experience and a voice's form, when the latter is individual. I may assume I will always have the chance to register an account of my life with others in some relatively durable form; 'my' voice may *seem* transparent. That it is not becomes clear in those terrible cases when individuals are denied control even over the individual form through which voice can be expressed. This happened in the Nazi death camps. As Primo Levi put it in *If This is a Man*, his account of Auschwitz: 'nothing belongs to us any more; they have taken away our clothes, our shoes, even our hair; if we speak, they will not listen to us, and if they listen, they will not understand'. The only outlet was dreams: 'why', Levi wrote, 'is the pain of every day translated so constantly into our dreams, in the ever-repeated scene of the unlistened-to story?'[44] The extreme Nazi denial of voice continued to the end of life, intensifying that denial's retrospective force. As Hannah Arendt put it:

> the concentration camps, by making death itself anonymous (making it impossible to find out whether a prisoner is dead or alive) robbed death of its meaning as the end of a fulfilled life. In a sense they took away the individual's own death, proving that henceforth nothing belonged to him and he belonged to no one. His death merely set the seal on the fact that he had never really existed.[45]

There are many less drastic ways in which voice can be undermined at the collective or social level through an inadequate fit between the forms of voice and experience: when collective voices or institutional decisions fail to register individual experience; when institutions ignore collective views; when distributed voice is not reflected in opportunities to redeem voice in specific encounters. Above all, voice is undermined when societies become organized on the basis that individual, collective and distributed voice need not be taken into account, because a higher value or rationality trumps them.

Voice is undermined by rationalities which take no account of voice and by practices that exclude voice or undermine forms for its expression. Voice can be undermined in subtle ways through the organization of social relations. Not just individual lives but social life and social space are organized in part by narratives that set reference-points, relevances and values. So models for organizing life that *place no value* on voice may, when applied, undermine voice not just by failing to acknowledge it, but also by blocking alternative narratives that would authorize us to value voice. Let's call a narrative of this sort a *voice-denying rationality*.

Once again, for the most extreme case of a voice-denying rationality we must turn to Nazi Germany and its health policy, because this worked not indirectly through a chain of partially intended consequences but directly, by organizing resources on the explicit basis that some individuals' voice and life had no value. Its clearest expression was the doctrine of 'Life without Value'

(*Lebensunwerten Leben*) from Nazi medical, legal and psychological thinking on which Giorgio Agamben and others have reflected.[46] As the historian of Nazi medicine Robert Proctor put it: 'the social policies ultimately favoured by the [Nazi] government equated value of life with ability to work ... the goal of occupational medicine likewise became a worker who would remain productive until retirement and then pass away shortly thereafter'.[47]

Much more common, thankfully, are rationalities that *do not* directly deny the value of voice outright (indeed, in some contexts they may celebrate it), but work in other ways to undermine the provision of voice at various levels. Is neoliberalism perhaps a voice-denying rationality in this different but important sense?

Countering neoliberal rationality

Neoliberal discourse emerges from an extreme generalization of the advantages of markets and the disadvantages of other modes of social and economic organization. Of course, markets are an important way of organizing human affairs and distributing goods. Few would deny that the operation of markets may provide opportunities for consumption that enable individual or group expression, under particular conditions, to have political consequences. The point therefore is *not* that markets, as they operate in practice, have *nothing* to do with voice; indeed, there are historians who argue that the development of consumer markets in early modernity was a key contributor to the gradual diversification of expression and voice,[48] while some cultural commentators stress the importance of everyday consumption as a site of identity and indeed action, particularly when opportunities for some traditional forms of politics are reduced or denied.[49] But neoliberal rationality relies on an excessive valuation of markets that goes much further than acknowledging these basic truths about markets, and it is this excessive valuation that must be rejected.

Neoliberalism insists that there is no other valid principle of human organization than market functioning. The tension between neoliberal doctrine and the value of voice becomes clear when we consider how markets work. Markets match inputs and outputs in regular ways at the level of individual transactions and at what the political economist Robert Lane calls the level of 'species' benefits.[50] All that matters for market functioning is this matching; it is no part of market functioning that a particular individual's sequence of inputs and outputs match in a particular way, let alone in a way that matches with that individual's reflections on that sequence. Markets do not therefore function to provide voice. The value of market functioning is not explicitly, or implicitly, equivalent to – or even isomorphic with – the value of voice. Market functioning does not require the exchange of narratives between reflexive, embodied agents; but voice does. Voice in our sense is what economists would call an externality of market functioning.[51]

This becomes a problem when, like the leading proponent of neoliberalism Milton Friedman, you argue that markets are the best (indeed the only good) model for social and political organization.[52] The consequence is to understand social and political organization, from the start, on terms that, without necessarily intending to do so, exclude the possibility that voice matters. From one perspective this might seem puzzling: the 'freedom' that neoliberalism celebrates can sound rather like a celebration of voice since what we do as participants in markets can, under some circumstances, contribute to voice, whether individual (the type of clothes I buy, the food choices I make), collective (fan communities or user groups) or distributed (consumer boycotts or buycotts).[53] But, as we will see in Chapter Two, the notion of freedom underlying neoliberalism is abstracted from any understanding of the social processes that underpin 'voice' in its full sense as an embodied process of effective speech. Market populism, which claims markets as the privileged site of popular voice, is based on a category error, confusing market functioning with the sort of process that in itself can provide the conditions for sustaining voice. As Thomas Frank points out, that error was ideologically motivated, since the rise of US market populism coincided with one of the most extreme periods of upwards wealth redistribution in democratic history.[54]

Political theorist Wendy Brown argued in 2003 that we were in the middle of an epochal shift towards a political order characterized by the absolute prioritization of market logics across the whole of social life, which 'while foregrounding the market, is not only or even primarily focused on the economy; rather it involves extending and disseminating market values to all institutions and social action'.[55] The force of this transformation, Brown argues, is that it does *not* operate through force, or political rule, but through the internalization of rationality. Its values come, as it were, pre-rationalized, as part of 'the given'.

Neoliberal rationality is reinforced not just by explicit discourse but through the multiple ways in which that discourse and its workings get *embedded* in daily life and social organization. Neoliberal rationality provides principles for organizing action (in workplaces, public services, fields of competition, public discussion) which are internalized as norms and values (for example, the value of entrepreneurial 'freedom') by individuals, groups and institutions: in short, they become 'culture'.[56] Through this process neoliberalism, over time, crowds out other rationalities, other ways of organizing. As neoliberal rationality becomes institutionalized culture, it shapes the *organization of space*. Some types of space become prioritized, others fall out of use and so stop being imagined; because voice is embodied, this matters hugely for the effectiveness of voice, since neoliberalism literally changes where we can and cannot speak and be heard.[57] Agents whose needs and interests once seemed necessarily linked (for example, by common conditions of work) become visible only as individuals, linked, if at all, by diverse networks. The result is what Zygmunt Bauman in another context called 'the social production of distance',[58] disabling particular types of group voice (for example, trade unions), and often leaving individual voices out of account. The only way of challenging such an all-encompassing rationality is, as Brown notes, through a 'counter-rationality – a different figuration of human beings, citizenship, economic life, and the political'.[59]

The value of voice is offered here as part of such a counter-rationality. Valuing voice means valuing something that neoliberal rationality fails to count; it can therefore contribute to a counter-rationality against neoliberalism. To succeed, it must have relevance and scope across the multiple domains where neoliberal rationality works. 'Voice' does more than value particular voices or acts of speaking; it values all human beings' ability to give an account of themselves; it values my and your status as 'narratable' selves.[60] This value does not derive from particular political forms or from the position one takes on the different models of democracy (liberal, republican, communitarian, deliberative, cosmopolitan, radical), or indeed from the practice of democracy at all. Articulating voice – as an inescapable aspect of human experience – challenges the neoliberal logic that runs together economic, social, political and cultural domains, and describes them exclusively as manifestations of market processes. It challenges the silences and gaps that arise when decisions on one scale – market functioning – seem naturally to 'trump' the potential exercise of voice on other scales. It challenges any form of organization that ignores voice, and rejects, as a starting-point, apparent forms of voice (for example, practices of 'self-branding' celebrated in recent marketing discourse)[61] which offer only the opportunity to compete as a commodity.

Articulating voice means challenging the distance that neoliberal logic installs between subjects and a key dimension ('voice') of what gives their lives meaning. It draws strength from thinkers who have worked to redefine the *ends* of contemporary economics or politics (the economist and philosopher Amartya Sen on the *ends* of economic life; social and political theorist Axel Honneth, echoing John Dewey, on the *ends* of democratic politics). It connects also to a broader tradition across philosophy, literary theory and sociology that emphasizes the role of narrative in human life, as the embodied form of our actions and reasoning about the world.

Structure of the book

The principles I have just outlined underlie the rest of the book. They generate an argument that falls into two parts: a critical account in Chapters Two to Four that identifies the neoliberal conditions that currently undermine voice and a positive account in Chapters Five to Seven of our resources for building a counter-rationality to neoliberalism.

The contemporary crisis of voice …

Within the *economy*, discussed in Chapter Two, contemporary labour conditions demand of workers an intense personal commitment (indeed, a narrative performance of commitment or 'passion'), as a condition of their having a place in the labour market, yet offer in return minimal security and minimal support to sustain employees' underlying capacities to work. Paradoxically, those conditions may deny voice in work-based decision-making, while appearing to mobilize voice via the commitments they demand from workers. At the same time, the market logics, which govern the distribution of work opportunities, offer precious little scope for the exercise of individual or collective voice.

Within *politics*, discussed in Chapter Three, there is increasingly a gap between individuals' or groups' capacities for voice and the process whereby policy gets made. When politics is dominated by external market forces, policies become not so much options for genuine disagreement than 'facts of life', what 'modernization' or 'global competitiveness' requires, in short, a matter of necessity. In neoliberal regimes the potentially authentic domain of political voice is translated back to voters as force, as the 'delivery' of decisions about which no choice has been possible. This outcome is reinforced by an ideology that installs neoliberal *economics* as the dominant frame for politics.

We can develop a parallel argument too within the *cultural* domain if, that is, we set aside the crude populism that automatically equates demand – as registered in markets for cultural goods – with the satisfaction of populations' need for cultural voice and expression. Cultural products such as reality TV may not only fail to deliver voice, but may normalize a framework of value that helps *undermine* voice's exercise across various domains. This process is reinforced from another direction when the organizational principles of neoliberal government become locked into a media cycle that requires fast outcomes and fast sanctions, not the slower, more uncertain process of genuine deliberation and consultation about public ends. While the market logics that drive media institutions' contributions to these processes are, of course, distinct from the dynamics of neoliberal *discourse*, market logic and discourse converge in their effects, leaving few routes in mainstream media through which the value of voice can be sustained: Chapter Four discusses these processes. This remains true, even when in other areas of media (particularly online) forms of individual voice are expanding.

My argument, then, will be that neoliberal doctrine, as embedded within economic practice, politics and culture, produces a series of painful contradictions, which I focus particularly through the case of contemporary Britain. Britain today, after 12 years of New Labour and 18 years of Thatcherism, embodies the *oxymoron* of 'neoliberal democracy', which had generated what Neal Lawson characterized as a '*social* recession'[62] even before the current economic recession. But the case of Britain only shows in clear ways the contradictions more widely present in the neoliberal notion of the 'market state',[63] and these contradictions are relevant wherever neoliberal doctrine is made into a principle of politics.

... and thinking beyond it

If the book's first part is devoted to laying out an analysis of the contemporary crisis of voice, its second part, more positively, reviews what resources we have to promote a counter-rationality of voice.

One key stage (Chapter Five) is to look back critically at our philosophical resources for understanding voice. Some versions of post-structuralism have been deeply sceptical of 'the subject', proclaiming that we must move beyond it. Such arguments, I will suggest, amount to an overreaction to the faults of Descartes' view of the thinking self as entirely disembodied. Instead, drawing on Bergson and Wittgenstein, Taylor and Ricoeur, our starting-point should be a self that is embodied, intersubjectively grounded, and predisposed to giving a narrative account of itself to others. I explore what this view can add specifically to larger frameworks for reinterpreting economics or politics in terms of the ends, respectively, of freedom (Sen) and recognition (Honneth). I also clarify the terms on which a 'distributed' voice can still count as voice, provided it is redeemable in satisfactory encounters.

Chapter Six explores the resources for a positive sociology of voice that can be gathered from a variety of writers – from Richard Sennett to Carol Gilligan, W. B. du Bois to Judith Butler, Bev Skeggs to Danilo Martuccelli – across sociology, cultural studies, psychology and philosophy. All of them have in various ways helped us understand the conditions that support or obstruct the practice of voice. I also consider the methodological commitment to listening that sociologies of voice involve. These approaches are important since they help us contextualize what is undoubtedly an online explosion of speaking, writing and exchanging (blogs, image and video exchange sites, social networking sites) that do not necessarily constitute social processes of voice, and need to be interpreted in the light of deeper exclusions.

The concluding chapter (Chapter Seven) turns more explicitly to the key questions that must be addressed if a post-neoliberal politics is to be built that more adequately embodies the value of voice. This is anything but easy because it involves articulating principles of voice that have become dormant or never been developed in neoliberal democracies and yet remain insufficiently developed even in new forms of transformative politics such as the anti-corporate globalization movements.

The role of critical sociology

Surely, you object, talk of a crisis of voice is exaggerated. But consider *The Good Childhood Report*, published in Britain in February 2009, whose lead author, Richard Layard, is an economist. This report discusses Britain's growing inequality and its education system focused more on government targets and market incentives than on the quality of the educational process. The problem requires, its authors believe, urgent solutions. So they look for an underlying factor that might explain '*both* income inequality and poor child outcomes'. They find this in a *moral* lack, in 'inadequate respect between people', tracing this moral lack to faulty values, 'excessive individualism'.[64] Another recent report by the Joseph Rowntree Foundation, based on consultations with more than 3,000 respondents, also identifies 'individualism' as the main 'evil in contemporary Britain'.[65] But excessive individualism has been the cry of modernity's reformers since at least the mid nineteenth century.[66] More important is the close fit between excessive individualism and the narrow market-based values that are the legacy of neoliberalism. We will look in

Chapter Two at Boltanski and Chiapello's subtle account of how apparently positive values (freedom, spontaneity, flexibility, the conviviality of the network) are tied up with social costs that the discourse of 'market freedom' fails to grasp. Meanwhile, in the wake of public outcry over excessive rewards paid to bankers and investment traders, even mainstream commentators such as economist John Kay argue for 'a comprehensive reappraisal of ... the economic *and political* role of the [UK's] financial services sector'.[67]

A crisis of values, then, is being registered in mainstream debates, but not yet answered. In such circumstances, the role of a critical sociology must be to provide some resources through which alternative values can be articulated. This book has no choice but to address an unstable mix of 'real world' and 'academic' issues, venturing beyond the safe boundaries of a single discipline. The book will trespass into other territories (political theory, philosophy, economic thought) far beyond my own area, sociology of media. This is dictated both by the lack of any distinct disciplinary area that examines the conditions for voice – reflections are scattered across sociology, political anthropology, feminist studies, media and cultural studies, literary theory, and philosophy – and by the pervasive challenge that neoliberal rationality poses. The result is a book that risks, as Raymond Williams once put it, 'an extension and variety of themes well beyond the limits of any kind of academic prudence'.[68]

For this I make no apology. Nothing less bold will address neoliberalism's affront to the very idea of a socially grounded democratic process, a democracy that is more than formalism. If this recalls Raymond Williams' vision of a 'full democratic process'[69] which animated cultural studies at its outset, this is no accident. While this book makes no claim to be 'cultural studies' – at most it is written *after* cultural studies – it does seek to 'reoccupy',[70] in a modest way, aspects of the original project opened up by Raymond Williams half a century ago when he articulated his dissatisfaction with the British democracy of his time.[71]

Just as important in providing the normative framework and imaginative provocations that have shaped my argument is recent social, political and economic theory. Axel Honneth's theory of recognition reconnects with, and regrounds, John Dewey's vision of democracy as a 'social ideal', a pervasive principle of social cooperation, addressing, unlike Habermas's more formal model of democracy, the wider 'field of moral-practical conflicts [that] ... lie hidden behind the façade of late capitalist integration'.[72] Meanwhile in economics, Amartya Sen has insisted on reconnecting economic discourse to ethical questions about the ends of human life through his notion of human capabilities (that is, 'the actual ability of [a] person to achieve those things that she has reason to value').[73] Behind this revival of normative frameworks lie broader calls for rethinking the basis and nature of politics. Political theorist Nancy Fraser argues that the partly transnational *constitution* of contemporary politics makes urgent new second-order questions about the justice of 'relations of representation', questions about 'who is included in, and who excluded from, the circle of those entitled to a just distribution and reciprocal recognition'.[74] Etienne Balibar, also influenced by the challenge of transnational politics, particularly in the contested space of 'Europe', suggests that we are in a moment of huge potential which requires a new 'civility', not mere politeness, but something more radical:

> a politics of politics [aimed] at creating, recreating, and conserving the set of conditions within which politics as a collective participation in public affairs is possible, or at least not made absolutely impossible.[75]

In a different way Pierre Rosanvallon insists on a new attention to indirect democracy, calling for the repoliticization of administrative and other procedural aspects of government that have fallen out of the political domain: this 'rediscovery of ordinary politics' approaches the question of voice, and the politics of politics, by rethinking the scope of everyday political action.[76] These attempts to reopen the normative horizon of politics are shared with other influential approaches, such as Hardt and Negri's writings on 'multitude'.[77]

There is always the danger, however, that once we define our aims at this abstract meta-level, we lose focus. As Zygmunt Bauman remarks in *The Individualized Society*, there is little value in general critiques of individualism that fail to note its interlocking with more particular processes: what he calls 'the political economy of uncertainty'.[78] It is here that historically more specific work – Michel Foucault's late lectures on the foundations of neoliberal thought, Boltanski and Chiapello's rich account of the 'new spirit of capitalism' and its networked hyperindividualism – provide essential resources. And behind all these lies a long-standing tradition that for three decades, in parallel to the strident discourse of neoliberalism, has quietly been insisting on the detailed role of narrative in human life (Charles Taylor, Paul Ricoeur, Alisdair MacIntyre, Adriana Cavarero).

In all these ways, a rethinking of politics and culture beyond the horizon of neoliberalism is now in progress to which a critical sociology of voice – an interrogation of the conditions for, and against, voice – can contribute. But this very project involves taking a normative stance. Neoliberalism's discounting of voice is so deeply embedded that alternative discourses that value voice will not simply emerge as if from a vacuum. They must be worked for, in opposition to forces that, even after what many regard as the worst financial crisis the world has seen in late 2008 (a crisis in which doctrines of market self-correction were acknowledged to fail even by their proponents), insist that nothing in neoliberal discourse, beyond perhaps a few superficial slogans, needs to change. It is here that Jonathan Lear's book *Radical Hope* provides inspiration. Lear reflects on the possibility of surviving absolute cultural loss, the sort of loss that faced American Indian peoples such as The Crow when the activities of inter-tribal territorial conflict that had oriented their way of living were made illegal by an arbitrary external power (the US government). As Lear makes clear, the point of his narrative is to illuminate situations *far beyond* that exceptional and tragic case,[79] and to ask how human beings in general face times of great uncertainty through 'radical hope ... directed toward a future goodness that transcends the current ability to understand what it is'.[80]

Radical hope rests, Lear explains, on at least three things: addressing a current crisis as openly and clearly as possible; facing the unknowability of the transformations which a current way of living will undergo; and finding some underlying principle from the past which can be sustained into a future period whose features cannot yet be anticipated. This returns us to voice's status as a *second order* value: its insistence that, whatever transformations social, political and economic structures undergo, none will be acceptable unless they are based on valuing individuals' ability to give an account of themselves and the conditions under which they live. Voice's apparent vagueness can, from this perspective, be seen as its strength, since it is only a flexible, second order value of this sort that can be expected to survive major transformations. Another strength is its link with the working principles of past democracy; something must be carried over from the past. And yet, in a crucial respect, voice is neither vague nor backward-looking: it articulates a direct response to neoliberalism's *own* second order value, market functioning, the card that trumps all considerations of voice. It is striking how Lear's vision of 'radical hope' is *itself* grounded in valuing a process much like voice:

> although we may be corrected in various ways by others, we take ourselves to have authority when it comes to the narratives of our own lives. ... in general, we think it constitutive of a person having a life that he or she claims some authority over saying what is happening in it.[81]

It is only from the perspective of humans as 'self-interpreting animals' with 'narratable lives',[82] that the depth of loss to which radical hope was for Lear a possible answer comes into view: so too for the losses generated by neoliberal discourse. Only by facing and naming those losses do we have a chance of developing, over time and from many sources, a counter-rationality that can succeed neoliberalism and a 'counter-expertise'[83] that generates new directions for policy and politics.

So if you expect from this book 'solutions' already to the political, social and infrastructural problems which the global financial and market crisis has generated, let alone proposals for the concrete forms in which, for example, markets can be better regulated in accordance with political values and social need, you will be disappointed. More specifically, this book will not address the extremely difficult question of whether implementing the value of voice requires some specific transformations of contemporary institutional structures, or even more broadly a transformation of contemporary structures of capitalism.[84] It may well do, but those questions go beyond the scope of this book. My hope, however, is that this book's attempt to develop some elements of a counter-rationality to neoliberalism will provide material for such discussions. We need first, I believe, to find the right starting-point from which such solutions and proposals might come into view, a different starting-point from that of neoliberal rationality. The task of this book is therefore modest, but for that reason perhaps more immediately helpful: to review our resources for describing the social world as if, once more, voice mattered.

Notes

1 Ricoeur (1984b: 28).
2 Deane (2004), Buckley et al. (2008), Tacchi et al. (2009). See also www.voicesindia.org.
3 Easton (1965) quoted in Delli Carpini and Keater (1996: 12).
4 Aristotle (1992: 60)
5 Hardt and Negri (2006); Benhabib (2004).
6 Agamben (1998).
7 Peet (2007: 111–112).
8 Peet (2007: 4). For broader sociological accounts, see Sklair (2001), Smith (2008: chapter 4).
9 Harvey (2005); Peet (2007: 77).
10 Peet (2007: 27).
11 For useful summary, see Peet (2007: 7–8).
12 Frank (2001).
13 Unger (1998), Stiglitz (2002), Soros (1996).
14 *El Pais* 21 November 2002, quoted Juris (2008: 295).
15 Hirschman (1969). For a recent discussion, see Flew (2009).
16 See Gray (2007: chapters 3 and 4).
17 Gramsci (1970). For discussion, see Gilbert (2008: 172–174) on Clarke (2004: 89). Compare Harvey (2005), Grossberg (2005), Giroux (2004a).
18 Boltanski and Chiapello (2005: 11).
19 Peet (2007).
20 See Background Note.
21 The first meaning of 'term' is 'a limit in space or time' (*Shorter Oxford English Dictionary*, 2000 edition).
22 Quoted Juris (2008: 120).
23 Juris (2008: 286).
24 Butler (2005).
25 Macintyre (1981: 194).
26 Taylor (1986).
27 Hirschman (1969: 30).
28 Taylor (1989), Ricoeur (1992), Butler (2005).
29 Marx (1973: 84), discussed by Harvey (2000: 118–119).
30 MacIntyre (1981: 203). Cf. Ricoeur (1992: 161).
31 Cavarero (2000: 88).
32 Arendt (1958: 193).
33 Discussed by Honneth (2007: 222, 233).
34 See Honneth (2007: chapter 11) for discussion of the differences between Dewey and Habermas.
35 Harvey (2000: 118, added emphasis).
36 Cavarero (2000: 41).
37 Bourdieu (1999) on the 'space of points of view'.
38 Cavarero (2000: 21).
39 Spivak (1987: 59).
40 Cf. Hannerz (1980).
41 For this general sense, see Ricoeur (2005).
42 Butler (2005).
43 Du Bois (1989 [1903]: 3).

44 Levi (2000 [1961]: 26, 69).
45 Arendt (2004 [1951]: 583).
46 Agamben (1998); Proctor (1999: 314 n179); and Hilberg (1985: 872).
47 Proctor (1999: 118).
48 Brewer and Porter (1993).
49 Willis (1990); McRobbie (1997).
50 Lane (2000: 95).
51 As mentioned earlier, economist Albert Hirschman had already noted this in the 1960s (Hirschman 1969).
52 Friedman (1982: 135).
53 On the history of politics focused on consumption, see Cohen (2003), Littler (2009).
54 Frank (2001: 7–8).
55 Brown (2003: para 7).
56 For a brilliant account of neoliberalism's consequences for public and private culture, see Giroux (2004a, 2008).
57 Cf. Harvey (2000: 130) on embodiment and spatial organization.
58 Bauman (1989: 192).
59 Brown (2003: para 42).
60 Cavarero (2000: 33–34).
61 Banet-Weiser (forthcoming).
62 Lawson (2007).
63 Bobbitt (2003).
64 Layard and Dunn (2009: 135, 4, added emphasis).
65 Joseph Rowntree Foundation (2009b).
66 Lukes (1973: 196–197).
67 Kay (2009, added emphasis).
68 Williams (1961: 9–10).
69 Williams (1958: 318).
70 Hans Blumenberg's term (1992).
71 Williams (1989: 152) distinguishes between cultural studies' 'project' and its detailed practice.
72 Honneth (1995a: 207).
73 Sen (2002: 10).
74 Fraser (2005: 75).
75 Balibar (2004: 114). On the 'politics of politics', see also Beck (1997: 99).
76 Rosanvallon (2006: 244, 250).
77 Hardt and Negri (2006).
78 Bauman (2001: 52).
79 Lear (2006: 68).
80 Lear (2006: 133, 103).
81 Lear (2006: 3, 56).
82 Taylor (1986); Cavarero (2000).
83 Peet (2007: 194).
84 See especially Gilbert (2008).

Chapter 2

The Crisis of Neoliberal Economics

> We've been through an extraordinary financial crisis. One doesn't have to ask questions about the 'worst since when', since it may be hard to find any period when it was actually worse than this. (Mervyn King, Governor of the Bank of England, speech on 12 August 2009)[1]

> The rules that make for a successful community are also necessary for the banking system. (UK Prime Minister Gordon Brown)[2]

If one narrative dominates our times, it is that of global economic crisis. I first sketched this chapter in early 2007, never expecting that, before I completed it, we would hear Alan Greenspan, former head of the US Federal Reserve Bank, acknowledge the failure of the market system and the 'intellectual edifice' underlying it.[3] As economic historian Robert Skidelsky noted: 'behind the efficient market idea lay the intellectual failure of mainstream economics. It could neither predict nor explain the meltdown because nearly all economists believed that markets were self-correcting'.[4] Even now we cannot tell the full extent of the current crisis: in spite of signs of recovery in some countries, UK economic experts in August 2009 pronounced the outlook for the UK economy as 'unusually unclear',[5] while in June 2009 the International Monetary Fund warned that the worst of the USA economic crisis may still be ahead.[6] The long-term consequences become more uncertain still when, for example, we consider long-term impacts on youth unemployment and global poverty: more than half of the UK jobs lost since mid 2008 were held by those under 25, while the World Bank recently estimated that following the financial crisis net private capital inflows to 'developing' countries would fall in 2009 to $363 billion, down more than threefold from $1.2 trillion in 2007.[7]

Whatever the ultimate outcome, the belief that markets *always work* has become unsustainable as public doctrine; it is no consolation that this discovery only repeats earlier such discoveries, and predictions of something like the current collapse more than a decade ago.[8] Debate rages about the lessons to be learned from the current crisis. These range from the outlawing of the more outlandish financial instruments (such as the $45 trillion credit-default-swap market) to the Bank of International Settlements' call for 'the comprehensive application of enhanced prudential standards'.[9] There is an important wider debate about the broader social forces that led to the current crisis, and in particular the role of 'financialization', that is, the prioritization across whole societies of financial risk-taking (whether in corporate governance or individual lifestyles).[10] However, it is not this chapter's aim to explore the causes of the 2008 financial crisis, including the regulatory failures that contributed to it: I leave that to those more qualified. I am more concerned with the issue of underlying values.

Some leading figures have indeed been prepared to draw striking conclusions about the financial crisis's implications for neoliberalism more generally. UK Prime Minister Gordon Brown spoke in March 2009 of the end of 'the Washington consensus in favour of free markets',[11] a consensus in which he had, of course, enthusiastically participated. Australian Prime Minister Kevin Rudd argued in a powerful article in February 2009 that:

> Two unassailable truths have already been established: that financial markets are not always self-correcting or self-regulating, and that government (nationally and internationally) can never abdicate responsibility for maintaining economic stability. These two truths in themselves destroy neo-liberalism's claims to any continuing ideological legitimacy, because they remove the foundations on which the entire neo-liberal system is constructed.[12]

If that paragraph identified all there was to neoliberalism, then this book would probably be redundant. However, as I will show, neoliberalism involves a broader range of *underlying principles*, ultimately political values that are deeply embedded and require much more if they are to be defeated. We focus here on the broad belief that *facilitating* market functioning should be the primary aim of economics, and implicitly therefore politics (the application of this belief to politics itself is discussed in Chapter Three). Clearly, once the practical assumption that markets always self-correct is disproved, this opens up questions about the values that assumption conceals: by what criteria are markets meant to 'work'? 'Work' for whom? And underlying this are wider questions about the criteria of economic success and the ends of economic activity. And it is here, rather than in the discredited faith that markets will always self-correct, that we reach the heart of neoliberal doctrine.

The day after President Obama's inauguration, the London *Times'* Anatole Kaletsky commented that 'there is likely to be recognition that many problems demand non-market solutions and that financial incentives are neither necessary nor sufficient to achieve social ends'.[13] But this leaves us no clearer what values will *replace* market fundamentalism; no set of alternative positive values has yet emerged. Recent talk of 'moral capitalism' from some European political leaders (Angela Merkel, Nicolas Sarkozy)[14] suggests so far only the development of new forms of market regulation and market stabilization, failing to articulate in what direction, beyond 'better' market functioning, such moral correction is aimed. Will the US or other governments be prepared seriously to limit the systemic risks that the banking sector generates and the moral and political questions that they raise (for example, concerning bankers' remuneration which *fell* (sic) to £7.6 billion for the UK financial intermediary sector in the depths of the financial crisis)?[15] We must wait and see.[16] Meanwhile, Gordon Brown's equation (quoted above) of everyday morality and the operating standards of the banking sector is fanciful. The debate about new economic norms and values has barely begun. It is an unresolved conflict that is one aspect of the contemporary crisis *of voice*.

By exploring some of the cracks in economic discourse, however, we can search for a route beyond that crisis of voice. If you doubt whether economic thought can be a useful resource for cultural critique, my reply is: *How else* can we begin to contest, for the long term, the 'strong discourse' of neoliberalism[17] than by turning first to the discipline on which it is founded?

The emergence of neoliberal economic theory

In the last chapter, I distinguished between 'neoliberalism proper' and broader 'neoliberal doctrine'. 'Neoliberalism proper' is the set of principles about the economy's workings, and the economy's relations to society, politics and government, that emerged originally in economic thought but, under particular circumstances, in the 1980s–2000s, developed into a dominant 'doctrine' for political and social organization. I leave consideration of the effects of that wider political doctrine to Chapter Three. In this chapter, we concentrate on the view of economics at the heart of neoliberalism.

'Neoliberalism proper' identifies something more than the spread of markets into new areas of life. At its simplest, it is the principle that market functioning is the privileged reference-point for organizing how *governments* – indeed, all modes of social organization – must operate. This overrides other political principles, whether of social welfare, non-market ('public') provision of goods, services or resources, or non-market modes of bureaucratic organization. Already, there is something curious about the idea that economic theory could generate such a *political* principle. Pierre Bourdieu characterized this in terms of the ideology of perfect, unfettered markets that is now shattered, defining neoliberalism as:

> the movement, made possible by the policy of financial deregulation, towards the neo-liberal utopia of a pure, perfect market takes place through the transforming and ... destructive action of all the political measures ... [that are] aimed at *putting into question all the collective structures* capable of obstructing the logic of the pure market.[18]

David Harvey makes clear that any 'pure' principle of market functioning is already complicated by the state's need to *create* market conditions. Here is how Harvey defines neoliberalism:

> A theory of political economic practices that proposes human well-being can best be advanced by liberating individual entrepreneurial freedoms and skills within an institutional framework characterized by strong private property rights, free markets and free trade. The role of the state is to create and preserve an institutional framework appropriate to such practices ... if markets do not exist ... then they must be created, by state action if necessary. But beyond these tasks the state should not venture.[19]

We will return to the notion of entrepreneurial freedom later, but for now note that even this very helpful definition may understate the elaborate structures for *continuously regulating* market functioning through governmental agencies that have been associated with neoliberal democracies such as the UK in the period since its major privatizations (of telecommunications, water, gas, railways, and so on). Here political scientists Levi-Faur and Jordana see a paradox: 'neoliberalism preaches deregulation but paradoxically seems to expand and extend regulation'.[20] So is neoliberalism proper contradictory from the start? To see why not, we need to understand in more detail what lies behind its approach to markets.

Here we must turn to Michel Foucault and his remarkable (and only recently edited and translated) lectures from 1978–79.[21] Paradoxically, Foucault's account comes as a detour from his account of the birth of biopolitics, which led him to consider the origins of neoliberalism in the radicalization of liberalism's view of markets, first, in Austro-German economic thought of the 1930s to 1950s (the so-called 'ordoliberal' school of von Mises, von Hayek, Röpke and others) and, second, in US economic thought of the 1950s to 1970s (the Chicago School of Henry Simons, Milton Friedman and, within broader social thought, Gary Becker).

Debate about the shift in the late twentieth century towards a different rationality for government had already been influenced in a looser way by Foucault's approaches to power and governmentality, sometimes using the term 'advanced liberalism'.[22] But two things must be noticed about Foucault's account of neoliberalism at the outset. First, it is an account of neoliberalism, as a deliberate approach to political practice, not just a series of governmental techniques.[23] Second, it emphasizes that the key issue at the root of neoliberalism was its rethinking of the scope of politics from the new perspective of a market economy: 'what is at issue', Foucault writes, 'is whether a market economy can in fact serve as the principle, form and model for a state'.[24] At stake in Foucault's account of neoliberalism are issues not just of how to regulate or manage markets, but what are the 'truths' about the world from which rationales for government can be built.

Foucault traces the roots of twentieth-century neoliberalism to the birth of liberalism in late eighteenth-century Europe and North America. At this point, the state's relationship to an abstraction called 'the market' came to be understood in a different way. It is Foucault's reading of the relations between market and state in early liberalism that allows him to identify certain 'crises of governmentality' within later liberalism in a way that goes beyond Marx's reading of history solely in terms of successive crises of capitalism.[25] In a sense, the contemporary crisis of voice can be understood as another such crisis of governmentality, operating alongside, but intertwined with, today's crisis of market capitalism.

Instead of the market being seen as one among many domains in which the state can be expected to intervene to control excesses and injustices – in accordance with the state's legitimacy and authority – the market became a form of organization whose legitimacy was independent of the state. Such a shift was not possible without what Foucault calls a new 'regime of truth' that gave the emerging discipline of political economy (represented by David Ricardo and Adam Smith) a privileged position. Under this regime of truth, the market became viewed as a *natural* domain, operating by natural law, whose functioning was distorted if the state intervened in its operations more than minimally.[26] The market became a particular and privileged site of knowledge for, and in relation to, society and government: as Foucault puts it, 'the market must tell the truth; it must tell the truth in relation to government practice'.[27]

It is this naturalism of markets that Foucault sees as informing the notion of 'freedom' in modern liberalism and enabling the later radicalization of liberalism in neoliberalism:[28] as we see at the end of the chapter, considerable effort is needed to *denaturalize* this notion of market-based freedom. For the value of freedom has already within neoliberalism been displaced to some degree onto a space beyond individual norms ('the freedom, honesty and efficiency *of the market*').[29] Even if in heavy disguise, we see here the origins of neoliberal thought's tendency to what Jacques Rancière calls oligarchy – 'the compulsion to get rid of people and of politics';[30] we might also see it as the point from which, whatever its rhetoric of freedom, neoliberalism was destined to be opposed to democracy. As Larry Grossberg noted in his insightful study of US neoliberalism, 'the free market ... is fundamentally an argument against politics, or at least against a politics that attempts to govern society in social rather than economic terms'.[31] For if, in one respect, democracy involves the principle of 'no body rules' (John Keane's reversal of Rancière's definition of oligarchy),[32] the basis for the later radicalization of liberalism was the principle that it is the market that rules.

How did this radicalization in neoliberalism come about? While both Austro-German and US neoliberalism emerged through opposition to the doctrine of state intervention in markets advocated by John Maynard Keynes in 1930s Britain – and applied in New Deal America and many other places – they have distinct features. In Austro-German neoliberalism, the principle of free market functioning that, as Foucault put it, 'does not ask the state what freedom it will leave to the economy, but asks the economy how its freedom can have a state-creating function'.[33] The 'natural fact' of market functioning became viewed as not just a condition that states should protect, but as the principle on whose basis *the state's own operations could be judged*. This followed from a broader understanding of markets as not just sites where individuals or companies needed to be free to exchange, but as a space whose growth required effective competition which it was the role of government to *actively produce*.[34] Under this model, governments became judged by the degree to which they 'govern[ed] for the market, rather than [just] because of the market'.[35] So the Keynesian social policy of correcting for bad market effects was seen from the perspective of Austro-German neoliberals before and after World War II as irrational, since it was trumped by a prior *non-social* principle of 'accord[ing] everyone [as individuals] a sort of economic space within which they can take on and confront risks'.[36] Within this perspective, the 'enterprise' and not government is seen as 'the formative power of society',[37] displacing government's role as a positive force for social transformation (except, and in so far as, it did so by allowing market forces to operate 'naturally'). At the root of this was Ludwig von Mises's radicalization of the principles of liberalism: 'the point of departure of all liberalism lies in the thesis of the harmony of rightly understood interests of individuals'.[38]

The introduction and sustaining of market principles of competition becomes, in this way, the reference-point for judging not just government operations, but also for evaluating *the social domain as a whole*. The principle of market competition comes to authorize 'a general regulation of society by the market' through the business enterprise.[39] The principle of market naturalism was in this way expanded into a mechanism for reforming the institutional basis of society and, by the same token, for assessing in a different way government's role in governing the social.[40] This market naturalism was based, in von Hayek's work, on a particular interpretation of the value of freedom.

What about US neoliberalism? Although this is closer to us in time, frustratingly Foucault's account is less detailed. But it illuminates some key points. The first is that, by contrast to Germany and Europe generally, the US state, from its formation, already depended for its legitimacy in part on its role as guarantor of market functioning:[41] US neoliberalism was linked to a pre-existing radical strand of US market liberalism, and so was not simply a twentieth-century invention. Whereas Austro-German neoliberalism emphasized in its original versions the need for a strong state to introduce and sustain market conditions, Milton Friedman's thought put greater emphasis on freedom itself, freedom conceived *against* the state. This notion of freedom generates an account of everyday life opposed to the very *idea* of social goals:

> To the free man, the country [any country including the USA] is the collection of individuals who compose it, not something over and above them. He recognizes no national goal except as it is the consensus of the goals that the citizens *severally* serve. He recognizes no national purpose except as it is the consensus of the purposes for which the citizens *severally* strive.[42]

The nation and society are conceived here literally like a market, as a device for aggregating individual wants. Freedom is the key reference-point: 'as liberals, we take freedom of the individual, *or perhaps the family*, as our ultimate goal in judging social arrangements': the equivocation about the family is revealing.[43] Political power, by contrast, is defined by Friedman as a power of coercion which must be eliminated 'to the fullest possible extent'.[44]

Friedman's emphasis on freedom from coercion and his suspicion of social goals was shared with von Hayek who grounded the latter, theoretically, in a sceptical insistence on the 'inevitable ignorance of all of us concerning a great many of the factors on which the achievements of our ends and welfare depends'.[45] This links, as we see later, to rational choice theory, and its policy-oriented extension, public choice theory,[46] and is based on the belief that freedom can be articulated sufficiently as a negative value (freedom from coercion),[47] without needing to specify its positive content. But von Hayek was concerned to emphasize, first, that this philosophy of freedom does not rule out the evolution of social ends; second, that the role of the state in ensuring public goods and sustaining the infrastructure of market competition may be quite extensive; and third, that other values, for example a cooperative spirit with neighbours, may be positive.[48] We will come back in Chapter Three to Friedman's more visceral hostility to state involvement and its implications for his intensely reductive view of the market-state.

A quite distinctive set of historical circumstances propelled von Hayek's and Friedman's ideas into the political mainstream in the USA and UK, and then globally in the late 1970s and early 1980s. The economic and political crises of the early 1970s (linked to sudden oil price rises, high inflation, the breakdown of agreement between governments and organized labour) generated an interpretation in elite policy circles that, as Richard Peet argues, made neoliberalism (and its delegitimation of the state's economic management) newly fashionable: 'the real crisis of capitalism in the 1970s was interpreted as the failure of Keynesian policy'.[49] Von Hayek directly influenced the new UK Prime Minister Margaret Thatcher, who appointed a follower of von Hayek, Keith Joseph, to be Secretary of State for Industry, while Friedman attained prominence as an adviser to the new US President Ronald Reagan.[50] There were quickly outcomes in terms of new constraints on the money supply to allow 'free market forces' to operate.

As the 1980s developed, neoliberal doctrine grew, from its distinctive US starting-point of historically strong hostility to the state, into 1990s 'market populism', generating many strange features: what Thomas Frank calls 'the fantasy of the market as an antielitist machine' (both the later von Hayek and the US radio talk show pedagogue Rush Limbaugh); the idea that 'suspicions of wealth' are a major *cause* of poverty (George Gilder, author of the 1981 book *Wealth and Poverty*).[51] Add in heavily overdetermined beliefs in the emancipatory power of technology, particularly the 'open' space of the Internet; add in also the management literature's and corporations' skill at marketing themselves as a zone of not only freedom but also compassion and sensitivity, and you had a powerful ideology that came to fit well with aspects of US culture, but even spread to the post-Marxist left in the UK.[52]

Foucault also brings out how, from its distinctive liberal base, US neoliberalism proposed extensions of classical economic thought that turned the principle of market competition into a tool for *reinterpreting social and even private life* in all its aspects, so expanding market principles' practical application in a way that Austro-German neoliberalism had merely implied. The result was not merely (as in Gary Becker's work) to analyse, for example, the family as a site for utility maximization,[53] but to reinterpret labour as an individual process of optimizing capital – the individual worker as the optimizer of her own capital (in the form of labour skills) for a potentially profitable return (salary). As a result, all levels of economic functioning, not just the level of corporate enterprise, came to be interpreted in terms of competitiveness.

These shifts had further radical consequences. US neoliberalism transformed the economic fiction of 'homo economicus' from a mere partner in exchange to the individual who is 'an entrepreneur of himself';[54] the individual market participant ceased to be a black box and became an internal site of competition, indeed of *self-transformation* for better competitiveness. In this way, neoliberalism became transformed into a tool for reforming every individual within society, and indeed the meaning of the term 'society' itself. There was no space left, on any scale, whether public or private, work-based or family, that was not amenable to reform in terms of producing more perfect competitiveness. As a result, every area of human life became subject to reorganization on economic principles, with economic thought becoming coterminous with rationality itself.[55] From this it followed that market rationality was not one principle of thought among many, but *the* general calculus by which all public and government action fell to be judged.[56] The recent school of US legal positivism, represented by Richard Posner, which makes market rationality and cost-benefit analysis into a key principle of legal thinking, represents the farthest development of this trend.[57]

If understood in this broader historical context, neoliberalism proper was much more than advocacy of free markets and privatization of public services. The result was to change understanding of the *ends* of government. As Graham Burchell put it in relation to approaches to government from the 1980s onwards:

> government must [now] work for the game of market competition and as a kind of enterprise itself, and new quasi-entrepreneurial and market models of action must be invented for the conduct of individuals, groups and institutions within those areas of life hitherto seen as being either outside or even antagonistic to the economic.[58]

This changes quite radically the *ontology* to which government is thought to respond (the market is now seen as a site whose 'truth' and natural processes depend on governments interfering with them as little as possible)[59] and the *epistemology* of government which becomes oriented towards a new type of 'fact': 'the limitation of [the state's] power is not given by respect for the freedom of individuals, but simply by the evidence of economic analysis which it knows has to be respected'.[60] Foucault thus uncovers the move by which economics itself became installed as a dominant reference-point in thinking about government. But this epistemology already excludes an alternative domain of facts – about the resources on which tolerable social interaction and individual integrity rely – and an alternative notion of freedom which might allow other values to be heard.

Within this radicalization of liberal thought, Foucault detects, however, the seeds of contradiction. For Austro-German neoliberal economists, at least, did *not* imagine that whole societies could operate on the basis of perfect competition alone. Foucault notes a debate among German economists in the 1930s and 1940s where many insisted on the need to place a political and moral framework above the economy. As Röpke warned:

> competition is a principle of order in the domain of the market economy, but it is not a principle on which it would be possible to erect the whole of society. Morally and sociologically, competition is a principle that dissolves more than it unifies.[61]

Here we suddenly see just how far US neoliberalism, which, in its popular forms, ignores that note of caution, has travelled from the basic idea of market freedom. It leaves us with an account of the social that lacks any of the features normally associated with social life.

What has been the impact of neoliberal principles within economic life? This cannot easily be disentangled from some wider transformations in the organization and culture of capitalism under way for the past 20–30 years.

Neoliberalism and the 'new spirit of capitalism'

A book which greatly enriches our understanding of how more broadly market principles have become embedded in social life is Luc Boltanski and Eve Chiapello's *The New Spirit of Capitalism*.[62]

'Living in a network'[63]

Boltanski and Chiapello's starting-point is also Max Weber's: that because capitalist accumulation demands large-scale loss of freedoms, capitalism always requires a set of ideas, norms and patterns of behaviour to 'justify engagement in capitalism', a 'spirit of capitalism'.[64] They argue that, alongside the growth of neoliberal discourse, there has been a wider transformation of the spirit of capitalism since the 1960s. A 'new spirit of capitalism' replaced the old commercial logic, which validated the reproduction of capital's interests principally through large corporations based in particular places, with a new *connectionist* logic, which in a world of expanding and interconnected markets validates mobility of capital, resources and labour. Mobility becomes 'a highly valued commodity' whose price 'is rising rapidly and is paid exclusively by the "slow"'.[65] As they explain:

> In a connectionist world ... it is not only the quality and scarcity of a product or service that are valued. The premium accruing from the mobility differential is added to the price paid. The most mobile can in fact threaten to 'exit' at any moment, with the opportunities open to them on account of their potential for variability.[66]

Yet Boltanski and Chiapello dismiss, in passing, 'denigrators of "neo-liberalism"':[67] fellow French sociologists Pierre Bourdieu and Alain Touraine are presumably among their targets.[68] Are we, then, disallowed from treating their argument as a critique of neoliberalism? This would be a mistake, since, as they develop their account of the distinctive forms of injustice associated with 'the new spirit of capitalism', Boltanski and Chiapello increasingly incorporate concerns that are highly relevant to wider critiques of neoliberalism: capital's indifference to the consequences of economic restructuring for families; the increasing indifference of new market logics to the costs that individuals must incur to enter and stay in the labour market. While drawing specifically on the shifts in working culture in France, Boltanski and Chiapello's account resonates importantly with transformations in the UK, USA and elsewhere.

Where Boltanski and Chiapello are most original is in insisting that contemporary critique of capitalism can only begin from the recognition that markets (and their hegemonic[69] resonance in contemporary cultures) have *themselves changed* as part of the wider transformations they identify. This broadens our appreciation of the shifts within work organization and capitalist culture of which US market populism is only an extreme manifestation; it also helps us understand the attraction, and potentially the limits, of recent celebrations of the intensified networking potential of Web 2.0 for culture, society and politics.[70] It links also to the positive value of 'entrepreneurial freedom' that, as Harvey notes, is one of neoliberal discourse's starting-points.[71]

The transformation of capitalism that Boltanski and Chiapello identify involves the increasing dominance of a new way of thinking about how capitalism is and should be organized, and how within it individuals should maximize their opportunities, as they conform to capitalism's needs for greater mobility and flexibility. Like neoliberalism proper (as analysed by Foucault), the new spirit of capitalism involves a new ontology and epistemology which Boltanski and Chiapello express through the language of the 'tests' which individuals and organizations must undergo to prove themselves. At the heart of 'the new spirit of capitalism' is a distinctive type of freedom for the networked individual in 'the new enterprise mechanisms':

... which demand greater engagement and are based on a more sophisticated ergonomics ... [and] precisely because they are more human in a way, also penetrate more profoundly into people's interior being. The latter are expected to 'give themselves' ... to their work, and the mechanisms permit an instrumentalization and commodification of what is most specifically human about human beings.[72]

Boltanski and Chiapello analyse well the attractions of consumer freedom and employers'/workers' freedom from ossified bureaucratic structures which are affirmed by the new spirit of capitalism, and the way that 'new spirit' incorporates many themes of political and cultural rebellion from the 1960s and 1970s (Nancy Fraser suggests the incorporation of some principles of feminism too).[73]

What is most important in Boltanski and Chiapello's analysis are the deeper contradictions in the new spirit of capitalism. To grasp these, we must note the difference from earlier forms of commodification of labour because of the growth of service industries and the long-term shift towards emotional or affective labour in all those service industries which require workers to contribute elements of their identity into their labour.[74] The Asda supermarket chain is part of 'the Walmart family';[75] when Asda employees were interviewed by Madeleine Bunting,[76] it became clear that they knew they *must* smile a *real* smile on the shop floor to keep their company's brand alive; they worked in a space whose performance rules were very difficult to oppose, since they seemed to confirm new values of identity and expression. This expansion of the modalities of labour can be related also to the explosion of informal symbolic labour that has led some writers to see a new paradigm of 'immaterial labour'.[77] The latter may be too simple: 'immaterial labour' continues alongside the grinding forms of older 'material' labour often in the same societies,[78] while, as Jack Qiu argues in relation to the huge Chinese working class, the impacts of 'immaterial labour' extend far beyond Western 'creative industries', changing our understanding of poverty and under-employment on a global scale.[79]

The debate over the material or immaterial nature of labour takes us to another key context which is the particular form of 'overwork cultures'[80] in a world of information technology and working from home or at a distance. The boundaries between the spaces, times and moral worlds of work and home become increasingly blurred under these conditions.[81] Meanwhile information technologies enable all work spaces (wherever they are) to become subject to forms of centralized surveillance and peer-to-peer surveillance that intensify work pressures and work's cycles of accountability and reporting.[82] For example, new IT-based 'enterprise systems' carry efficiency and rationalization down to the level of the smallest detail of everyday conduct, inspired by the idea that continuous monitoring of workers is a basis for their positive self-transformation into more efficient agents.[83] Take this example of how 'management systems' are offered as a positive tool for efficiency (it comes from a recent piece on UK schools and teachers in the *Guardian* Education pages):

> The real business end of the school's management information system (MIS) is – or should be – in the classroom. That's where teaching and learning happens ... The MIS, then, is vacuuming up data from around the school at a phenomenal rate ... however everything that goes in must emerge and work for its living.[84]

Little consideration is given here to the impacts on *individuals'* space for reflecting (instead it is data that is anthropomorphized). Meanwhile in UK universities, a widely circulated internal document for Leeds Metropolitan University indicated that it was seeking to improve its performance management systems to effect 'sustained organizational change':

> through establishing what behaviours and values we expect staff to demonstrate in everything they do. ... By ensuring that staff are recruited, developed, assessed and rewarded in relation to a set of core behaviours, we can align individual performance and organizational culture.[85]

The normative framework within which such developments might appear desirable (or not) is never raised.

The conflicts of value within the new spirit of capitalism are, however, complex. Boltanski and Chiapello analyse how management literature has, since the 1980s, given huge emphasis to the necessity of adaption to competitive market pressures, while also 'taking the maximum distance from hierarchical principles [of organization], promising formal equality and respect of individual liberties'.[86] Since markets inevitably create hierarchies of success, we cannot get far by taking the new spirit of capitalism's claims of liberation at face value. Its freedom from hierarchy is inseparable from individual commitment to learning how to 'live in a network'.[87] This brings benefits of flexibility and speed which may often feel exhilarating, whether to new market entrants or successful and well-established networkers. But the accelerated mobility that network culture involves brings as a cost, as Boltanski and Chiapello persuasively argue, a distinctive form of *anomie* (in Emile Durkheim's late nineteenth-century term), disrupting various evaluative reference-points on which self-esteem and group affiliation had previously relied.[88] In the following characterization of the 'commandments' of the contemporary workplace, stable values only enter via the notion of brand:

> I am available and organize my work accordingly; at a minimum, I participate in a work group; I make an effort to be mobile (versatility, switching, etc); on the outside, I contribute to the firm's good brand image.[89]

Other values are in play of course, as tools through which mutual monitoring can occur in an intense 'audit culture',[90] but they are unstable and themselves the site of competition.

This competition takes its most corrosive form when those who are more mobile 'extricate themselves from the forms of control on which the stability of the domestic world is based', by shifting relationships, friendships, work partnerships.[91] Networks are only possible because of underlying practices of meaning, which themselves require some element of what Boltanski and Chiapello call 'fixed capital' (resources, places, people and, above all, trust). Yet it is precisely the possibility of *fixing* capital that is threatened over the long term by a connexionist world. As they conclude, 'the generalization of a connexionist world without checks of any sort upon exploitation is such as to destroy the social fabric'.[92]

So the new spirit of capitalism, while rich in cultural resources, is likely to be no more stable in the end than previous spirits of capitalism. At the level of the self, the conflict is between the pressure towards 'adaptability' and the need in transactions at least to 'be someone', to be an entity that some other person might find it meaningful to trust on more than one occasion.[93] As in previous stages of capitalism, fundamental contradictions converge on the person and body of the worker, even, or especially, as an increasing percentage of contemporary labour consists in symbolic production.

Michael Pusey's survey- and interview-based study of how Australians experienced the economy during neoliberal reforms in the 1990s offers important insights here into this strange human calculus:[94] 'the family seem[ed] to be running out of the capacity to absorb the externalities of economic reform'.[95] This did more than corrode families and the social and civic spaces with which affected families interacted. It *cut off* the all-important world of work from broader processes of moral regulation (Durkheim).[96] The result 'threaten[ed] to crush [families'] capacity to hold onto moral choices'.[97] This creates, as Boltanski and Chiapello note, a distinctive inertia. Connexionist logic, by placing a premium on being mobile, undermines over the longer term some of the social conditions (stable contexts for affiliation, cooperation and organization)[98] required for articulating *alternative* values. As a result:

> the network presents itself as the *negation of categories to which people are attached on a permanent basis*, and thanks to which they can construct collective norms setting limits on their individual passions.[99]

At this point Milton Friedman's equivocation, noted earlier, on whether it is the individual *or the family* that is the reference-point for judging freedom and value becomes crucial. Market and network demands, unless limited by other considerations and values, become over time literally *unliveable*. As one Australian worker interviewed by Pusey put it, 'you give it all you've got, and they still want more'.[100]

Voice, then, as a minimal practical achievement – having the basic resources from which you can give an account of oneself on which trust might be built – is increasingly an essential resource for capitalism but its sustainability is systematically ignored by neoliberal discourse and undermined by the new spirit of capitalism, unless, that is, ways of disguising this contradiction can be found. It is significant in this context that the pressure towards 'commodifying the human' inherent to a connexionist world[101] is now being developed into practices of self-promotion and 'self-branding' that, as Sarah Banet-Weiser shows, ally an entrepreneurial vision of the self to the neoliberal value of freedom.[102] The result is an *apparent* expansion of 'voice' as cover for the increasing penetration of market values into the space of self. To contest this requires a different normative framework.

Alienation network-style

Developing a *counter-rationality* to connexionist logic – and neoliberalism in general – is then not simply a matter of using a different language; it means rethinking the principles on which human cooperation is currently organized, and establishing what Boltanski and Chiapello call new 'limits to commodification' based in a new approach to issues of 'liberation and authenticity'.[103] What hurt the workers interviewed by Madeleine Bunting[104] in her vivid study of the UK's overwork culture was that they discovered how their own values – of family, individual wellbeing and health, the time for social networks – *count for nothing* within the new borderless workplace. The result is potentially a loss of 'coherence' between work and the rest of our lives, generating what Richard Sennett has called the 'corrosion of character'.[105]

In spite of all the transformations since Marx wrote, his account of alienation still has much of importance to tell us. First, workers may sense a lack of meaning in their work, because one dimension of meaning they *do* know as important is regarded as meaningless at work, trumped by the overriding value of profit and market position. This is what Jon Elster calls 'spiritual alienation', alienation at the level of meaning.[106] Sennett sees this disconnect in ethical terms when 'the qualities of good work' cease to be 'the qualities of good character'.[107] As a result, the necessary conditions of work become detached from the conditions of voice. Marx provides the most eloquent commentary: 'the worker therefore only feels himself outside his work, and in his work feels outside himself. He is at home when he is not working, and when he is working he is not at home'.[108]

Second, these workers are suffering the type of alienation Elster calls 'social alienation', because it is linked to how social assets are legally owned.[109] Marx's key idea is that 'under capitalism the products of man gain an independent existence and come into opposition to their makers'.[110] We can pass by the old debate about whether the relationship between labour and capital is intrinsically alienating, since there is something *distinctively* alienating about contemporary conditions of work which require the entire creative commitment of workers – the creativity Marx and many others have seen as human – in a structure which cedes *control over* that creativity to external forces, understood in the form of impersonal markets.[111] Increasing levels of emotional performance and display at work only deepen the alienation. As under other forms of capitalism, workers lack control over the conditions by which work commitment is, in the long term, sustained – bodily and emotional health, companionship (a sense that you matter to others), meaning – but with the added paradox that more and more of those same emotional and symbolic resources must be used up within everyday work performance.

These contradictions never go away in the digital world of 'continuous, updatable work'[112] which, as Boltanski and Chiapello argue, also enable 'the costs of maintaining and reproducing labour [to be] transferred largely onto private individuals and public systems'.[113] A core mechanism here is internal markets and outsourcing which both corporations and governments have developed in neoliberal democracies. Such shifts are often justified by external market necessities with the market seen as 'an uncontrollable external factor'.[114] Add this to the increasing uncertainties of labour markets as corporate management focuses almost exclusively on short-term shareholder value or public asset value[115] (the average length of time a middle-aged US male can expect to stay with the same employer fell between 1978 and 2007 from eleven to seven and a half years)[116] and Marx's circle of alienation is complete.

A strategy for disguising this alienation is to efface the self that is a potential site of alienation (because it has an inherent capacity to develop its own projects and voice) and replace it with a different self whose fulfilment is pre-defined by reference to whatever it takes to market oneself successfully. As Sarah Banet-Weiser and Alison Hearn point out,[117] recent US marketing discourse takes Gary Becker's theoretical concept of the entrepreneurial self and converts it into a popular morality – the *duty* to brand ourselves – that in social networking sites has a ready-made space for performance and mutual evaluation. At this advanced stage of neoliberal discourse's cultural embedding it is not enough, of course, to oppose markets or 'flexibility' as such. We need, as Boltanksi and Chiapello argue, *values* that can seem meaningful within the connexionist world in which neoliberal principles have become deeply embedded, even down to the level of the individual's evaluations of what developing the self involves. There is no way out of the expanding domain of neoliberal logic unless we start out from the contradictions involved in seeing markets as providing a self-sufficient logic for the social that have been exposed within neoliberalism's home territory of economics.

The cracks within classical economics

Economics' hegemony within the politics and culture of neoliberalism affects all of us, whether we have technical facility in economics or not. From this perspective, recent debates among economists that challenge the principles of neoliberalism are an important resource for cultural critique. Those critiques come from a variety of positions within and around economics, and yet ultimately converge in a powerful rejection of the fundamentals of neoliberal ideology, above all in the work of development economist Amartya Sen.

Less radical critiques

Let us start from the important argument of the UK economist and 'happiness' theorist, Richard Layard. Philosophically, Layard appears to be an unabashed utilitarian[118] and focuses on whether economics helps us maximize a particular good ('happiness'), which for him must be clearly measurable and countable.[119]

Layard's criticism of economics is that for a long time it has been measuring the *wrong good* (gross national product). In spite of its radical tone, this is hardly a radical attack on markets or the techniques of economics. Layard insists that most people want more income, and that becoming richer than others does make people happier.[120] But he is interested in the 'paradox of happiness' (paradoxical perhaps only to economists!),[121] namely that when you compare one society to another – so abstracting from the relative differentials within those societies – you find that 'when *whole societies* become richer, they have not become happier'.[122] The explanation is that a number of factors important to happiness are ignored by economics, and consigned to the status of 'market externalities': fulfilment at work, friendship, a sense of mutual social trust, a sense of community.[123] None of these are 'goods' within market economics, yet they are all important to happiness. Aggressive neglect of these externalities in new regimes of 'flexible' labour makes things, Layard argues, much worse and is strongly criticized in the policy recommendations at the end of his book, which offer a notable stand against New Labour's market rhetoric (on which see Chapter Three).[124] But Layard's conclusion goes even further:

> Humans are deeply social beings ... to a large extent our social ties define our personal identity and give meaning to our life. So it is a deep fallacy of many economists to think of human interaction as mainly a means to an end, rather than also an end in itself.[125]

So Layard's book is important for my wider argument because, from premises that are hardly radical, he comes to conclusions which pose a significant challenge to the primacy of market functioning in economic and political reasoning.

Part of the historical background to Layard's work, and the recent growth of happiness research in economics, is Tibor Scitovsky's earlier book *The Joyless Economy*. Although mainly concentrated on consumer satisfaction, this book posed early on a broad challenge to the principles of market fundamentalism. First, Scitovsky challenged the assumption that economics actually *knows* what its postulated rational consumers want. Challenging the methodological principle of 'revealed preference'[126] – the idea that people's real preferences are identical with their preferences actualized in the market place – Scitovsky opened the possibility for psychological research into what consumers 'really' want, and its relation to what market economies provide. Scitovsky concluded that 'economic activity ... is only one of many sources of satisfaction, perhaps not a very important one'.[127] This leads to Scitovsky's second challenge to market fundamentalism, when he contests the assumption that freedom of market participation is the consumer *sovereignty* market liberals claim it is; for Scitovsky, 'the consumer is [only] sovereign insofar as his choice influences the nature and quantity of the goods and services provided',[128] which is rarely the case. In looking, as Layard does much later, for desires and needs not necessarily satisfied by or within markets, Scitovsky identified various 'externalities' in mainstream economics whose relevance need to be addressed: 'the comfort of belonging', 'the comfort of being useful', and 'the comfort of sticking to our habits'.[129]

The US political scientist and political economist Robert Lane is helpful here, building on Scitovsky's insight that many of the things we value most are mere 'externalities' within economics. Once again, Lane's is not prima facie an argument against neoliberalism. First, he praises the success of markets in generating wealth, and the success of economic modelling in helping them do so.[130] Second, the empirical research on markets' relationships to happiness that he analyses covers the past 30–40 years, so in part predating neoliberalism. But his argument is nonetheless more radical than Layard's. He notes the paradox of happiness – that higher gross national product does not *increase* societal happiness – but goes on to note a more disturbing negative correlation: richer societies may have higher levels of *depression* than poorer societies.[131]

Lane's list of what economics misses out, while consistent with Layard's, is also broader. The key factor ignored in economics for Lane is 'companionship', defined as 'both family solidarity and friendship (social support, to social scientists)'.[132] Lane goes further than Layard or Scitovsky in his dissection of what may be wrong in contemporary workplaces, insisting on the importance of affiliation at work and people's sense that 'they belong to a network of communication and mutual obligation'.[133] Lane's criticisms of both mainstream economics and political science are also sharper. For in Lane's diagnosis, economics is misguided precisely because it looks to *markets* for the source of human values, when markets are just general mechanisms for achieving 'species benefits', not individual benefits.[134] The work values that market fundamentalists associate with market behaviour (that is, individualized competition) are *inimical* to happiness, because they inhibit companionship.[135] Indeed, 'the principal sources of happiness *and unhappiness* are market externalities';[136] necessarily these are 'things that markets may casually ignore, make better or make worse without endogenous correction'. Recall the argument in Chapter One that voice itself is, from the point of view of economics, an externality.

It is here that Lane develops a major challenge to neoliberal values as they shape the experience of work. Work, Lane argues, is the site of profound misunderstanding in economic thought:

> There is a deep reason for the undervaluation of the psychic income and enjoyment of work: in market accounting work is a cost, whereas consumption is a source of benefit ... The

> underlying assumption is that people work in order to earn
> in order to consume; work is a disutility for which income
> and consumption are the compensating utilities. But even in
> a market economy, this is often, perhaps usually, not true ...
> rather work and work mastery are the sources of very great
> pleasure.[137]

It follows that the *absence* of opportunities for 'work mastery' is a source
of great displeasure and discomfort. As a result, Lane argues, mainstream
economics ignores key factors in (un)happiness – job (in)security, work (dis)
satisfaction, the effects of labour market participation on family and friends.
Lane's fundamental criticisms of the assumptions, methods and values of
economic thinking cast an ironic light on the current dominance of narrowly
based market thinking in contemporary politics and culture: '"the end of history" is not the triumph of the market, but only the end of a particular history
of one paradigm [of the market] and perhaps the beginning of the next'.[138]

Layard's, Scitovsky's and Lane's work clearly resonates not only with
aspects of Boltanski and Chiapello's account of injustice within the 'new spirit
of capitalism', but also with the empirical work on the suffering within neoliberal economies discussed earlier. But it does not yet amount to a critique of
neoliberal rationality itself.

Sen's radical critique

For this we must turn to the development economist and philosopher Amartya
Sen. Sen's writings on rationality, justice, the philosophy of action, development economics and the role of ethics within economics are voluminous, and
it is well beyond my capacity to cover them. Some brief points will be enough
to illustrate the radical nature of Sen's challenge to the economic reasoning
underlying neoliberalism. Yet surprisingly, his work has received little attention from those engaged in the cultural critique of neoliberalism, apart from a
brief mention by Hardt and Negri.[139]

If other approaches argue that economics should incorporate within it a
consideration of the wider purpose (or good) at which economic activity is
directed – implying that, once this adjustment is made, a redirected economics
or 'happiness studies', as Layard calls it, can get on with its work – Sen poses a
deeper challenge by insisting that mainstream economics has floundered from
the moment it separated itself from ethics. This, he argues, has 'substantially
impoverished' the subject, reducing economics to an 'engineering' approach
divorced from ethics.[140]

For all its claims to social relevance, Sen argues, contemporary economics
fails to satisfy the very different demands that ethics makes: for ethics 'cannot stop the evaluation [of economic activity] short at some arbitrary point
like satisfying "efficiency". The assessment has to ... *take a broader view of the
good'*.[141] So by this move, Sen reintroduces into the 'normal science' of economics all of philosophy's uncertainties about what constitutes the good. Against

economists and politicians who would see this as a betrayal of Adam Smith's foundational belief in the 'invisible hand' of the market (operating without regard to good notions of ethics), Sen insists they make a profound misreading of Smith's work and the importance within it, precisely, of 'moral sentiments' extending far beyond the rational calculations of market-players.[142] Indeed, for Sen, the closeness of economics to ethical considerations of value is not something exceptional or surprising. It goes right back to Aristotle, an intellectual tradition from which it is modern 'value-*neutral*' economics that is the aberration.[143]

But what about rationality? Doesn't rationality demand (whether in economics or elsewhere) a sharp distinction between its own demands (from market logic) and the fuzzier area of sentiments and emotions (in play as always, no doubt, but simply not economists' concern)? In response, Sen argues that this account of rationality is also impoverished. Rational choice theory – the offshoot of abstract economic models of choice within social and political science that, from a radical account of uncertainty within social life, reinterprets all action in terms of individual utility-maximization – is a classic case in point.[144] Sen's attack on the definitions of 'rationality' within rational choice theory is too elaborate to be fully considered here, but in broad terms Sen argues that 'RCT' offers only 'one very narrow interpretational story' of how human beings think.[145] More specifically, two assumptions at RCT's core are flawed:

1   the 'self-welfare goal': a person's only goal is to maximize her own welfare; and

2   the 'self-goal choice': a person's choices must be based entirely on the pursuit of her own goals.[146]

Sen acknowledges that some forms of RCT[147] are subtle enough to allow that humans do rationally choose to avoid the pain caused *to them* by seeing others whom they care about suffer: so in practice rational agents do not seek *only* their own wellbeing. But even this more sophisticated RCT stops short of acknowledging that I might rationally choose to maximize the welfare of some group of people larger than myself (against assumption [1]) or that I might rationally choose to act so that others' goals, not just my own goals, are satisfied (against assumption [2]).

Rational choice theory, and neoliberal principles more widely, rules out the possibility of wider social, ethical or political *commitment*. In this way, Sen argues, these approaches miss completely any broader consideration of how humans reflect on *what* goals they should pursue, for example the goal of constraining one's own individual goals for some greater collective good.[148] They are therefore, Sen argues, blind to a key subset of human values, that is, 'values about values'.[149] Sen goes further and insists that individual rationality becomes meaningful only within a *social* context, paralleling Charles Taylor's critique of the 'punctual self' of Enlightenment philosophy (John Locke, David Hume and others).[150] Here Sen's critique has relevance not just for economics, but for the wider spread of RCT principles, for example in 'public choice theory'. As Colin Hay argues, 'public choice theory' has had wide impact in legitimating, as 'rational', the neoliberal limitation of public policy to quasi-economic ends.[151] So Sen's challenge to RCT's foundations has implications also for neoliberalism's adoption as politics (see Chapter Three).

Important, too, is Sen's questioning of economics' notion of freedom. Sen notes that it is only by bringing ethics back into economics that we can develop an adequate account of what freedom, for example the market 'freedoms' so beloved of neoliberal economics, might mean.[152] Mainstream economics' definition of freedom (the freedom to maximize one's preferences in a market setting) is divorced from any broader consideration of *why we value* freedom, or indeed what the *content* of freedom is. This absence of ethical and normative reference-points is particularly emphatic in US neoliberalism. Here is Milton Friedman:

> In a society, freedom has nothing to say about what an individual does with this freedom ... it is not an all-embracing ethic. Indeed, a major aim of the liberal is to leave the ethical problem for the individual to wrestle with.[153]

The issue here is whether excluding ethics from our notion of freedom is coherent. According to Sen, there are two dimensions to freedom, and both are fundamental: the 'process' aspect and the 'opportunity' aspect.[154] Freedom of process is important of course (eg. the basic freedom to sell or buy your goods at a market, free from interference), but the problem is that market liberalism is interested *only* in the process aspects of freedom, and ignores its opportunity aspects. What are those 'opportunity aspects' of freedom? Sen defines them as 'the actual ability of [that] person to achieve those things that *she has reason to value*'.[155] Yet surely this is part of understanding what freedom is for. Even if your fundamental value *is* 'freedom', you must ask: freedom to do what? This means that in defining freedom you cannot exclude debate about values other than freedom. So freedom in the abstract is not fully coherent as a value. Here Sen boldly rejects the much vaunted 'negative liberty' tradition derived from Isaiah Berlin,[156] and allows, implicitly, a return to the idea of freedom linked to questions of social justice that von Hayek rejected in John Dewey.[157]

We are back to the question with which we began the chapter: if we want a more moral capitalism, we have to identify the new values on which that morality will be based. Neoliberal doctrine's espousal of market freedom as an absolute value is exposed as hollow, since, as Sen puts it, 'freedom cannot be fully appraised without some idea of what a person ... has reason to prefer'.[158] It follows that *a fundamentalist notion of market freedom, divorced from wider values, is empty*. The same point would apply to more recent visions of freedom expressed within the connexionist and exhibitionist logics that Boltanski and Chiapello and, more recently, Banet-Weiser identify: if no ends are specified, the logic is empty – *network for what? Brand ourselves for what?* In reopening economics to ethics, and so opening economists' concepts of rationality and freedom to new considerations of value, Sen argues he is merely 'reclaim[ing] for humanity the ground that has been taken from it by various arbitrarily narrow formulations of the demands of rationality'.[159] Nonetheless the foundations of neoliberal discourse are shaken.

Sen's arguments have an implicit connection with the concept of voice. Note Sen's remarks about his mentor Kenneth Arrow, whom he praises for *reinserting voice* into economics, that is, achieving 'the recognition of the "voice" of members of the society in the formulation of social choice and the role that this voice gets in influencing social decisions'.[160] Sen's own work does something similar: the second order value of voice (a 'value about values' in his phrase) blocks the aggregate logic of the market, insisting on the distinctive perspective individuals have on the world in which they live. I develop the connections between Sen's thought and the concept of voice further in Chapter Five.

A new economics?

If modern economics' starting-point need no longer be the competitive individualism of market-players considered in isolation from any other value, new models of economic decision-making are possible. Economists are beginning to take into account different goods, such as the pleasures of 'mutual fellow-feeling' and the importance for humans of relationality and reciprocity,[161] and considering within a framework of economic reasoning the effects of markets on the contexts that sustain those other goods, such as social interaction aimed at helping or cooperating with others.[162] Stefano Zamagni questions whether the narrow instrumentalism of economic reasoning fits how people – especially happy people – actually think:

> The reduction of happiness to the category of utility generates serious explanatory problems, for the simple reason that a large number of social interactions and the great majority of practical decisions *acquire meaning* only thanks to *an absence of instrumentality*.[163]

On this view, far from market operations correcting for a faulty social logic, as US neoliberal doctrine has it, it is the anti-*society* rhetoric of neoliberal doctrine that constitutes bad *economics*.

The increasing divorce discussed by the French sociologist Alain Touraine between 'the economic system (and especially the financial economy) and the social whole to which it should belong'[164] can be seen as the result of a deeper intellectual and moral breakdown: first, the failure of economics not only to predict market malfunction, but *to care about markets' limits* and, second, the failure of whole societies, or at least political systems, to maintain a political grasp on those limits. But Sen's arguments demolish the intellectual respectability of those who would oppose a more 'moral' capitalism on grounds that morality or ethics 'shouldn't interfere with markets'.

This groundswell against neoliberal economics is beginning now to be felt at the level of policy advice. Against the background of profound long-term economic uncertainty – as the head of the European Central Bank put it, 'we live in non-linear times – the classic economic models and theories cannot be applied, and future development cannot be seen' –[165] a report by the New Economics Foundation in the UK, endorsed by Richard Layard, called in January 2009 for new national accounting measures of 'wellbeing',[166] while at an international level the OECD launched in 2008 a global project for 'measuring the progress of societies'.[167] Even those seeking to preserve the lineage back to von Hayek must now emphasize the broader ethics within which he framed his arguments. Here is Nobel Prize winner Edward Phelps:

> It is important to make explicit what Hayek must have believed but did not say ... in a significantly unknown world, an individual's freedoms to experiment, to learn, to explore, to act on impulse, and to test ideas offer personal benefits ... under the heading of *personal growth*: expansion of 'talents' and 'capabilities', widening experience and self-discovery.[168]

Phelps was speaking at a 'New World, New Capitalism' symposium co-chaired by President Sarkozy and Tony Blair. Amartya Sen's reflections from the same symposium – emphasizing economics' basis in a consideration of justice and inequality – were rather different.[169] The symposium was part of the deliberations of the Commission on the Measurement of Economic Performance and Social Progress, reporting to French President Sarkozy and formed in early 2008 with Joseph Stiglitz as Chair, and Amartya Sen as Chair-Adviser. The recommendations of this Commission, published just as this book was being completed (September 2009) are the most important contribution so far to these debates.[170]

Four things are particularly striking about the Commission's final report, leaving aside the important links it opens up between economic measurement and the broader question of environmental sustainability. First, it proposes that gross domestic product, the traditional measure of economic activity which 'mainly measures market production', is not a good measure of '*economic* wellbeing' (Recommendation 1), and should be replaced for many policy purposes by measures of income and consumption. Second, and from that basis, measures of income and consumption should include a valuation of services provided by governments including health care and education (Recommendation 2). Third, more emphasis should be given not just to aggregate figures but to the 'distribution of income consumption and wealth' (Recommendations 4 and 7). Fourth and most radically, a multidimensional definition of broader wellbeing should be used which includes not only material living standards, as just discussed, but many other goods which traditional economics has not measured, including: health, education, personal activities such as work (compare Lane), social connections (compare Layard, Boltanski and Chiapello) and 'political voice and governance'.[171]

Market fundamentalism always claimed underlying values of economics were non-negotiable. But now, from some directions at least, debate about those values has become imaginable, prising open the gap between economics and politics that, as Wendy Brown noted, neoliberal doctrine had slammed shut. Unanswered questions arise about whether our *political* institutions can sustain the debate about economic goals that now seems necessary. As the French forum FAIR ('Forum pour d'autres indicateurs de richesse'), formed in response to the new French Commission, argues in its manifesto:

> To redefine the menu of our national wealth implies, as a pre-condition, an interrogation and the opening up to debate of [questions about] what makes our values, what really counts, what is the meaning in economic exchanges, and about the place granted to the democratic dimension of 'living well together'.[172]

A better economics, in other words, requires a better politics, a politics which has a place for debate about the political (and social) ends of economic processes.

This has further implications for the role of 'voice' and participation not just in economic thinking and (relatedly) in development practice,[173] but in the mainstream political process. However, the critique of neoliberal doctrine cannot safely stop with economics. We must consider also the second, political dimension of the contemporary crisis of voice. This means looking closely at how, for various reasons, neoliberalism proper became embedded not just as an economic but as a *political* ideology, with disturbing consequences for the very practice of democracy. That is the subject of Chapter Three.

Notes

1 Quoted in *The Guardian*, 13 August 2009.
2 Interviewed in *Time*, 6 April 2009.
3 Quoted Skidelsky (2009: 36).
4 Skidelsky (2009: 36).
5 Expert forum convened by Fathom Consulting, quoted in *Financial Times*, 7 August.
6 IMF statement 15 June 2009, quoted in *The Guardian*, 16 June 2009.
7 Blanchflower (2009); World Bank (2009).
8 See Polanyi (1975 [1944]) for classic argument. For recent predictions, see Gray (1998), Soros (1996).
9 Soros (2009), compare Soros (2008); BIS (2009).
10 Finlayson (forthcoming).
11 Quoted in *The Guardian*, 17 March 2009.
12 Rudd (2009).
13 Kaletsky (2009).
14 *The Guardian*, 8 January 2009.
15 Office for National Statistics figures quoted *Sunday Telegraph*, 16 August 2009.
16 For debate, see Chakrabortty (2009), Plender (2009), Elliott (2009b).
17 Bourdieu (1998: 95).
18 Bourdieu (1998: 96), emphasis in original.
19 Harvey (2005: 2).

20 Levi-Faur and Jordana (2005: 7).
21 Foucault (2008).
22 Barry, Osborne and Rose (1996).
23 See also Barry, Osborne and Rose (1996: 10–11), Rose (1999: chapter 4).
24 Foucault (2008: 117).
25 Foucault (2008: 70).
26 Foucault (2008: 28–31).
27 Foucault (2008: 32).
28 Foucault (2008: 63).
29 Foucault (2008: 162).
30 Rancière (2006: 81, 55).
31 Grossberg (2005: 117). See also Giroux (2008).
32 Keane (2009: 856).
33 Foucault (2008: 94–95).
34 Foucault (2008: 121).
35 Foucault (2008: 121).
36 Foucault (2008: 144).
37 Foucault (2008: 148).
38 Von Mises (1983: 182), quoted in Peet (2007: 73).
39 Foucault (2008: 145).
40 Foucault (2008: 148).
41 Foucault (2008: 217).
42 Friedman (1982: 2, added emphasis).
43 Friedman (1982: 12, added emphasis).
44 Friedman (1982: 15).
45 Von Hayek (1960: 29), cf. (1949: 14–15).
46 Hay (2007: chapter 3).
47 Von Hayek (1944: chapter 2; 1960: chapter 1). Cf. Berlin (1958).
48 See respectively, von Hayek (1944: 44), (1949: 107–118) and (1960: chapter 15); and (1944: 158).
49 Peet (2007: 83).
50 Peet (2007: 77–78).
51 Frank (2001: 30, 21).
52 See Frank (2001: chapters 2 and 6).
53 Becker (1991: ix).
54 Foucault (2008: 226).
55 Foucault (2008: 243, 269).
56 Foucault (2008: 246).
57 For example, Posner (2003).
58 Burchell (1996: 27).
59 Foucault (2008: 30).
60 Foucault (2008: 62).
61 Quoted in Foucault (2008: 242–243).
62 Boltanski and Chiapello (2005).
63 Boltanski and Chiapello (2005: 85).
64 Boltanski and Chiapello (2005: 7–8).
65 Boltanski and Chiapello (2005: 371).
66 Boltanski and Chiapello (2005: 372).
67 Boltanski and Chiapello (2005: 371).
68 See Bourdieu (1998), Touraine (2000).
69 See Background Note.
70 Benkler (2006), Jenkins (2006), Leadbeater (2008a).
71 Harvey (2004: 2).
72 Boltanski and Chiapello (2005: 465–466).
73 Fraser (2009: 110–111).
74 Hochschild (1983), Illouz (2007).

75 See www.about-asda.co.uk/inside-asda/our-history.asp.
76 Bunting (2004: 102–107).
77 Virno (2004).
78 Greenhouse (2009), Ehrenreich (2002).
79 Qiu (2009). See also Background Note.
80 Schor (1992).
81 Boltanski and Chiapello (2005: 422), Beck (2000a: 77).
82 Boltanski and Chiapello (2005: 247).
83 For review, see Head (2007).
84 Haigh (2008).
85 Quoted in *Times Higher Education Supplement*, 23 March 2007, 6. For the US university, see Giroux (2007).
86 Boltanski and Chiapello (2005: 71).
87 Boltanski and Chiapello (2005: 85).
88 Boltanski and Chiapello (2005: 421ff).
89 Boltanski and Chiapello (2005: 331 n56).
90 Boltanski and Chiapello (2005: 432), drawing on Power (1997).
91 Boltanski and Chiapello (2005: 379).
92 Boltanski and Chiapello (2005: 377).
93 Boltanski and Chiapello (2005: 461).
94 Pusey (2003: 4).
95 Pusey (2003: 89).
96 Durkheim (2006 [1897]).
97 Pusey (2003: 78).
98 Boltanski and Chiapello (2005: 432), referring to Taylor (1989).
99 Boltanski and Chiapello (2005: 432).
100 Pusey (2003: 63).
101 Boltanski and Chiapello (2005: 471).
102 Banet-Weiser (forthcoming): for an earlier history of self-promotion, see Wernick (1991).
103 Boltanski and Chiapello (2005: 466, 468).
104 Bunting (2004).
105 Sennett (1998: 10).
106 Elster (1985: 74–78).
107 Sennett (1998: 21).
108 Marx (1959: 72).
109 Elster (1985: 100–107).
110 Elster (1985: 100).
111 Hardt and Negri (2006: 111).
112 Terranova (2004: 90).
113 Boltanski and Chiapello (2005: 251).
114 Boltanski and Chiapello (2005: 245–246).
115 Boltanski and Chiapello (2005: 224–225, 231); Aglietta (1998: 69).
116 US Bureau of Labor Statistics, quoted in Lardner (2007: 62).
117 Banet-Weiser (forthcoming); see also Hearn (2008).
118 Layard (2005: 22, 118–125).
119 Layard (2005: 17–18).
120 Layard (2005: 3).
121 Cf. Bruni and Porta (2005: 1).
122 Layard (2005: 31, added emphasis).
123 Layard (2005: 67–69, 137).
124 Layard (2005: 175–180).
125 Layard (2005: 225–226).
126 Scitovsky (1976: vii).
127 Scitovsky (1976: 80).
128 Scitovsky (1976: 8).
129 Scitovsky (1976, chapter 6), cf. Layard (2005: 226).

130 Lane (2000: 324, cf. 94).
131 Lane (2000: chapter 2).
132 Lane (2000: 77).
133 Lane (2000: 81).
134 Lane (2000: 95).
135 Lane (2000: 137).
136 Lane (2000: 159).
137 Lane (2000: 162, added emphasis), cf. Scitovsky (1976: 90).
138 Lane (2000: 328).
139 Hardt and Negri (2006: 157).
140 Sen (1987: 4, 7).
141 Sen (1987: 4, added emphasis).
142 Sen (1987: 22–23), cf. Sugden (2005: 91–94), Rothschild (2001).
143 Sen (1987: 2–3).
144 See Chong (2000); for critique of RCT in political science, see Green and Shapiro (1994).
145 Sen (2002: 28),
146 Sen (2002: 34, numbers added),
147 Becker (1991).
148 Sen (2002: 36–41).
149 Sen (2002: 6).
150 Taylor (1989).
151 Hay (2007: chapter 3, especially 97–99).
152 Sen (2002: 628, cf. chapter 17).
153 Friedman (1982: 12), cf. Downs (1957: 5).
154 Sen (2002: 10, cf. chapter 20).
155 Sen (2002: 10, added emphasis).
156 Sen (2002: 586).
157 See further Chapter Seven below.
158 Sen (2002: 5).
159 Sen (2002: 51).
160 Sen (2002: 591).
161 Sugden (2005) and Zamagni (2005).
162 Sugden (2005: 109).
163 Zamagni (2005: 327, added emphasis).
164 Touraine (2000: 18).
165 Jean-Claude Trichet, quoted in *The Guardian*, 23 February 2009.
166 See www.nationalaccountsofwellbeing.org/public-data/files/national-accounts-of-well-being-report.pdf.
167 For its mission statement, see www.oecd.org/document/5/0,3343,en_40033426_4003734 9_40038469_1_1_1,00.html.
168 Phelps (2009: 5, added emphasis).
169 Sen (2009).
170 Commission on the Measurement of Economic Performance and Social Progress (2008 and 2009).
171 Commission on the Measurement of Economic Performance and Social Progress (2009: 14–15).
172 See www.idies.org/index.php?post/De-la-societe-du-beaucop-avoir-pour-quelquuns-a-une-societe-de-bien-etre-durable-pour-tous [my translation].
173 Tacchi et al. (2009).

Chapter 3

Neoliberal Democracy: An Oxymoron

> There is a strong argument to be made that neoliberal capitalism, in its millennial moment, portends the death of politics by hiding its own ideological underpinnings in the dictates of economic efficiency, in the fetishism of the free market. (Jean and John Comaroff)[1]

> The attempt by institutionally conservative social democrats to reduce progressive politics to the reconciliation of social protection with market flexibility leaves democracy unrealized and fails in its own objective. (Roberto Mangabeira Unger)[2]

Neoliberal doctrine matters beyond the domain of economics because at varying paces and scales over nearly three decades it has been promoted, and then implemented, as a principle for social and political organization. I shall call countries where this has happened systematically and over a long period 'neoliberal democracies'. The consequence has been to install certain fundamental contradictions into the practice of politics and government. This chapter's task is threefold: to explore the contradictions at the heart of the fiction of 'neoliberal democracy'; to explain the multiple forces whereby this fiction has nonetheless come to be lived out in countries such as the UK and the USA, exploring some of the implications for everyday life; and, on the basis of that analysis, to consider how we might think about politics beyond the horizon of neoliberalism.

The story of how 'neoliberalism proper' (the legacy of von Hayek, von Mises and Friedman) grew into a wider hegemonic reference-frame of 'neoliberal doctrine' is hugely complex.[3] On a global scale, the spread of neoliberal doctrine in the form of the Washington consensus provoked a much broader range of resistances than in the UK case, including over the 'globalization' and 'modernization' enforced by the structural adjustment programmes (SAPs) of the World Bank and IMF from the 1980s onwards.[4] We must therefore, as Aiwha Ong insists, allow for the unevenness of neoliberalism's spread on a broader, global scale.[5] But that global complexity does not undermine an important general point: the *paradoxical nature* of neoliberal politics. Take two examples. Writing in the late 1990s, Roberto Unger (then Harvard Law professor and now Brazil's Minister for Strategic Affairs) characterized neoliberalism's global expansion thus: 'this unity [of neoliberal doctrine] is social and political rather than narrowly economic and technical. It is the negative unity of the *disempowerment* of government; it disables the state from interfering with the established order of society'.[6] Writing from South Africa, Achille Mbembe's characterization of the outcome of international creditor demands is, if anything, bleaker: 'the developments now under way ... in Africa are *creating systems* in such an original way that the result is not only debt, the destruction of productive capital, and war, but also the disintegration of the state ... and the radical challenging of it as a "public good", as a general mechanism of rule'.[7]

We find, then, an overlapping set of paradoxes, whether we look to the difficulty of developing alternative forms of modernity in Brazil, or the threat to the stability of African states, or the corrosion of long-existing democratic forms in the UK, and that potential commonality is surely important. It is the third of those specific paradoxes on which I will concentrate here.

Why the UK case matters

The UK case matters for a number of reasons. First, it is a country where neoliberal principles were pioneered as political doctrine by Margaret Thatcher from the late 1970s and applied over nearly three decades, but in increasing tension with other principles, leading to something like political breakdown by the end of the 2000s. Second, the UK has been centrally involved in the global economic and market crisis, as the proposer of 'solutions' and, many argue, one of the key sources for the policies that encouraged the crisis.[8] It is the country most exposed to the long-term costs of addressing that crisis, investing the equivalent of *nearly 20%* of its gross domestic product in supporting its banking sector in the 2008 global financial crisis, more than three times the percentage in the USA or any Western European country except Norway (13.8%).[9] Third, the UK is facing a growing crisis of trust in the political system (most recently, with a long-running scandal over MPs expenses claims) yet, in spite of a widely unpopular government, it remains completely unclear whether the next national election will offer genuine choice beyond the various disguises of neoliberal orthodoxy on offer. The UK therefore provides a good example of what goes wrong when neoliberal doctrine is embedded within established democratic systems.

In British politics over the past three decades – I leave aside Northern Ireland, most political statistics quoted below being compiled on that basis – two processes have been prominent: first, the emerging neoliberal consensus among major political parties, with New Labour from 1997 continuing in many ways (privatization, marketization, the abandonment of wealth redistribution as a political aim, priority given to labour market flexibility) the essential shape of Thatcherite neoliberal policy; second, the shrinking range of effective political actors, resulting from a sharp decline (shared with other countries) of trade unions and large-scale political parties combined with the weakness (distinctive to Britain) of religious and civil society institutions and local government.

The result is a drastically *foreshortened* democratic process whose inadequacies have not escaped the attention of British citizens. Recent national surveys found that as many as 60% agreed that 'people like me have no say in government' (only 25% disagreeing), with more denying than agreeing (42% to 31%) that 'people like me' can change how the country is run *even when they get involved in politics.*[10] Turnout in the 2001 UK general election was at its lowest ever (59%), marginally improving in 2005 (61%). This disenchant- ment particularly affects young people: in the 2005 UK general election only 37% of 18–24 year olds and 48% of 25–34 year olds voted, and *substantially less than 50%* of those age groups said they were certain to vote at the next election.[11] While minority turnout among the young is not unique to the UK,[12] its 'generation gap' in voting propensity is particularly wide.[13] Concerns arise about other groups too: less than half of those in unskilled manual labour or who are unemployed or retired consider themselves certain to vote,[14] while only 47% of ethnic minorities voted in the 2005 election.[15] The problem is reflected more generally in basic levels of contact between British citizens and their political representatives: in 2008 only 15% had 'presented their views to a local councillor or MP in the past two or three years', while in 2006 only 14% had *ever* contacted their MP.[16] One online survey reported that 72% of UK citizens felt 'disconnected' from their political representatives.[17] Yet this is not because British citizens *want* no say in politics: 69% indicate they want a say in 'how the country is run', with only 12% saying they do not.[18]

The British political system now satisfies almost none of its citizens: 92% regard 'the present system of governing Britain' as needing improvement (62% indicating a need for major improvement);[19] note these figures *preceded* the 2009 crisis over MPs' expenses. The problem goes wider than a decline in trust in politicians, bad though the British figures are on that too (71% trust- ing politicians 'not very much' or 'not at all', only 8% generally trusting 'any politician to tell the truth').[20] Between 2003 and 2006, with Sonia Livingstone and Tim Markham, I conducted a study on 'Public Connection' at the London School of Economics. We concluded that the British political system provided insufficient bridges between people's practices of engagement – including their continued (if declining) sense of a duty to follow media – and their sense that government *recognized* that engagement. The result was not so much a crisis of citizen motivation, as 'a recognition crisis, a gap between what citi- zens do, or would like to do, and the state's recognition of what they do'.[21] The outcome is a political process largely unconnected from daily realities, as one of our most civically active 'Public Connection' respondents noted:

> the be all and end all is putting out the story. It isn't delivering anything. It's putting out the perception ... It's all a top thing – it's not at the bottom at all. The reality at the bottom is still totally different. ... But that's of no concern to politicians.[22]

This democratic deficit is most neatly encapsulated by a recent finding that 74% agree that 'government does not spend enough time listening to the views of individual members of the public' (only 7% disagree).[23] Marketing-based politics,[24] as a perceptive ex-marketer (Leon Mayhew) pointed out, risks corroding the communicative trust between government and voters.[25]

A system that provides formal voice for its citizens but *fails so markedly to listen*[26] exhibits a crisis of political voice of the sort we identified in Chapter One: it offers voice (having no choice but to do so) yet retracts it as a reality, so engineering what Manuel Castells has recently called 'a systemic dissociation between communicative power and representative power'.[27]

Where does this leave the legitimacy of political power in Britain? Not surprisingly, the policy community has become worried by this question. The Power Report in March 2006, led by Dame Helena Kennedy QC, expressed concerns at the atrophy of UK local government and low involvement in the British formal political process, rejecting Robert Putnam's idea – that the problem is a decline of social capital and through that civic activism – to reach a more disturbing conclusion: that UK civic engagement *remains healthy*, but the civically engaged are themselves disengaged from, indeed despairing of, the formal political process.[28]

How did the British state react? Neoliberal doctrine after all *requires* a state that can sustain conditions of market competitiveness so the Power Report's criticisms could not safely be ignored (as Foucault made clear, neoliberalism is *not* the same as nineteenth-century *laissez faire*).[29] The UK government's response, however, has been constrained by a neoliberal view of how democratic politics works. In July 2008 New Labour's Department of Communities and Local Government published an outline of potential legislation or 'White Paper' (*Communities in Control: Real People, Real Power*). Two gaps in the White Paper are striking. First, while it contains much detail on how local decision-making might be made more inclusive – participatory budgets and more local negotiation of police crime reduction priorities[30] – no attention is given to how such reformed local government might connect or challenge with *other levels of government*, whether national or regional. In a political system whose local government commentators from all sides consider very weak[31] – in 2004–5 almost three-quarters of local government income came from central government distributions[32] – this is surely the essential point. Second, the role that the White Paper imagines for local citizens is largely confined to that of local services *user*: little attention is given to how local citizens might challenge local policy, let alone debate national policy and the way *that* impinges on local decision-making:

> Unless we empower citizens to exercise the same level *of choice* in our democratic system and have the same rights *to demand the best*, then we will oversee a further erosion of trust and participation in democracy.[33]

Consumerist language conveniently pushes the possibility of direct challenge to politicians' decisions out of view: the only issues at stake are 'value for money' or 'passing the delivery and ownership of [that is, responsibility for] services directly to voters themselves'.[34] The impoverishment of this thinking emerges vividly when the White Paper claims as a success for democracy the high percentage of parents in one of London's poorest boroughs who apply *online* for secondary school places for their children![35] Yet parents' need to apply for secondary school places was *imposed* by government through the introduction of a quasi-market system. Only a neoliberal doctrine which reduces governments' responsibility for social policy to according 'everyone [an] ... economic space within which they can take on and confront risks [as individuals]'[36] sees citizens' exercise of required 'freedoms' in new ways as an extension of democracy.

Recent UK government proposals for people to leave comments about doctor, police and childcare services on government-sponsored websites are equally superficial.[37] The legitimacy of a political system cannot be rescued by allowing small elements of 'interactivity', or even devolved decision-making, while paying only symbolic attention (for example, through e-petitions to the Prime Minister)[38] to whether the political system *as a whole* offers adequate accountability of government to citizens. 'Communities in control' is at best a convenient fiction,[39] when trumped by the neoliberal imperative to centralize power in a state that guarantees or extends market competition.

These tensions would be of limited interest if they were the peculiar result of one nation-state's tensions. But they are exactly the tensions that constitutional theorist Philip Bobbitt sees as inherent to the 'market-state'. Writing in 2003 in the immediate aftermath of entry into the Iraq war, Bobbitt announced the superseding of the nation-state by the 'market-state' as world markets are restructured on supra-national lines. The nation-state is reduced, Bobbitt argues, to the status of 'a bear chained to a stake, trying to chase a shifting beam of light'.[40] National governments' aims shift from maximizing the welfare of citizens to maximizing populations' opportunities for participation in a global market; policy aims such as employment and currency stability become subsidiary to enhancing individual economic opportunity within that larger global space.[41] The result is drastic: the state for Bobbitt becomes 'largely indifferent to norms of justice, *or for that matter any particular set of moral values* so long as law does not act as an impediment to economic competition'.[42]

However, Bobbitt is sensitive to the political contradictions that result. For the offer of participation in government cannot be completely abandoned. Instead it becomes contradictory: 'there will be more public participation in government, but it will count for less'.[43] Yet the market-state still needs legitimacy for its coercive power required to sustain security and markets.[44] More than that, the market-state must still, somehow, produce what Bobbitt calls the 'public goods' that the market 'is not well adapted to creating or maintaining': these public goods are 'loyalty, civility, trust in authority, respect for family life'.[45] So Bobbitt lets in through the back door the whole domain of the social that orthodox neoliberalism had expelled through the front door.

And so we reach the underlying paradox of neoliberal politics: that neoliberal doctrine requires a politics that its principles simultaneously disable and disavow. The resulting *oxymoron* 'neoliberal democracy' is not a simple or predictable set of contradictions, as Unger notes,[46] but the contradictions are no less important for all that.

Let us now explore in greater detail how in Britain the oxymoron of neoliberal democracy developed, noting along the way the paradoxical consequences for social policy and justice. My claim will not be that everything that has gone wrong in Britain over the past three decades is neoliberalism's fault – or that everything *has* gone wrong in Britain – only that important connections exist between the contradictions of neoliberal democracy and the state of Britain today (I come to the USA later).

The historical emergence of neoliberal politics

How did the principles of neoliberal economics get transformed into a model for politics and government?[47]

Principles

Milton Friedman's approach to government wears its paradoxes lightly. Friedman's philosophy of freedom was not just an affirmation of market principles but, drawing on the long tradition of US liberalism, a challenge to the legitimacy of the state and the governance of the social. In *Capitalism and Freedom*, Friedman gives a non-exhaustive list of things that governments actually do but *should not*: some are expected (import quotas, rent controls, detailed industry regulation), others are more chilling (compulsory social security programmes or national insurance, public housing programmes, publicly owned roads, a legal minimum wage).[48] Friedman's restricted notion of government rests on two normative principles. First, there is no end at which governments can aim beyond the freedom of each individual citizen to pursue his or her own benefits within markets; there is, accordingly, *no meaning* to the notion of public or social goals. Second, even if there was a 'social interest', it is unknowable, so there is no point either individuals or corporations aiming at it.[49] This is a bold normative position which, as we saw in Chapter Two, hesitates only at the point of whether it is the individual, or perhaps the family, that is the ultimate reference-point for the value of freedom.

The normative confidence of US neoliberalism was not necessarily shared by the earlier Austro-German version. In post-World War II Germany a number of factors combined:[50] the gathering of German and Austrian economists who had been sceptical since the Weimar period of the effectiveness of state interventions in markets; the need of politicians to renew the German state *ex nihilo* and to find in the 'free market' principles of state operation which could command wide acceptance in the ruins of Nazi Germany, in part by rejecting the subordination of economy to state under Nazi rule.[51] In this exceptional context, the political options for economic policy became polarized into a choice, as Foucault puts it, between liberal 'free-market' politics and 'any other form whatsoever of economic interventionism', with a rejection of free market principles being identified with the risk of returning to the worst excesses of the state under Nazism.[52] On this basis, the market was seen as a more plausible source of social order than a discredited German state,[53] but, as we saw in Chapter Two, von Hayek's defence of market freedom was less extreme in its hostility to the state than Friedman's.

The early impetus behind US neoliberalism had been the growing criticism among economists from the mid 1930s of Roosevelt's interventionist policy in the New Deal era. Intellectual connections just before the outbreak of World War II between German and US economists and political scientists (including even the non-neoliberal US political theorist, Walter Lippman) were important, Foucault argues. But neoliberal thought remained isolated from the US political mainstream during the 1950s and 1960s, as Friedman notes ruefully in the preface to the second edition of *Capitalism and Freedom*. It was only in the mid to late 1970s that neoliberals, led by Milton Friedman and Friedrich von Hayek, acquired prominence among right-wing politicians such as Ronald Reagan and Margaret Thatcher. One important part of that context, at which Foucault hints, was the increasing concern in the early 1970s, particularly among conservative thinkers, at the 'ungovernability' of democracy.[54] This was the time of final crisis for Keynesian pacts of social and economic planning,[55] as labour–state conflicts came increasingly to impinge upon political order and state legitimacy.

Neoliberalism and long-term processes of rationalization

Let's examine the paradoxical form of democratic governance that emerged from this shift, approaching it first from the point of view of techniques of government. At first sight, neoliberal doctrine in its Friedmanite form is about the withdrawal of government, not its extension. So the market is imagined as a space of 'unconstrained' choices by 'autonomous' rationally calculating agents who are simply seeking the best way of satisfying their *individual* ends, while the actions of the state and state agencies, whether or not grounded in popular representation, are seen as the imposition of power on the space of individual choice. As Milton Friedman put it:

> The fundamental threat to freedom is power to coerce ... the preservation of freedom requires the elimination of such concentration of power to the fullest possible extent ... By removing the organization of economic activity from the control of political authority, the market eliminates this source of *coercive* power.[56]

What cannot be avoided, however, even for neoliberalism, are the consequences for freedom of the means through which marketization is introduced.

Neoliberalism's prioritization of market logics *as a principle of government* could not have been effective if it had not, paradoxically, built upon a longer-term process of intensified rationalization, in the course of which new techniques of power emerged whereby market discourse could more easily be actualized as a mode of governance or government-at-a-distance. Neoliberal doctrine was not the only force behind the shift from 'state provision' to 'market functioning' in the 1980s. There were broader factors: the increasing unmanageability of government's practical challenges as then defined, the profound discrediting of elaborate models of state economic management owing to the collapse of state communism in Eastern Europe in the late 1980s. The 'degovernmentalization of the state'[57] required techniques, and one was the increasing reliance on *numerical targets* which we discuss in more detail in Chapter Four in connection with the mediatization of government.

Behind this shift lies not only a broader growth in calculability across social life which has been developing since the nineteenth century,[58] but more distinctively the installation of *auditing* – and the monetization on which it is based – as the key tool of government. Michael Power's analysis of the 'audit explosion'[59] in Britain from the late 1980s (from the height of Margaret Thatcher's political influence) links not only to the increasing prevalence of public choice theory within the policy domain,[60] but also to neoliberal doctrine's need, discussed in Chapter Two, for increased, not decreased, regulation as the means of securing market conditions. But Power goes further and identifies audit as the key *cultural* mechanism through which abstract market norms are translated into wider social practice. Auditing, Power notes, 'works by virtue of *actively creating* the external organizational environment in which it operates'.[61] The result has been to transform every level of public resource provision, through a 'managerial transformation of organizational governance which must assume *a priori* the efficacy of different forms of auditing'; the resulting dominance of 'value for money' discourse enabled a wider shift of 'evaluative culture' in UK government 'away from social scientific towards managerial knowledge bases'.[62] The rationales for this transformation were of course multiple: aspects of the transformation could be defended on the grounds of greater transparency in government, even democratization. But this, Power argues, ignores the bias towards norms of calculation when auditing is installed as the dominant reference-point for government:

> The audit process requires trust in experts and is not a basis for rational public deliberation. It is *a dead end in the claim of accountability* ... more accounting and auditing does not necessarily mean more and better accountability ... this promise is at best ambiguous ... audit is in this respect *a substitute for democracy* rather than its aid.[63]

The resulting transformations reinforce the role of non-deliberative techniques in the governmental process. This becomes of much wider importance for democracy when, as happened intensively in Britain, the shift towards marketization is driven by wider transnational pressures.

Market-driven politics

Neoliberal doctrine has, over the past 20 years, become embodied in a new form of transnational politics that Colin Leys calls 'market-driven politics'.[64] By 'markets', Leys first means global investment markets, but the outcome of market-driven politics is practices of directed marketization under which whole fields of society and government action are made ripe for transformation in accordance with market principles. This shift in the global context of national government is hugely complex[65] and I can only give here the barest outline, drawing on Leys' brilliant account. Leys identifies two explicit political factors which drastically reduced the possibilities of national politicians adopting principles other than those that supported the functioning and extension of global markets.

First, there are the structural factors which have drastically reduced the influence of national governments over national economies, leading to what Leys calls an 'internationalised state'.[66] Such a state is, in most situations, considerably weaker in bargaining power and financial muscle than most transnational corporations, and in all situations massively weaker than global capital and foreign exchange markets. (Let's defer for the moment the question of how far, and in what sense, the global financial crisis has changed this.) Many factors coincided in the emergence of market-driven politics in the UK case: the liberalization of capital flows in the late 1970s, in which the Thatcher government played a leading role; the liberalization of ownership of national financial sectors (following London's Big Bang in 1986), the huge growth in capital markets linked to the growth of ever more complex speculative investment instruments; huge growth of overall dealings on global financial markets. Foreign direct investment became not only easier (through increased mobility of capital and faster transnational communications) but also more 'necessary' to spread risks and minimize costs in a liberalized trade environment.

More important than increases in international trade (comparisons with the early twentieth century are ambiguous)[67] is the increasing *transnationalization of national economies*. This process was particularly acute in Britain. Leys draws on UNCTAD figures from the late 1990s which show the UK as then having the highest percentage among what he calls 'major OECD countries' of productive capacity and fixed capital investment sourced from foreign transnationals.[68] More recent figures intensify the pattern Leys identified. If we look at foreign direct investment (expressed as a percentage of gross domestic product), by 2007 this had grown in the UK to *nearly 50%* from 19% in 1997; among the major OECD countries Britain remains, by this measure, the most dependent on transnational investment, having long since overtaken Australia and Canada (the comparable US figure incidentally was a mere 15%). If we consider inward transnational investment as a percentage of fixed capital formation, the widening between major countries is even more dramatic: in the UK by 2007 this had trebled since 1997 to 45%, a percentage to which only one other large OECD country came close (France, 29%).[69] Other factors (for example, the high dependence of the UK economy on the intensely internationalized banking and finance sectors) only reinforce these trends.

The overall outcome of all these shifts was both the steadily diminishing influence of national governments such as the UK over their domestic economic policy and the growth of specific pressures towards adopting policies specifically favourable to markets: remember Bobbitt's image of the chained bear chasing a light beam. Equally, policies that go in a direction markets 'won't like' attract a political premium on the bond markets, with immediate and drastic consequences for national governments' costs of borrowing.[70] These various influences are non-negotiable, operating seemingly beyond the margins of national political deliberation. The resulting conflict between the logic of capital accumulation and the political requirement of legitimation[71] is barely registered on the surface of everyday politics. Instead, under market-driven politics, the nature of politics itself changes. As Leys puts it, 'politics are no longer about managing the economy to satisfy the demands of voters, they are increasingly about getting voters to endorse policies that meet the demands of capital'.[72]

Even so, the transformation of the political field requires a *second* set of transformations in specific sectors, especially those involved with state resource provision. Social relations in specific sectors need to be 'adapted' if they are to be marketized. In Britain, once again, this was a complex process: the divestment during the 1980s and 1990s of many state assets; the dispersal of the state's regulatory and management resources into a mass of state agencies; the decline, hastened by government, of trade unions which might otherwise have resisted these changes; and the huge cultural and political work necessary, often against the resistance of relevant professionals, to implement the marketization of particular sectors of public provision. The latter included shifts at the level of discourse – for example, addressing recipients of public services as 'customers', not 'patients', 'travellers', 'students', and so on; renaming providers of public services (for example, groups of doctors) as 'purchasers' 'free to buy' from other health 'providers' – but they also included the shifts, already noted, in techniques of government. Only strong mechanisms, such as audit culture, could explain how in the lengthy, still incomplete reforms of the UK national health service, dentists were at one point given precisely 18 minutes maximum to treat any filling for a child; or consultants were discouraged from entering into research or even sharing information with 'competitors'.[73]

Yet the marketization has arguably led to increased costs and reduced cost controls. In the UK National Health Service, the benefits for patients are at least unproven and widely doubted.[74] In the schools sector, the introduction of comparative data on school performance – and the resulting 'league tables' that media generate from those figures – were criticized in Layard and Dunn's *Good Childhood* report (quoted in Chapter One) for getting in the way of educational provision,[75] even though market-based consumer 'choice' precisely *requires* such information flows. Meanwhile, in spite of some attempts to generate 'a stronger local voice' (to quote the title of one Department of Health document),[76] government language for public services remains dominated by the consumer-based discourse of 'interactivity' and competitive 'choice', a bizarre hybrid of Friedmanite market liberalism and management-speak. Writing here are the advocates of the new strategy of making public services more 'personal':

> In the 1990s management techniques borrowed from the corporate sector were introduced to drive improvement in public services through target-setting and tighter performance management. These initiatives rely on the know-how of a small group of central policy-makers and target-setters to redesign a service ... [But] *self-directed services* instead mobilise thousands of people *to set targets* that are relevant to them.[77]

But what if this whole approach to organizing public services generates different priorities from those that people want? What if it ignores the insight of economist Kenneth Arrow that 'media care cannot conform to market laws because patients are not ordinary consumers and doctors are not ordinary vendors'?[78] And what if underlying it is a shift away from the model of a 'democratically accountable public service' to 'a full health-care market' on which voters have never been consulted at all?[79] Such questions fall outside neoliberal logics of consumer choice entirely. Instead, 'market mimicry'[80] is imposed on public service provision, occluding other policy priorities.

You might argue that the global financial crisis has already stopped market-driven politics dead in its tracks. Certainly the crisis of the global financial markets has placed governments and central banks in the place of lenders of last resort to shore up commercial banks' and finance corporations' damaged balance sheets, purchase tainted assets and, in many cases, take over majority ownership of large market players. In the short term, this gave national governments some (limited) bargaining power over large transnational corporations, but for the longer term governments' capacity to act independently of market pressures has *reduced*, not increased; the imperatives of policy – and the destinations of vast amounts of state resources – have become ever more closely tied to market expectations. And none of this reversed the progressive marketization of public services in the UK under way for two decades. Indeed, the depletion of state funds (now drastic in the UK) can only intensify future competition among public services for what is left of government finances.

The social costs of neoliberal politics

We have seen how market-driven politics, once installed in the UK, has brought various paradoxes of accountability in its wake under both Conservative and New Labour governments. But what of the distinctive paradoxes in which a social democratic party (New Labour) became embroiled when it pursued a strategy of ameliorating marketization's consequences for 'social protection' (see Unger quote at the start of this chapter)? For New Labour *did not* simply continue the policy of Conservative administrations (Margaret Thatcher, John Major); it presided over a large *increase* in public expenditure in areas such as health and education and has introduced important innovations in social policy, for example the much praised Sure Start programme, which attempts to coordinate better the childcare and other services available to parents and children.[81] The most authoritative analysis of the impacts of New Labour on UK inequality insists that they were at least uneven, with some significant successes.[82] However, this was within a policy framework that in other ways insisted on free market principles and an increasing push towards marketization. The resulting paradoxes are again not accidental but inherent to neoliberal democracy, and so deserve wider attention.

Legal theorist Philip Bobbitt, as we saw, noted that, unless the market-state *corrects* for the limits of the market by producing various public goods, it will lack the legitimacy and authority on which its effective running depends.[83] The UK New Labour government from 1997 provides a particularly interesting example since, on the one hand, its key advisers were unquestionably influenced by market populism and neoliberal doctrine generally;[84] on the other hand, its social democratic history required New Labour, when they continued the neoliberal project, to adopt a different balance from the Thatcher, Reagan or Bush governments.

From the beginning, New Labour emphasized its commitment to aspects, at least, of social justice and adopted a minimum wage policy that went directly against Friedmanite doctrine. In looking back on the outcome of neoliberal politics under UK's New Labour, what matters is to bring out long-term trends of wider significance, rather than pay close attention to the historic debates out of which New Labour policy emerged. A few qualifications, however, must be made. First, even if retrospectively we are entitled to emphasize the continuities of the Blair/Brown governments with the preceding Conservative neoliberal project, a key mediating process was the development on the left of 'Third Way' thinking which, after the fall of European communist regimes, cleared new ground for left politics, but from the starting-point of capitalism's inevitability.[85] Second, the political strategies of New Labour were informed from the start by a pessimism about the future of traditional party politics that, in some respects, connected with the deep scepticism towards the rationality of political participation in neoliberal and public choice theory.[86] Third, the interface between New Labour's inherited social democratic principles (for example, that of social justice) and neoliberal doctrine was sometimes quite complex.[87] While von Hayek and Friedman insisted that social justice was not a legitimate aim of the state,[88] New Labour was explicit in maintaining some links to its historic aim of social justice, for example in welfare policy, where continuities can be found between the 1994 Labour-sponsored Commission on Social Justice and its regime a decade later for encouraging (many would say pressurizing) welfare-receivers into work.[89] But the overlaying of market and social democratic discourse needs careful unpacking. Ruth Levitas's detailed analysis brings out how the social justice element in New Labour's 'social exclusion' policies was limited to the principle that everyone should have, indeed should be required to take up, the opportunity to enter the job market; any wider redistribution to correct for the *consequences* of the functioning of labour or other markets was missing from this thin principle of social justice.[90]

Such tensions become more acute in other areas. Let's start with labour market flexibility. This has been a key emphasis of the New Labour government from the beginning, which continued the UK's opt-out from the Social Chapter of the European Union's Maastricht Treaty that provided various social protections against the unfettered operation of labour markets. We have already touched in Chapter Two on the social costs of the overwork culture endemic in intensely marketized economies. Britain has one of the highest percentages of workers working over 48 hours per week;[91] by 2007, the numbers of such workers had started rising steeply again, while almost 25% of UK workers were considering or already taking a sabbatical from work.[92] Respect for family is one of the key goods Bobbitt argues states must still protect, so we are entitled to ask: what are the consequences of this for 'family life'? Various statistics suggest considerable disenchantment: in early 2007, 82% of respondents to a survey by the Equal Opportunities Commission said it was difficult for parents to balance work with home life, most expecting the problem to get worse, while the British Social Attitudes Report found that more than 80% of full-time working men and women wanted to spend more time with their family, and 77% of full-time working men (67% of women) wanted to spend more time with their friends.[93]

How can we not connect this with the 'pervasive anxiety about the current educational and social contexts' which Cambridge University researchers found in parents of UK primary school children in 2007?[94] There are worrying indications in relation to other age-groups: a Nuffield Foundation report found a nearly 40% rise between 1986 and 2006 in the UK of 16 year-olds who said they had no best friend; one South Tyneside teacher referred to a 'culture of pessimism' among 11–12 year-old pupils just starting secondary school;[95] while mental illness among young people is not only rising, but three times as likely among 'unskilled' families as among 'professional' families.[96] Most prominently, a much cited 2007 UNICEF report placed the UK *bottom* out of 21 rich countries on a multidimensional indicator of child wellbeing, noting that in 2001 Britain was one of only two countries where less than half of children found their peers 'kind and helpful'.[97] To New Labour's credit, on some of the UNICEF indicators, including peer helpfulness,[98] there had been *improvements* by 2005–6. Meanwhile one former New Labour adviser, Geoff Mulgan, is working with economist Richard Layard to develop a 'Local Wellbeing Project', which will include work with school children.[99]

A second area is inequality. Here the tension has been acute. While inequality was unquestionably a target of New Labour policy from the outset, reductions in inequality were pursued in a limited form: New Labour's market principles forbad the pursuit of social justice or greater socioeconomic equality at the expense of interfering with market functioning at the top end of the income range. And so New Labour has resolutely stood out *against* increasing taxes on high-income earners on the good neoliberal ground that it would discourage wealth creation. Indeed, the UK in the 2000s saw a continued increase in the spectacle of wealth. A simple index is the 75% increase in helicopters registered in New Labour Britain, the helicopter being the transport method of choice for the super-rich in the UK and elsewhere.[100] More substantively, there were many indicators even before the revelations of the current financial crisis that executive pay was out of control. In the year to November 2007, CEOs of some companies listed in the second tier of the London Stock Exchange ('AIM') were paid more *in a year* than their companies' *stock market valuation*.[101] But trends of this sort did not alarm the New Labour government, notwithstanding the worrying parallels with the USA, where CEO pay rose after 1997 to a multiple of 150–300 times that of average worker pay.[102] On the contrary, Business and Enterprise Secretary John Hutton argued five months later that:

> Rather than questioning whether huge salaries are morally justified, we should celebrate the fact that people can be enormously successful in this country. Rather than placing a cap on that success, we should be questioning why it is not available to more people ... I believe a key challenge for New Labour over the coming years is to recognise that, far from

> strengthening social justice, a version of equality that only
> gives you the opportunity to climb so far, actually subverts the
> values we should be representing.[103]

So by this impeccably Friedmanite logic, *greater* inequality becomes a sign of *stronger* values. The Minister had the grace to add that New Labour's target for halving child poverty by 2010–11 would not be abandoned.

However, by this point many believed that target had little chance of being attained. New Labour's early announcement of targets for the reduction of child poverty was deservedly praised. But the policy of child poverty reduction has had limited success: not only has the percentage of children living in poverty (those with working parents, or a sole working parent) risen by a third since New Labour came to power, but the number of UK children in poverty has started to rise again since the mid 2000s (the UK continues to have one of the highest rates of child poverty in Europe, the only 'improvement' between 1998 and 2006 being that Italy and Spain's rates caught up with the UK's).[104] Even if social mobility is not declining, as many have argued, Britain's leading analyst of class stratification suggests that *downward mobility* predominates over upward mobility.[105] Most importantly, overall economic inequality in Britain has *increased* under New Labour, using a technical measure of inequality that the New Labour government itself recognizes: the Gini coefficient.[106] This has increased from 33 to 36 since New Labour came to power (a small increase compared with that under the previous Conservative government, but an increase nonetheless). Behind those figures lies an increase of the richest fifth's share of the UK population's total disposable income from 40.5 to 43.1 since 1996/7, all other groups suffering a fall in their share.[107] In terms of income distribution, the UK had (based on slightly older figures) twice the level of inequality in Germany and Sweden and three times that in Japan, with the top decile's purchasing power being nearly 14 times more than that of the bottom decile.[108] Major inequality remains a significant social fact about the UK, which has followed an 'enlightened' neoliberal policy framework, even if on some measures it can be argued that focused action by the New Labour government has had beneficial effects.[109]

However, the stubborn fact of inequality is often dismissed by neoliberal commentators on the ground that wealth creation takes priority. This ignores the growing evidence (particularly Wilkinson and Pickett's much-cited research) that the more unequal societies are, the worse their *general* health and other problems.[110] Certainly, more unequal societies (the UK and the USA) have lower life expectancy, and lower expectancy of years in good health, than less unequal societies (Germany, Sweden, Japan).[111] Inequality in life expectancy has *increased* under New Labour (and especially for men) after a period of reducing inequality since the mid 1970s which *continued* during the Thatcher years.[112] Geography is important here too. Percentages of the population reporting themselves in 'poor health' were, in 2007, considerably higher in North East England (10.4%) compared with South East England (5.9%).[113] And while there was an overall fall in suicides across the UK between 1991 and 2004, that figure masks significant variations: the suicide rate for every

100,000 men fell in England from 19.8 to 16.7, but *rose* in Scotland (from 29.1 to 30) to nearly double the rate in England.[114]

It is when we turn to the links between inequality *and social values* that the paradoxes of neoliberal politics become most apparent. First, recall the UK concerns mentioned at the end of Chapter One at excessive individualism, which Layard and Dunn relate to greater social inequality.[115] If we want other signs of a reduction in cooperative values – remember 'civility', another of the essential 'public goods' Bobbitt identifies – they are not hard to find. There is the 'pervasive anxiety about a deterioration in the everyday interactions between [adult] strangers' that UK social commentator Madeleine Bunting notes; the evidence of reduced inter-adult tolerance in a *fivefold* increase in complaints against noisy neighbours recorded by the Office for National Statistics Social Trends survey over the past two decades;[116] while cash-strapped local authorities in the UK are unable to provide basic levels of care to the elderly, with three-quarters planning in late 2007 to *refuse* care unless elderly people's needs were 'substantial'.[117] In various ways, then, the UK has become not only a bad place in which to bring up children, but a society where social interaction and care at all levels are being corroded.

Finally, Bobbitt argues, government in a market-state needs to find ways of generating 'loyalty' and 'trust in authority'. In January 2009 the New Economics Foundation reported, using European Social Survey figures, that 'trust and belonging' among all UK age-groups under the age of 50 was the lowest in Europe.[118] Similar concerns arise with contemporary Britain's 'culture' of government. Not only do UK citizens mistrust their government (that has been growing also in many developed countries), they mistrust each other, a measure which has increased markedly in the UK in recent decades.[119] Even more striking is the UK *government's* increasing suspicion of its own population.[120] Both national and local UK government have increasingly based political management less on cooperation and consent than on the mechanisms of a 'surveillance society', relying on the world's most extensive public surveillance system, which extends not just to streets and other public spaces but even into school classrooms.[121] This risks undermining still further public trust, and possibly the effectiveness of public services too: some argue that service workers retreat from 'engaging with others because official restrictions discourage it',[122] a sign both of intense work surveillance and of the impacts of targets within that control culture (on which see Chapter Four).

There is plenty of evidence, then, that neoliberal democracy, even *or especially* in its enlightened, 'softened' forms such as in New Labour Britain, is contradictory. Worse, if we follow Bobbitt's analysis, it is *self-harming*. This might be tolerable, if neoliberal democracy allowed a wide range of political options, some of which explicitly contested neoliberal policy: the issue then would be why those policy alternatives had been rejected by the electorate. In countries where neoliberal doctrine has been embedded less intensively, this remains possible, as in France where the consistent resistance to President Sarkozy's market-based reforms (on civil service pensions, universities, the economy generally) shows that no social pact yet exists to authorize neoliberalism as normal. As a banner of the *lycée* pupils union in January 2009 demonstrations put it vividly: 'We refuse to be the children of the financial crisis!'[123] But, as we saw earlier in the chapter, the hegemony of neoliberal doctrine in the UK has long since marginalized such alternatives. If the market-state fails even to generate the critical opposition that it needs to rescue itself from its own contradictions, then there is nothing, it seems, to interrupt neoliberalism's crisis of voice.

Neoliberal democracy: US style

Although my main attention has been on the UK as a symptomatic case, we must also discuss the USA, if more briefly, because it represents not only the principal recent source of neoliberal doctrine, but in the Bush era the radicalization of the tendencies experienced in the UK without any attempt to ameliorate the consequences. For the sake of argument, I will focus on the more extreme trends: it is not my claim, however, that the dominance of market rationality in the USA is total, since the spread of neoliberal hegemony meets a variety of resistances in every country.

In the USA of George W. Bush, against the background of a much longer history of market liberalism, it was possible by outright denial almost to ignore for eight years neoliberalism's crisis of political voice. In the economic sphere, until the mid 2008 crisis, the Bush regime relied on a claim of economic growth in a country where levels of poverty and inequality far outstripped anything experienced in the UK or indeed in any other major OECD country.[124] The result over time was that popular dissatisfaction at the direction of American society came, by August 2008, to reach unprecedented proportions (90%), for which Edward Luce, US correspondent of the *Financial Times*, offered this explanation:

> [P]art of [the reason] was because the latest period of economic growth failed to create jobs at nearly the same rate as in previous business cycles and even led to a *decline* in the number of hours worked for most employees. Unusually for a time of expansion, the number of participants in the labour force also fell. But mostly it was because the fruits of economic growth and soaring productivity rates went to the highest income earners.[125]

Reliance on economic statistics which only measured overall GDP, and ignored social factors such as inequality, wealth distribution, and even employment levels, had created a complete disconnect between government discourse and working people's experience of the economy, in a period from the late 1990s and 2000s when the latter gained little or nothing (as Paul Krugman put it laconically: 'economic growth' became 'a spectator sport').[126]

But that was not the worst. Under the special circumstances of the 'War on Terror', the Bush regime sought increasingly to act as if its initial, and highly contested, political legitimacy overrode any need for legal legitimacy. Its culture of illegality (or 'exceptionalism')[127] has been extensively analysed. Leaving aside the wide use of torture[128] both by US agents and other states selected for the purpose through 'extraordinary rendition' – in which many suspect the UK government was shamefully implicated – there was also a disturbing attitude to questions of legality in general. On the one hand, torture committed in Guantanamo Bay was argued to be exempt from a federal statute (on torture committed overseas) because Guantanamo was part of US territory, yet in cases from Guantanamo inmates before the US courts, the US administration argued that Guantanamo lay outside the USA (under Cuban sovereignty).[129] John Yoo of the US Justice Department's Office of Legal Counsel achieved notoriety through his August 2002 memorandum stating that the President could not be barred from ordering torture in wartime because under the US Constitution, acts of the President 'Commander-in-Chief' committed in pursuit of war cannot be restricted by any law or treaty.[130] Bush, meanwhile, had abrogated to himself the power to designate any American citizen as an enemy combatant and imprison him or her in solitary confinement without access to legal advice.[131] More generally, while every President can issue 'signing statements' overturning aspects of passed legislation, Bush exercised it more than 800 times in his first six years in office, against 600 exercises of that power by all previous presidents taken together.[132]

Where did this leave democracy in America? Neoliberal legal theorist Richard Posner argued that with few exceptions – he drew the line at the arbitrary naming of US citizens as enemy combatants – all was fine. Bush's actions were justified through a *cost-balancing* exercise that weighed an overwhelming threat to national security versus the speculative costs to individuals of constitutional impropriety.[133] Other commentators have taken a different view. Historian Tony Judt is worth quoting at length:

> There is a precedent in modern Western history for a country whose leader exploits national humiliation and fear to restrict public freedoms; for a government that makes permanent war as a tool of state policy and arranges for the torture of its political enemies; for a ruling class that pursues divisive social goals under the guise of national 'values' ... for a political system in which the dominant party manipulates procedural rules and threatens to change the law in order to get its own way ... Europeans in particular have experienced such a regime in the recent past and they have a word for it. That word is not 'democracy'.[134]

Judt wisely avoids specifying that other word. Robert Paxton's book *The Anatomy of Fascism* made clear that the Bush regime fell far short of any definition of fascism, not least because fascism subordinated economic policy to national politics, as the Austrian ordoliberals recognized.[135] Meanwhile, Sheldon Wolin provoked controversy just after the invasion of Iraq by arguing that the US system had spawned an 'inverted totalitarianism', with corporate power appropriating the state for its own authoritarian ends.[136]

Maybe the exact word we choose for the outcome of neoliberal politics, whether in the UK's conflicted version or in Bush's supercharged version, matters little. For the key point is simple: whatever other name we give it, *'democracy' operated on neoliberal principles is not democracy*. For it has abandoned, as unnecessary, a vision of democracy as a form of social organization in which government's legitimacy is measured by the degree to which it takes account of its citizens' particular voices. Interestingly, Richard Posner makes this explicit: 'democracy is not ... self-rule'; 'politics is ancillary, not ultimate', mere 'jawing in the agora' that is unproductive beyond intermittently monitoring to check government isn't doing anything completely out of line;[137] political apathy, by contrast, may be a good thing, disguising a broad acceptance of 'the system we have'.[138] There is, I acknowledge, an important sceptical line of argument that might support Posner's position: the argument that a minimalist 'monitorial' democracy is all we are ever likely to get and so, notwithstanding its limitations, should be celebrated for its realism.[139] Rational choice theory (whose underlying flaws we discussed in Chapter Two) provides technical support for the details of this argument,[140] but at the cost of a new flaw: it assumes that what we have here *is* democracy, that citizens *can* rely on their ability to influence governments' actions through the exercise of political voice. But my argument in this chapter has been that the contradictions of neoliberal democracy run so deep that it cannot be safely monitored from a distance. Neoliberal democracy is not a version of democracy at all, but an example of how a particular *illusion* of democracy can be sustained.[141] That illusion works not just in general terms, but in a highly racialized way, as the profound unconcern of US government on various levels at the distress of the poor, mainly black population trapped in New Orleans during the Katrina catastrophe of August 2005 demonstrated to the world.[142] The formal democratic process, meanwhile, as under Bush and Cheney's extremism, becomes prey to ever more alarming neoconservative adaptations.[143] Neoliberalism, in Colin Crouch's succinct phrase, risks installing an era of 'post-democracy'.[144]

The importance of this neoliberal trajectory away from democracy is not altered by the hope invested in the presidential candidacy of Barack Obama and his new presidency. Even if our starting-point is not the alienation from government in the Bush era, but instead the striking rise in engagement and participation in the 2008 election by young people and African-Americans,[145] on many policy issues Obama's stance towards neoliberalism remains ambivalent.[146]

We return to whether the Obama mobilization of autumn 2008 offers signs of a permanent reversal of neoliberal politics in Chapter Seven. Meanwhile I want to ask: do theoretical resources exist for rethinking democracy beyond the horizon of neoliberalism, for imagining democracy *in the present* once more?

Rethinking democracy

Let's start with some recent attempts to reconsider the mechanics of government. Behavioural economist Richard Thaler and law professor Cass

Sunstein's book *Nudge*, published in the run-up to the 2008 US presidential election, sought to shift thinking about how governments influence their populations. From the premise that people's choices are complex and must always be made on the basis of fallibility and limited information, Thaler and Sunstein propose the value of 'libertarian paternalism': governments should 'nudge' their citizens through better design of the 'choice environments' in which they act. In effect, this argument is addressed to 'softline' neoliberals, suggesting that the Friedmanite position of governments holding back entirely from market operations may advance the cause of freedom less well than subtly helping people to choose better, that is, 'better ... as judged by themselves'.[147] There can, in other words, be paternalism – environmental management of people's means and contexts of choosing – 'without coercion'.[148] But this takes us no further towards addressing the contradictions of neoliberal politics: on the contrary, if perhaps tactically, Thaler and Sunstein take care to affirm Friedman's value of freedom as primary: 'there is all the difference in the world between senseless opposition to all "government intervention" as such and the sensible claim that when governments intervene, they should usually do so in a way that promotes freedom of choice'.[149] The very different context in which neoliberal discourse was put to work in the UK becomes clear when we read the reflections on government of former lead adviser to Blair, Geoff Mulgan. Published two years earlier, he focuses on softening, not extending, government's connection with wider society, calling both for 'an ethic of service and humility' in government and for the encouragement of a 'dynamic civic culture'.[150] Once again, these welcome reflections on the ethics of government practice fall short of addressing directly the paradoxical consequences of neoliberalism for political culture.

A second approach rethinks the means by which creative (and potentially therefore political) innovation occurs. Charles Leadbeater, another major influence on New Labour policy from the mid 1990s and the leading advocate of the 'personalization' of public services, also starts out from the complexity of everyday practice, and in particular the information overload in the digital age. But drawing on Yochai Benkler's important book *The Wealth of Networks*, Leadbeater argues that the digital age enables new forms of distributed collaboration and production that potentially make a positive contribution not only to business and leisure, but also to 'democracy, equality and freedom'.[151] True, unlike Benkler (who is not a neoliberal thinker), Leadbeater puts less emphasis on the potential of such collaborations to move beyond market-based production into a new sphere of *social* production.[152] Yet he offers some convincing examples of collaborative production. Particularly helpful is Leadbeater's discussion of the 'finely balanced conditions' in which 'we-think' works, one of which is recognition:

> The currency that draws people to these [online] communities ... is recognition. We-think communities provide their participants with what they most value: recognition for the worth of their contribution, the value of their ideas, the skills of their trade.[153]

Drawing on Charles Taylor, Amartya Sen and others, Leadbeater sees 'we-think' as a way in which people can 'add ... their voice to the mix'.[154] But what Leadbeater fails to question is the relation between the implementation of neoliberal doctrine and these ideal conditions of collaboration. As Leadbeater admits, not all, even most, work operates so collaboratively. Nor does he ask whether neoliberal politics in its ordinary course can acknowledge and recognize people's 'freedom to be creative'.[155] In a recent piece, Leadbeater goes further and argues for the renewal of family and friendship networks without commenting on their relation to the market logics emphasized in his earlier work.[156] But these are key contradictions that contemporary thinking about democracy must confront if it is to address the paradoxes of neoliberal politics. Indeed, it is only when we step beyond the limitations of the neoliberal framework that the potential of Leadbeater's and Benkler's ideas can be fully developed.

It would be misleading, however, to suggest that the only pressures towards a rethinking of democracy's workings come from the contradictions of neoliberalism. There is also the question of political scale, what John Ruggie identified as the problematic 'territoriality' of the modern state,[157] and the resulting uncertainty about the *meaning and feasibility* of democratic politics when its dynamics are stretched beyond national borders. But even finding more adequate forms of representation on a transnational scale would be of no avail as long as neoliberal doctrine, which devalues the very idea of voice, remains dominant. There is no option, then, but to go further in our challenge to the rationality of neoliberal democracy and to identify the fundamental good on which the practice of democracy (however and wherever constituted) is based.

We need here to address the fundamental conflict between freedom and control on which neoliberal politics founders. There are multiple ways in which this conflict can be approached, whether through Max Weber's analysis of the inevitable tendencies towards bureaucratization in modernity[158] or as a paradox of complexity, following Alberto Melucci's insight that:

> on the one hand, complex societies distribute resources with which individuals can identify themselves as autonomous subjects of action; on the other, they ask the same individuals ... to function as dependable and effective terminals in complex information circuits. Systematic demands are thus contradictory, since the same resources must be distributed *and* withdrawn, entrusted *and* then placed under control.[159]

But both these analyses would miss the more fundamental point that neoliberal politics *inevitably* generates conflicts between freedom and control because its notion of freedom (see Chapter Two) is purely individualist and makes no reference either to people's socially oriented goals or to the conditions of social cooperation necessary for any meaningful notion of freedom. The problem is that, for neoliberalism, democracy is merely the instrument for achieving individual 'freedom'; neoliberalism has therefore no conception of the social, let alone political, ends that democracy might serve.

At this point, we need to turn to an understanding of democracy as a social ideal that is shared between the German social theorist Axel Honneth, the US political theorist of the early twentieth-century John Dewey, and the contemporary US political theorist, Nancy Fraser. Let me start with Honneth's theory of recognition.

Honneth's aim is not to confront neoliberal democracy as such, but to reground the possibility of critical thought about the social world.[160] Honneth is the latest representative of the Frankfurt School of Critical Theory. He rejects left critique based either on a utopianism of alternative social organization remote from everyday realities (Adorno) or an abstract standard of communicative rationality that applies to any and all social life (Habermas).[161] Instead, Honneth looks to rebuild critical theory on the basis of norms and reference-points that can be found in everyday experience under specific historical circumstances. The result, however, is far from banal; from this modest starting-point Honneth provides a basis for rethinking not just Critical Theory, but democratic theory too.

Honneth's starting-point, derived from Hegel, is that the intersubjectivity of human life on all scales makes possible *moral* injuries – we can damage each other's 'personal integrity' by how we talk with and treat each other. So any notion of 'the good' must include the *absence* of such moral injuries and, more positively, the recognition of our status as human agents. It follows that any notion of justice must cover the distribution not only of material goods, but also of opportunities for recognition.[162] In this framework, morality is seen as a structure for sustaining mutual recognition and political action seen as in part aimed at correcting those social conditions that interfere with the possibility of recognition, linking morality and ethics with democratic theory. Honneth distinguishes multiple levels of recognition. First, basic care and love for 'the person as such'; second, respect for the person as a moral agent with responsibility; and third (of greatest interest to formal democracy) what Honneth calls social esteem or solidarity, that is, the recognition of someone 'as a person whose capabilities are of constructive value to a concrete community'.[163] From here Honneth is able to specify what a project of democratic politics might be about: the broader good of mutual recognition. This principle would, however, be insufficient, as Honneth realizes, if 'recognition' were merely a matter of mutual acknowledgement divorced from institutional practices and social organization. Here two points are particularly helpful: Nancy Fraser's intervention in debates about recognition and Honneth's own analysis of John Dewey's theory of democracy.

In relation to Fraser, my interest is not so much in her detailed debate with Honneth about whether material 'resources' are a separate dimension of justice, or whether a fair distribution of material resources is better seen as a precondition to the primary good of recognition,[164] but in her more fundamental intervention against *uses of* the principle of recognition that reduce it to a simple politics of group identity-claims.[165] Such an understanding of recognition not only detaches the achievement of recognition from institutional settings (for example, political mechanisms of representation), but it detaches failures of recognition (misrecognition) from the often socioeconomic dynamics that generate them.[166] Fraser makes a powerful argument not only that the just distribution of resources is a fundamental precondition for effective recognition, but that the identity model of recognition misreads what is at stake in this principle: by 'treat[ing] misrecognition as a freestanding cultural harm' or a 'psychic deformation', that inadequate understanding of recognition ignores that the *point* of recognition is 'establish[ing] [a] subordinated party as a full partner in social life, able to act with others as a peer'.[167] Indeed, it is only in this sense that the concept of recognition is useful to our wider argument about voice.

However, Honneth's approach to recognition easily accommodates this move: there is a principle of social cooperation implicit in the third dimension of recognition already discussed and this principle becomes explicit in Honneth's very helpful unpacking of the contemporary relevance of John Dewey's theory of democracy.[168] Dewey's theory is based, in its mature form, not in a sense of mutual common feeling or (as with Habermas) in certain norms of intersubjective discourse, nor (as Honneth points out was the fault of Dewey's early work, influenced by Hegel) in some natural resonance between individual and community, but in the *achieved good of acting together*. On this view, democratic institutions become 'the medium through which society attempts to process and solve its problems',[169] and our understanding of how they work includes thinking about the social and family hinterland of people's engagement with (or detachment from) formal politics, and particularly the way in which people are treated in their place of work, if they have one. This is, as Honneth notes, an understanding of democracy as a 'social', not only a 'political', ideal.[170] It broadens our appreciation of the achievements of democracy, which become more than a specific set of representative mechanisms, but instead an open-ended process that will be 'the outcome of the experience that all members of society could have if they related to one another cooperatively through a just organisation of the division of labour'.[171]

On this understanding of democracy – based in Dewey but reinforced strongly by Honneth's own theory of recognition as further interpreted by Fraser – there is no gap, indeed there is a direct *relationship*, between a democratic form of life and how, in general, we are able to realize our capacities as human beings. It is interesting to note the similarities here with Raymond Williams' argument half a century ago in *The Long Revolution*: 'if man is essentially a learning, creating and communicating being, the only social organization adequate to his nature is a participating democracy, in which all of us, as unique individuals, learn, communicate and control'.[172] Such an approach also has a major impact on the boundaries of political theory. Purely economic principles can no longer trump accounts of the ends of politics from the outside, while markets' success or failure in sustaining public goods ceases to be an 'externality' of economic reasoning and becomes a central issue for political thought.

Conclusion

Implementing neoliberalism proper as a principle of government leads to major contradictions for the practice of democracy. As a result 'neoliberal democracy' is an oxymoron. Yet neoliberalism, as formula, remains a powerful ideology in the UK and elsewhere, and this feeds into the wider hegemony of neoliberal doctrine: we have seen the multiple ways in which in the UK and the USA it has been embedded as the 'new politics', 'the way things are', 'the modern'. In response, a fundamental reassessment of democratic workings is required.

The work of Honneth and Fraser, and before them, John Dewey, helps us here by rethinking democracy as a mode of *social* organization – on any scale, not only the national – that is oriented to providing the recognition due to all human agents. As Ann Phillips notes,[173] the main term implicitly at stake in struggles for recognition, on Nancy Fraser's interpretation of the recognition principle, *is* political voice. I will adopt Phillips' point, even though in Chapter One I defined voice more widely than formal politics. This reframing of democratic theory enables a rebalancing of economic and political theory, mirroring Sen's work on economics (discussed at the end of Chapter Two). Once we define the ends of politics substantively again, those ends can no longer be trumped by abstract economic principles that ignore the dimension of mutual recognition; by the same token, so-called 'democratic' processes driven only by the 'prior' demands of market functioning are, in reality, not democratic at all.

Notes

1   Comaroff and Comaroff (2001: 31).
2   Unger (1998: 277).
3   See Chapter One for this distinction.
4   Unger (1998: 52–58).
5   Ong (2006).
6   Unger (1998: 58, added emphasis).
7   Mbembe (2001: 73, original emphasis).
8   See from different points in the political spectrum, Hutton (2009b), Kay (2009).
9   International Monetary Fund (2009).
10   National Centre for Social Research (2006); Hansard Society (2008: 21).
11   Electoral Commission (2005); Hansard Society (2008: 16).
12   Keater et al. (2002).
13   It is also wide in Japan: Electoral Commission (2004: 8–9).
14   Hansard Society (2008: 16).
15   Electoral Commission (2005: 25).
16   Hansard Society (2008: 17), National Centre for Social Research (2006).
17   Coleman (2005).
18   Electoral Commission (2007: 37): question not asked in 2008.
19   Hansard Society (2008: 22).
20   Electoral Commission (2007: 42); question not asked in 2008; National Centre for Social Research (2006).
21   Couldry, Livingstone and Markham (2007: 189, original emphasis).
22   Couldry, Livingstone and Markham (2007: 127).
23   Hansard Society (2008: 33–34).
24   Scammell (1996).
25   Mayhew (1997).
26   On listening, see Bickford (1996), O'Donnell, Lloyd and Dreher (2009).

27 Castells (2009: 298).
28 Power Report (2006).
29 Foucault (2008: 121).
30 Department of Communities and Local Government (2008: 72).
31 Jenkins (2007), Lawson and Harris (2009), Lucas and Taylor (2009).
32 See House of Commons Select Committee on the Office of the Deputy Prime Minister (2004).
33 Department of Communities and Local Government (2008: 128, added emphasis).
34 Department of Communities and Local Government (2008: 73–74).
35 Department of Communities and Local Government (2008: 74).
36 Foucault (2008: 144).
37 PM Gordon Brown speech, reported in *The Guardian*, 10 March 2009.
38 See Background Note.
39 See Rose (1996b) for an early critique of the term 'communities'.
40 Bobbitt (2003: 220–221).
41 Bobbitt (2003: 229).
42 Bobbitt (2003: 230, added emphasis).
43 Bobbitt (2003: 234).
44 For an economic perspective on this, see Wolf (2009).
45 Bobbitt (2003: 814).
46 Unger (1998: 54–58).
47 Cf. Harvey (2004: chapter 3).
48 Friedman (1982: 35–36).
49 Friedman (1982: 133–135).
50 Foucault (2008: Lecture 4).
51 Foucault (2008: 111).
52 Foucault (2008: 111).
53 Foucault (2008: 116).
54 Crozier , Huntington, and Watanuki (1975), cf. Foucault (2008: 69 and 73 n29).
55 Harvey (1990).
56 Friedman (1982: 15).
57 Barry, Osborne and Rose (1996: 11).
58 Rose (1996a: 54); Beniger (1987).
59 Power (1997).
60 Hay (2007: chapter 3).
61 Power (1997: 3, 4, 13).
62 Power (1997: 42, 67).
63 Power (1997: 127, added emphasis). Cf. Rosanvallon (2008: 289).
64 Leys (2001).
65 See also more recently Sassen (2006).
66 Leys (2001: 13).
67 Hirst and Thompson (1996).
68 Leys (2001: 16 and n25), quoting UNCTAD World Investment Report (1999).
69 UNCTAD (2007).
70 Leys (2001: 22–23).
71 Leys (2001: 26).
72 Leys (2001: 68).
73 Leys (2001: 181, 198, 202).
74 Pollock (2008), Healthcare and Audit Commission report, quoted in *The Guardian*, 12 June 2008.
75 Layard and Dunn (2009: 104–106, 160), cf. Ball (2007).
76 Department of Health (2006a), cf. (2006b).
77 Leadbeater, Bartlett and Gallagher (2008: 14).
78 Relman (2009), summarizing Arrow (1963).
79 Pollock (2005: 237–238).
80 Marquand (2004: 114).
81 www.surestart.gov.uk/.

82 Hills et al. (2009: 350–352, 357–358).
83 Bobbitt (2003: 814).
84 See Frank (2001: chapter 10) on Geoff Mulgan and Charles Leadbeater.
85 Giddens (1998).
86 Mulgan (1995); for discussion, see Gilbert (2009).
87 In relation to the UK education sector, see Ball (2007).
88 Von Hayek (1960: 232), Friedman (1982: chapter 8); cf. Bobbitt (2003: 230).
89 Finlayson (forthcoming).
90 Levitas (2005: especially 164–169); Finlayson (forthcoming). See also Boltanski and Chiapello (2005: 354–355).
91 Chartered Institute of Personnel Development (2008).
92 TUC report, quoted in *The Guardian*, 6 June 2008; Global Vision International report, quoted in *Oxford Times*, 18 January 2008. For links between poverty and overwork culture in the USA, see Greenhouse (2009: 5–6).
93 Equal Opportunities Commission press release, 23 January 2007, www.eoc.org.uk/; British Social Attitudes Survey press release, 24 January 2007, www.netcen.ac.uk/.
94 The Primary Review (2007).
95 Reported in *The Guardian*, 30 April 2008, Society section.
96 Nuffield Foundation, 'Youth Trends' report, quoted in *The Guardian*, 5 June 2007; Office for National Statistics (2004: fig 12.5).
97 UNICEF (2007).
98 Stewart (2009: 285–287).
99 www.idea.gov.uk/idk/core/page.do?pageId=8617217.
100 Civil Aviation Authority figures, quoted in Henley (2008). On the UK's new super-rich, see Toynbee and Walker (2008).
101 Market surveys, quoted in *The Guardian*, 21 November 2007.
102 Guerrera (2009), quoting Economic Policy Institute figures.
103 Speech 17 March 2008, trailed by *The Guardian*, 16 March 2008.
104 Joseph Rowntree Foundation (2009a); Layard and Dunn (2009); Stewart (2009: 270), quoting figures for the 15 countries who were EU members as at 1998.
105 Goldthorpe and Jackson (2007).
106 This uses a scale of 0 (perfect equality) to 100 (perfect inequality).
107 Institute of Fiscal Studies figures, reported in Giles (2009).
108 UNDP (2007 and 2008).
109 Hills et al. (2009: esp. 342–344).
110 Wilkinson and Pickett (2008).
111 World Health Organization (2008: 36–48).
112 Sassi (2009: 142).
113 Department of Health figures, reported in *The Guardian*, 23 October 2007.
114 See Background Note.
115 Layard and Dunn (2009: 134).
116 Bunting (2008); ONS survey, reported in *The Guardian*, 11 April 2007.
117 Commission for Social Care Inspectorate, quoted in *The Guardian*, 22 November 2007.
118 www.nationalaccountsofwellbeing.org/. For commentary, see Bunting (2009), Easton (2009).
119 Pharr, Putnam and Dalton (2000: 9, figs), Layard (2005: 81).
120 Toynbee (2005); Elliott (2009a).
121 House of Lords (2009); on surveillance cameras in classrooms, see Shepherd (2009).
122 Russell (2009), cf. Jones (2009).
123 Quoted in *The Guardian*, 27 January 2009.
124 Greenhouse (2009: 7).
125 Luce (2008, added emphasis).
126 Greenhouse (2009: 4–7), quoting Krugman (2006) at p. 7.
127 Agamben (2005); Sassen (2006); and for a brilliant legal and institutional analysis, see Sands (2008).
128 See, for example, Cole (2009).

129 Lewis (2004).
130 Discussed in Cole (2005), Sands (2008).
131 Lewis (2004).
132 Didion (2006: 52).
133 Posner (2006), discussed in Cole (2006).
134 Judt (2005: 15).
135 Paxton (2004: esp. 218–220 and 145–147).
136 Wolin (2003).
137 Posner (2003: 130, 144, 387).
138 Posner (2003: 192–193, 207).
139 Schumpeter (1950 [1942]: Part IV), Lippman (1925), Downs (1957) and for recent reflections on 'monitorial democracy', see Schudson (1998: 310).
140 Downs (1957: 239, 258–259); Lupia and McCubbins (1998).
141 Schattschneider (1960).
142 Dyson (2005); Giroux (2006); Holmes (2009).
143 Gray (2007).
144 Crouch (2000).
145 Discussed by Castells (2009: 294, 364).
146 Castells (2009: 364–372).
147 Thaler and Sunstein (2008: 5, 9).
148 Thaler and Sunstein (2008: 9–11).
149 Thaler and Sunstein (2008: 253).
150 Mulgan (2006).
151 Leadbeater (2008a: 36, 24).
152 Benkler (2006).
153 Leadbeater (2008a: 21).
154 Leadbeater (2008a: 6, 194–195, 215).
155 Leadbeater (2008a: 114, 221).
156 Leadbeater (2009).
157 Ruggie (1993).
158 For discussion, see Held (1996: 168).
159 Melucci (1996: 93).
160 Honneth (2007: 66).
161 Honneth (2007: 65–70).
162 Honneth (2007: 130).
163 Honneth (2007: 138–139).
164 Fraser (2000); Honneth (2004); Fraser (2005).
165 Fraser (2005).
166 Fraser (2000: 111).
167 Fraser (2000: 110, 113, 114).
168 Honneth (2007: chapter 11).
169 Honneth (2007: 234).
170 Honneth (2007: 236).
171 Honneth (2007: 235).
172 Williams (1961: 118).
173 Philips (2003: 264).

Chapter 4

Media and the Amplification of Neoliberal Values

The individualism of self-realization ... has ... become an instrument of economic development, spreading standardization and making lives into fiction. (Axel Honneth)[1]

We no longer had ... the time or the capability to be thorough enough to explain *to ourselves*, to Parliament and the public just what we were attempting, and therefore to make reasonably sure what was practical and would work. (Christopher Foster)[2]

So far we have tracked the contemporary crisis of voice in the principles of neoliberal economics and in the multiple ways that neoliberal doctrine has become embedded in democratic politics. I have concentrated on neoliberal economics' denial of voice as a value and the contradictions of democratic political systems organized on the basis of neoliberal doctrine.

In this chapter, by contrast, I want to explore a more tangled version of voice's crisis within the domain where we often look to *find* voice: media. What if, under particular conditions (themselves connected to neoliberalism), the general space for 'voice' that mainstream media provide works in important respects to *amplify* or at least normalize values and mechanisms important to neoliberalism and, by a separate movement, to embed such values and mechanisms ever more deeply within contemporary cultures of governance? That will be my argument for the contrasting cases of reality TV entertainment and contemporary forms of government that operate under ever more intense media pressure. Let me emphasize, however, that I am not making claims about the relation of mainstream media in general to neoliberalism, which is much more complex than I can hope to cover here. My point instead is to isolate two important domains where media might be expected to increase voice, but where on closer inspection they do not.

I will suggest that the worlds of individual lifestyle and contemporary governance suggested by my opening quotes resonate with each other in unexpected ways. Recall Philip Bobbitt's diagnosis of the market-state: 'the role of the citizen qua citizen will greatly diminish and the role of the citizen as spectator increase'.[3] It follows that the solution to the contemporary crisis of voice cannot simply be 'more voice', if by 'more voice' we mean more media voice of the sort discussed in this chapter: more 'reality'-based presentations of social processes, more intense media monitoring of how government works at every level, are not, in themselves, the answer.

Deliberately, I do not discuss in this chapter the positive potential of the wider space of media (from blogging to citizen journalism): there is no doubt that the 'alternative media infrastructure'[4] emerging online will generate new voices, new conditions for voice. I return to that potential in Chapter Seven. For now, however, let's remember that the 'alternative media infrastructure' is still not the media most people consume or with which most governments, on a daily basis, engage; the particular crisis of voice that mainstream media embodies in neoliberal democracies such as the UK and the USA cannot simply be ignored.

The question, put bluntly, is whether particular operations of mainstream media's institutional voice contribute to the *closing down* of today's language of social explanation and policy-making, indirectly reinforcing the dominance of neoliberal discourse. In Chapter Three we saw in passing how elite concerns about 'governability' formed part of the context for neoliberalism's spread among 1970s political elites in the USA, the UK and elsewhere. The details of those long-forgotten reflections cast an ironic light on our question. In the early 1970s the US-based Trilateral Commission asked three leading political commentators to report on the 'governability of democracies'. One of them, French sociologist Michel Crozier, commented with concern on media's role in making government more difficult:

> Television has ... made it impossible to *maintain the cultural fragmentation and hierarchy* [sic] that was necessary to enforce traditional forms of control ... the more this [media] sounding board emphasizes the emotional appeal of the actors' 'life experience', especially as biased by the technique of the media, the less easy it is to force a real analysis of the complex game on which political leadership must act.[5]

Such an elite perspective would operate under heavier disguise today, but in the 1970s another Commission member, Harvard political scientist Samuel Huntington (later notorious for his 'clash of civilizations' thesis), could write directly:

> We have come to recognize that there are potentially desirable limits to economic growth. There are also potentially desirable limits to the indefinite extension of political democracy.[6]

Such concern at *too much* democracy resonates throughout the history of neoliberalism;[7] within this perspective, media's 'voicing' of populations' life experience was problematic from the outset.

Crozier's analysis of the resulting problems for effective government illustrates a much earlier stage of government's mediatization. For Crozier, the problem is that the gap will widen between 'the decision-making system, distorted by public relations problems' and the bureaucratically constrained 'implementation system'.[8] From the perspective of contemporary UK and USA, the problem appears to be just the opposite: that media's institutional voice leads towards the *merger* of media, topline decision-making and policy implementation into a common space of public relations (or, as it is often called, 'spin').

If so, the questions raised by the materialization of voice through media are particularly complex and admit of no easy resolution. Let's begin with the spotlit area of reality TV, before moving on to the less well-charted question of how media pressures are transforming government and policy formation.

The false dawn of reality TV[9]

In the mid to late 1990s I became interested in reality TV as a site where, potentially, the huge concentration of storytelling resources in mainstream media institutions was being challenged. This remains my main interest, raising, as it does, fascinating questions for comparative analysis as reality TV proliferates across the world. Over time, however, I became interested also in the specific types of social rhetoric that US and UK reality TV foregrounded, for example rhetorics of surveillance.[10] In early 2005, while reading campaigning journalist Madeleine Bunting's excellent account of the contradictions of UK overwork culture,[11] I was struck forcibly by the overlaps between the performance norms of contemporary work cultures and those of reality TV: how can we understand media culture's relation to these norms, which can hardly be one of simple imitation? What follows should not, incidentally, be taken to imply that neoliberalism is the only, or in many countries even a major, lens through which reality TV should be interpreted.[12]

There are, of course, many types of 'reality TV'. Some – the singing or dancing competitions based on popular voting (*Pop Idol, American Idol, Britain's Got Talent*) – lend themselves to be interpreted as providing 'voice' to audiences. Depending on political context, this entertainment-focused voice may have greater or lesser political resonance; in China a successful regional show produced in Hunan (*Super Girls Voice*) reached an audience of 200 million.[13] It is, however, reality TV as a broader phenomenon, whose possible relationship to social or political voice in a neoliberal democracy such as Britain, I want to consider.

Reality TV and neoliberal work norms

First, we need to recall some of the detailed norms of the contemporary workplace shaped by the 'new spirit of capitalism' and their contradictions. Chapter Two already approached some of these issues from another angle. Employers' requirement of passion from their staff can be seen as a way of masking (through excessive performance) contradictions that are beyond resolution. 'Passion' becomes a necessity in the neoliberal workplace because its work of denial erases contradictions and legitimates the extended appropriation of the worker's time.

The requirement of passion builds on a more general trend in contemporary work, the increasing requirement for emotional labour.[14] As Ann-Marie Stagg, chair of the UK Call Centre Managers Association, commented to Madeleine Bunting, 'service sector employers are increasingly demanding that their employees deep act, work on and change their feelings to match the display required by the labour process'.[15] While the requirement for acting is hardly surprising, the notion of *deep* acting is more surprising: surely acting out the required emotion is enough? First, however, we have to remember that in many forms of service industry, such acting must be performed under the permanent possibility of employer surveillance. Work-based surveillance is used to monitor every aspect of performance, including the length of toilet breaks, and is certainly not designed specifically to monitor emotion. Equally surveillance is so entrenched a practice that it is difficult to imagine any performance required of employees without a surveillant audience to monitor it. The surveillant audience (employer) wants assurance that the performance's features will be reproduced beyond the (necessarily limited) moment of active surveillance. This is where deep acting, based on internalized performance norms, becomes a necessary value, not an optional extra.

To see the problems here, it is not necessary to assume a simple view of human 'authenticity'; authenticity is a process of performance, as Judith Butler has shown.[16] It is the conflicts over which *types* of authenticity hold sway in these pressured performance environments that matter. As Bunting suggests, media performance standards and workplace norms may merge in a general circulation: 'when a human resources director gives out instructions that staff are to "*be themselves and be natural*" with customers, the staff's understanding of self or naturalness can be drawn from a disparate range of pop psychology, television, magazines and friends'.[17] Bunting describes her time spent talking to employees of the supermarket chain Asda. Even the spatial layout of that workplace (a supermarket in northern England) played with the myths of performance. On the stairs leading to the entrance to the supermarket floor, Bunting reports 'a full-length mirror and above it a big sign reading: "Are you ready for the Asda stage?"'.[18] The authenticity of performance on the supermarket 'stage' was assessed regularly, but in secret, by 'mystery shoppers'. The result was a permanent monitoring in work of authentic performance, justified by an appeal to overarching 'values':

> The 'colleagues', as staff are known, are exhorted to exhibit 'miles of smiles'. 'It's got to be a *real* smile', says Smith [head of Human Resources at Asda's UK headquarters]. ' ... We do have a sense that people in the Asda family live the values – it's gregarious, off the wall, a bit wacky, flexible, family-minded, genuinely interested in people, respect for the individual, informal. That's what makes the business go – *we've gone into personality, a family and community feel.*[19]

In this quotation, we see the employer reappropriating not so much the private time of the employee, but also the *values* normally associated with private time. Little wonder that, as Zygmunt Bauman has argued, the bridges between private life and public world are missing from political discourse: many of them are already occupied by corporate values.[20]

Some have seen these shifts as a 'humanization' of the workplace, for example sociologist Paul Heelas: 'work ... is taken to provide the opportunity to "work on oneself"; to grow ... to become more effective as a person ... . salespeople are not simply working for the sale; they are also working to be/become *themselves at work*'.[21] If Heelas intends irony here, it is well disguised. Indeed, he goes further, noting the overlap between new management and 'New Age' spirituality: 'one is now working on oneself to experience that spirituality which is integral to one's very nature or essence. The workplace is valued ... as a vehicle to the end of self-sacralization'.[22] The symbolic violence of this process is almost palpable: a 'self-sacralization' that can, at any time, be terminated by an employer's removal of one's job is fragile indeed, a fragility which perhaps *needs* the camouflage of emotional performance.

What of the other side of the comparison, reality TV? It is particularly to the 'gamedoc' sub-genre of reality TV ('reality'-based games such as *Big Brother*) that we must turn to understand how the irrationality of being *required* all day to 'smile for *real*' is transmuted on screen into something plausibly positive. Let me concentrate on the key points of the *Big Brother* format, indicating its links with the rituals of performance in the contemporary workplace.

The specific performance 'values' of *Big Brother* fit well with the demands imposed by contemporary working practices, once we factor out the features intrinsic to the entertainment form. First, *absolute external authority*: gamedoc reality TV shows such as *Big Brother* comprise a space governed by an external authority whose validity or rationality can never be questioned. There have no doubt been occasions where such authority was questioned in private, but this rarely surfaces in the broadcast output. Second, *team conformity*: while *Big Brother* is based on competition between individuals, a basic rule of the competition is acceptance of compulsory teamwork. Many of the set tasks in the *Big Brother* house are team-based, and the ability to 'get on with others' is one criterion by which it is assumed audiences will evaluate participants in voting them in or out. Dissent from this required gregariousness is not accepted. Third, *enforced authenticity*: the necessity to perform (with an unseen audience in mind) is balanced by the common claim that in the end your 'real' self must come out. This is the ludic version of the Asda personnel manager's insistence every day on a 'mile of smiles' where every smile must be real. Fourth, *being positive*. One potential source of convincing authenticity in performance under national television cameras – doubt, reflexive uncertainty – is normally excluded, or at least highly controlled. Contestants *must* be positive, banishing any thought of contradiction, in the same way that employees must be 'passionate' to ward off reflections about the contradictions which their performance entails. Fifth, *acceptance of arbitrary decisions*. Ultimately, you are 'in' or 'out' of the house, your 'exit' determined by the 'voice' of the unseen audience (to echo Hirschman); there is no basis for challenging the national vote, any more than we can individually challenge a corporate decision to downsize. Barbara Ehrenreich's comments in her study of underpaid work in the USA are worth recalling by way of analogy: 'when you enter the low-pay workplace ... you check your civil liberties at the door ... and learn to zip your lips for the duration of your shift'.[23] Sixth, *individualization*. Whatever the social dimensions of the *Big Brother* house (including its compulsory socialization), it is as individuals that contestants are judged against each other. Since the norm of teamwork cannot be challenged, its falsity (in this light) cannot be challenged. The game's consequences must in all cases be borne individually.

In these various ways, the 'as if' of reality TV tracks with striking fidelity the dynamics of the contemporary workplace: it is a place of compulsory self-staging, required teamwork, and regulation by unchallengeable external authority that is mediated via equally unquestionable norms or 'values', to which the worker/player must submit in a 'positive', even 'passionate' embrace, while enduring, alone, the long-term consequences of the 'game'.

Some might want to argue that in reality TV difficult social tensions are being addressed through the narrative voice of television. This, however, ignores the *absence* of reflexive connection between the much-watched surface of *Big Brother* and the intensely-lived realities of the neoliberal workplace. Gamedocs' refraction of neoliberal norms is largely unwitting, a theatre of spectacle whose real reference-point is displaced.[24]

I will come shortly to the underlying market dynamics of reality media. Before that, I want to consider some cases where the relation between reality text and social norms is more direct.

Reality TV and the social norms of neoliberal democracy

Other forms of reality TV, particularly those with a clear pedagogic intent, more directly reproduce norms of social management. What is striking in the UK is the convergence between reality TV's norms and the social consequences of neoliberal democracy. Laurie Ouellette and James Hay's study of US reality TV as a handbook of neoliberal governance has opened an important line of inquiry here that I will follow.[25]

Reality TV in Britain, in a curious version of the BBC's Reithian imperative, often claims an authority to social knowledge based on a claim to re-present '"real" experience':

> *Castaway 2000* is a unique experiment to discover what happens when a group representative of British society today is stranded away from modern life.[26]
>
> For the first time, these children will be forging relationships that are no longer about what music they like or what trainers they wear. They will change so much during these few weeks that going home to their old friends could be quite difficult for them.[27]

In 2004 Daisy Goodwin, editorial director of Talkback, production company of the BBC's *Apprentice*, said it was 'the first entertainment show to have a real point – to show what it really takes to get ahead in business'.[28] In

2008 Channel 5 trailed a reality programme called *Banged Up*, featuring ex-Home Secretary David Blunkett as the head of an imagined prison parole board and aimed to teach potential criminals about the harsh 'reality' of prison. Jim Dawkins, ex-prison officer and key participant, commented: 'I was amazed ... at how well everyone came together to give the kids as real an experience as possible'.[29]

It is common to dismiss such claims, however, on the ground that the word 'reality' here is just a dead metaphor, long since deconstructed by audiences. Of course audiences discount such claims. But that does not mean audiences (any more than TV marketers) treat these claims to 'reality' as trivial.[30] On the contrary, as recent research by Bev Skeggs, Helen Woods and Nancy Thumim brings out,[31] whether or not people say they discount such 'reality' claims does not affect whether they *act on* these claims, by treating reality shows as sources of knowledge or as presenting real moral choices. And authenticity in performance is something people look for in reality TV, as Annette Hill's extensive audience research has brought out.[32] Indeed, the genre roots of reality TV go back to an earlier documentary tradition.[33]

We need to understand the intersection of economic pressures and cultural adaptations that underlie the form of reality TV, whether gamedocs or instruction shows. Both versions result from various simplifying pressures linked to markets, as production cost pressures in a more open multi-channel field of television production intensified in the late 1980s and 1990s, linked in the UK to the Thatcher government's insistence on the BBC outsourcing an increasing proportion of its programme production to a wider production market.[34] Because the point of reality TV is to attract regular audience attention without the support of a formal plot, it needs a *temporal structure*, targeted at events which 'cannot' be missed. It is not accidental that reality programmes which a few years ago tried to impose narrative structure on to what was basically observation (observing staff at an airport, a hotel, and so on) have largely been replaced by programmes that, as John Corner puts it,[35] 'build their own social' within event-structures constructed for the purpose (*Big Brother, Survivor, X-Factor, American Idol*). Those event-structures require a way of generating critical moments: how better than through *judging* behaviour between characters, who thus become 'contestants'?

Those practices of judgement in turn require recognizable *criteria* of judgement (otherwise why take part?) and recognizable *forms of authority* through which decisions are ratified. As Espen Ytreberg's research on reality TV in Norway makes clear, we should not underestimate the capacity of editing and staging to 'script' apparently improvised performance.[36] In reality productions, media draw on various external forms of authority: the psychologist as judge of the 'facts' of general human nature, the industry expert, whether as guide of individualized instruction (*Masterchef*) or as final arbiter in collective spectacles (*Pop Idol*). Technical authority is sometimes wielded offstage (the *Big Brother* psychologists) but often in direct interaction with contestants on camera. When this happens, there can be considerable aggression. So nutritionist Dr Fi Ramsden on *Fast Food Junkies Go Native* announced to contestants: 'you can go on to an early grave or turn your life around'.[37] Or take this dialogue with a contestant on *Ben Fogle's Extreme Adventures* who had just explained that, after bringing up a family, she now had more free time:

> [psychologist Cynthia]   Have you ever done *anything* for
> yourself in your life?
>
> [contestant]   No
>
> [psychologist, smiling]   So you've devoted yourself to
> others?[38]

We see here the potential of reality TV to normalize a particular type of individualism, a self-improvement project that does not necessarily rate caring for others as a high priority. Jo Littler and I have elsewhere explored how aggression on reality TV, for example the UK version of *The Apprentice*, resonates with other norms of the neoliberal workplace.[39] If you find that connection far-fetched, the New Labour government provided some confirmation when, apparently without irony, it appointed the show's celebrity entrepreneur, Sir Alan Sugar, in June 2009 as its adviser on business based in the House of Lords!

UK reality TV, then, offers a culture of judgement: judgements meted out on particular bodies in front of large, unseen audiences. This emphasis on judgement distinguishes recent reality TV from the longer history of media-based instruction and lifestyle presentation, but also fits it more widely with the culture of management surveillance and self-disciplining in neoliberal workplaces and governance.[40]

Much more could be said about how this culture of judgement intersects with other social divides. Popular BBC programmes such as *Trinny and Susannah* (on clothing choice) and *Changing Rooms* (home decoration) have offered barely disguised judgements of *class* as if they were entirely unproblematic.[41] It is surely not coincidence that these programmes emerged in the New Labour period when, in spite of Blair's early vision of a classless society, a large majority of the UK population still regard themselves as judged by their class.[42] Indeed, a new English language of class abuse became acceptable: around 2004 in the UK the word 'chav' became a youth culture term whose US equivalent might be 'white trash who are also conspicuous consumers'. Not that reality TV only focuses on downward-directed class judgement. As Skeggs and Wood point out, reality TV in the UK has increasingly become a site for working-class women's judgements of their peers,[43] but this selective application also reflects how reality TV texts are structured by class from the outset. UK reality TV's saturation with class signals is hardly innocent in a Britain of increased inequality, increased downward mobility, significant child poverty, and low interpersonal trust. An equally strong argument can be made in terms of gender. As a number of writers have pointed out, reality television programmes (for example, those which prima facie offer 'democratic' routes into popular careers such as modelling) reproduce for young women norms of behaviour which fit well both with neoliberal ideals of competitiveness and new demands for a sexualized female body in a post-feminist era.[44]

In both these ways, a rationale of 'self-improvement' is actively worked upon in reality media and reflects, while rarely resisting, the wider features of neoliberal culture.

Reality TV and distorted recognition

There is no space here to discuss reality media's context in the broader phenomenon of celebrity culture – the category of 'celebrity' is, after all, crucial to the form of reality TV – but we should note a principle common to both: a version of Honneth's concept of recognition introduced in Chapter Three. One reason reality TV cannot easily be dismissed as a social form is that, at some level, it promises to fulfil *claims for recognition* that are not fulfilled elsewhere: Stephen Coleman's research is important for taking this possibility seriously.[45] The type of claim (and fulfilment) involved will vary greatly in different programmes in different parts of the world, but the general frame of 'reality'-based media, however discounted its authority at particular times and places, still links back potentially to individuals' and groups' claims to be seen and recognized. Luc Boltanski and Laurent Thévenot's analysis of the six 'languages of justification' in contemporary life, among which they include the 'world of fame',[46] rightly places the language of celebrity within wider social contests over value in complex societies.

However, the route from mediated visibility to recognition is not simple.[47] Indeed, it is already structured by the material *lack* of voice that characterizes social organization for many reasons. The sociologist Karin Knorr-Cetina once asked a tantalizing question: what 'fills in' the 'texture' of the social world, if older belief and value systems are withdrawing from the scene?[48] Her answer was interesting: not a positive set of values but 'unfolding structures of absences'[49] sustained by media. Can our lack of (desire for) celebrity be understood as one such 'unfolding structure of absences'? A *Times Educational Supplement* report from November 2006 suggests as much:

> Most pre-school children want to be a celebrity when they are older, according to a survey out today ... almost a third (31%) [of parents] said their sons and daughters wanted to be a famous performer.

At the same time, as Axel Honneth recently observed,[50] individuals operate in a social world with fewer clear signals about values, more incitements to mark themselves off from others through consumption, and increasingly abstract measures of their 'performance'. It is this conflict that Honneth claims is 'making [individual] lives into fiction'.[51] The fiction results from the gap between people's lives and the narratives available, indeed required, for making sense of them. That gap, or lack, determines that many available forms of voice work in detachment from people's wider needs or interests.[52]

It is difficult to deny the continuity of reality media with the 'commodification of the human' that Boltanski and Chiapello see as inherent to, and damaging in, the new spirit of capitalism.[53] The expanded zone of self-display – without the interception of media institutions – provided by 'reality media' such as YouTube only deepen the connection. *YouTube* provides a platform where page views and positive commentary on people's postings of themselves performing or simply 'being themselves' can literally be counted and monetized as part of the process of 'self-branding' that Sarah Banet-Weiser and Alison Hearn have identified (see Chapter Two). Extending the ways in which networked capitalism engages 'human persons ... more deeply than before in the profit dynamic',[54] the new range of reality media, for all its counter-hegemonic promise, provides a suitable performance space for publicizing and normalizing neoliberal democracy's demands on its citizens. Neoliberal logic can now rely on a pedagogic machine installed deep within the dynamics of contemporary media culture. The words of the late Jade Goody, the former UK *Big Brother* star who lived out her final cancer-ridden months under intense camera scrutiny, provide a suitable testimony for this ambivalent process of empowerment: 'the day before I left the *Big Brother* house I went into the diary room and was asked how I'd like to be remembered. I said: "As the person who let everybody see every single side of her, and they either liked her or they didn't". Well, I think I've achieved my aim.'[55]

Neoliberal management and the media/politics cycle

At this point, we need to move away from media texts and consider how, in more general ways, media authority and prestige takes its place alongside other forms of authority which serve neoliberal governance.

So far I have argued that, under conditions of intensified market competition in television and media industries, 'reality' entertainment emerged and stabilized as an important space of amplifying social values. In a neoliberal democracy such as the UK, that media form has developed in a particular way; it offers a displaced version of norms in the 'flexible' neoliberal workplace, or alternatively as a form of pedagogy that fits with neoliberal governments' particular expectations of their subjects and the general features of the neoliberal social landscape (increasing inequality, intensification of class differentials, and so on). The outcome is not a *simple* reinforcement of neoliberal values, let alone an explicit reproduction or legitimation of neoliberal doctrine as such: we know too little about audience reactions to this aspect of reality TV. But if media do offer 'voice' through reality productions, it hardly encourages the development of a counter-rationality to neoliberalism.

A similarly complex process of reinforcement of neoliberal culture can be seen at work in media's entanglement with everyday politics. There is no need to repeat Chapter Three's discussion of the multiple ways in which market rationality became embedded in political doctrine and administrative practice in the

UK and elsewhere. But we have to ask: where is the voice of media in this? Since media's role has historically been to hold governments accountable and since many aspects of neoliberal reforms have been controversial, why has media not provided a place where neoliberal doctrine's advance could be halted?

Many would seek answers in the pressures towards conservatism and capitalist values in a largely commercial media that works at high speed and with limited resources. Toby Miller has recently offered a devastating account of such pressures within US media, while James Curran and Jean Seaton's analysis of 'power without responsibility' within the UK media remains fundamental.[56] Instead I want to focus on a narrower point about the mechanisms through which media influence politics. This will help us see the *elective affinity* between a media-saturated politics and the specific contradictions of neoliberal democracy. Vague complaints that, for example, 'television' has ruined democracy because of its bias towards imagery and consumerism[57] tell us nothing about how policy gets made and implemented by particular governments in concrete domains of practice. Much more helpful are accounts of how media have transformed politics not by evacuating the 'general will', but by 'colonizing' politics 'at the "production" level', as German political scientist Thomas Meyer puts it.[58]

Let us for the moment bracket out the particular policy landscapes in which media intervene in different countries. Meyer argues that, *regardless of policy context*, the close practical symbiosis of media and politics, noted by countless commentators in the past 40 years,[59] has precise and damaging effects on politics as a distinctive space of deliberation. First, the very different timecycles of politics and media tend to merge. In principle, politics – the complex balancing of multiple persons, groups and ends – requires an 'extended time-horizon', whereas both the technological capacities and the economic dynamics of media tend towards an ever-accelerated cycle of news production and the exchange of news as commodity.[60] The conflict is 'resolved' by political time increasingly mimicking, indeed becoming virtually identical to, media time. This does not just involve producing news faster (making it increasingly difficult to retain a hold on a media-saturated past, although here online archiving may be a counter-factor), but more destructively leads, Meyer argues, to a *foreshortening of the future*. Instead of the political future remaining open for as yet undetermined deliberation, the future is swallowed up in the needs of the present:

> The media take on an interest in events that are both 'current', i.e., going on now, and yet completed, having a definite beginning and end, such that their whole course can be surveyed and understood.[61]

As a result, the multiple temporalities inherent to politics (short- and long-term) collapse into one temporality, the immediate.[62] A senior UK civil servant who worked in the New Labour and previous Conservative governments provides a vivid example:

> More than their predecessors, the Prime Minister [Blair], Campbell [his press secretary] and his staff hunted for new policy initiatives as the best source of good news stories. However, for the media and number 10 [Downing Street], a new idea or scheme reported in the media was as good as done.[63]

Second, the context and boundaries of politics are transformed by this intense symbiosis of media and politics. This goes beyond the often noted personalization of politics and blurred boundaries between formal politics and entertainment.[64] There is a more insidious shift in those policy areas foregrounded as *sites for* effective political intervention, and those which correspondingly fade into the background: some topics for policy are selected in, others selected out. We saw in Chapter Three how, for larger reasons, a bias towards market-friendly and market-creating policies developed in the UK (and in many other places) and was reinforced by the mechanisms of audit culture. We saw also how neoliberal governance, far from being *laissez-faire*, has a particular need for regulation to impose and sustain the conditions of supposed market competitiveness, even as other markets (global financial markets?) are allowed particular freedoms. What if the workings of the media/political cycle themselves, far from increasing politics' accountability via media to voters, favour a shift away from political deliberation and towards what Theda Skocpol calls politics as 'management',[65] or even worse a more violent 'preemptive politics' based on the manipulation of fear?[66]

At this point, it is useful to turn to a UK insider's account, already quoted, of how the behind-the-scenes practice of politics has changed in the past two decades. Christopher Foster was a very senior UK civil servant under both the John Major and early Tony Blair governments. He retired to write a book called *British Government in Crisis*.[67] His starting-point is similar to Meyer's, that issues of media presentation have become overwhelmingly important in contemporary government, resulting in a huge speeding up of the rhythms of policy development: fewer written papers submitted to Cabinet, shorter Cabinet meetings usually without formal agendas but with the PM's press officer present at all Cabinet meetings.[68] He sums up the shift thus: 'The considerations that moved Blair ... tended to be political or presentational. The two were much the same to him. Issues of presentation featured large at all his meetings.'[69] There is clearly a degree of personal distaste here, which we must discount to grasp what is important in Foster's analysis. The constant battle for positive media attention affected policy development, with announcements of proposed policy change used to get media attention *ahead of policy formalization*; that battle for media attention was itself a source of contention, with 'leaks' to media from government insiders reinforcing the trend against discussion based on full written documents.[70] Most importantly, the need for constant media attention risked reducing government to doing whatever was likely to obtain media attention. Foster's judgement is damning:

> The notion – central to the Prime Minister's [Blair's] conception of
> his role and by delegation that of his ministers – that they should
> intervene in the day-to-day working of any part of government
> or the public services *whenever news management seemed to*
> *justify it* – without reckoning the cost – was the antithesis of
> good management and not conducive to improved efficiency.[71]

The result, in Foster's view, was a transformation of government culture into something quite similar to the de-layered, charisma-driven authority that, according to Richard Sennett, characterizes the contemporary corporate environment.[72]

In this intensely mediated style of government, the time for political deliberation evaporates: not only at the highest levels (see this chapter's opening quote), but more forcibly – because directed from above – at other levels. As we saw in Chapter Three, local government in the UK is not allowed much of a deliberative voice, any more than a middle manager is free to negotiate targets deemed essential for an upcoming corporate stock market announcement. Indeed, politics that operates only in the immediate term is *necessarily* top-down, for two reasons: first, deliberation and debate takes time, which is not available; second, when the results of policy have already been anticipated (as the price of central government getting media attention), implementation lacks any exploratory dimension and becomes simply 'delivery'.[73]

The costs of this transformation depend on your standpoint. For strict neoliberal doctrine that *already* discounts political voice, there is no tension; indeed the costs of democracy have been reduced at a stroke. But outside the paradoxical world of neoliberal doctrine, we cannot be so relaxed. The shift does not affect political cultures alone, but also the sectors and agents that government seeks to regulate. Neoliberal governments need to change and monitor behaviour in many sectors, and often within government administration itself, so that they begin to conform more closely to market competition. One way of doing this from a decision-centre is by creating conditions of competition oriented to targets, with financial or other penalties as sanctions. There are, of course, strong arguments for *some* targets as democracy-enhancing; at the level of governments, they convert political accountability into clear criteria that the electorate can easily monitor, or appear at least to monitor, while at other levels (for example, targets for trains to run on time) they can provide useful measures of the progress of multiple actors in key areas of reform. The problem comes when, as notoriously in New Labour Britain, they are translated into the dominant mode of organization within government and within the organizations which government seeks to regulate.

In a target-*saturated* environment, the complexity of organizational culture is reduced to dimensions whose monitoring is ready-made for reinforcement in media reporting: just as targets were originally developed by New Labour to provide media-readable signs of government by success, so they equally offer media-friendly tools for the top-down exercise of government control. This undermines the time for, and habits of, reflexivity, and so risks creating rigidity, not adaptiveness,[74] in those who must implement 'delivery'. In more than one UK sector, it has been argued that government targets have reduced flexibility and effectiveness of services. A major report on the UK Primary School curriculum argues that government 'micro-management' (involving, for example, targets and the release of competitive information about individual schools) has contributed to the inadequacy of the current curriculum;[75] a high-profile report on the failure of UK social services to adjust to criticism of earlier failings argues that this was, in part, because good social work is hampered by 'an overemphasis on process and targets';[76] while, paradoxically, *less than half* of National Health Service staff think that caring for patients is their top priority.[77] As I write, New Labour's response to plummeting voter support has been to announce the end of 'target culture' and its replacement with 'rights' (for example, the right to receive hospital treatment within a particular period) that simply translate targets into a different syntax.[78]

As in Chapter Three, I have used the UK case to bring out a wider story. The workings of mainstream media voice in any country cannot be assumed to correct for the contradictions of neoliberal democracy, since they may work precisely to amplify those contradictions or the tendencies that generate them. We might argue that this tendency is determined as much by contemporary pressures towards what Pierre Rosanvallon calls 'counter-policy' (that is, a culture of political complaint without any basis in constructive political debate)[79] as by neoliberal doctrine itself. But whatever the underlying cause, the symbiosis of mainstream media and neoliberal government appears to strengthen the tendency for government mandates or policy directives to operate below the level of normative debate, at the level of what economic sociologist Laurent Thévenot calls 'decentralizable objectives'.[80] The *loss of a wider deliberative language for politics* may be neoliberal democracy's most far-reaching legacy. Government by targets, far from repairing, actualizes neoliberalism's failure to provide a working model of democracy. The result is a political *perpetuum mobile* running on at great speed, but with few reference-points, whether from past, present or future, to interrupt its futility.

Interrupting neoliberal democracy?

The global economic crisis has rendered some core assumptions of market fundamentalism counter-factual, yet the embedding (surveyed over these past three chapters) of neoliberal doctrine in economic, political, social and cultural life is too profound to suddenly be reversed. The building of a 'counter-rationality' to neoliberalism, as Wendy Brown put it, and the embedding of *that* alternative rationality as effectively as neoliberal rationality has come to saturate life in the UK, the USA, and many other countries, will without question be a long-term process.

Our predictions for media's contribution to that process depend on our view of media institutions' future. To close this chapter, let's briefly reflect on where the same set of neoliberal transformations has left media themselves.

Many aspects of the crisis currently affecting media institutions relate to dynamics that have nothing to do with neoliberal *doctrine*: the multiplication of digital media interfaces; resulting uncertainties about the source and volume of advertising income. Others, such as the shifting 'work–life' balance on habits of media consumption, are side-effects of neoliberalism's main effects on labour conditions, but uncertain in their scope. They require detailed treatment, but in a very different book. But we should at least note here that the marked recent decline in institutions' news-gathering resources[81] creates difficulties for government in communicating with its population; government responses to that problem are unlikely to help reverse neoliberalism's assault on conditions of recognition, although a UK minister recently put a positive spin on the issue:

> Tabloid newspapers ... sell 22m fewer copies than in 1997, while views on TV news channels have collapsed. The growth is in new media, with 100 million on *Facebook*, *YouTube* and freesheets, and it is these people the government has to reach ... the idea that the *Daily Mail* sets the agenda for government is in the past.[82]

How this takes account of the 30–40% of the UK population who remain without easy or effective Internet access,[83] let alone the novel task of using social networking sites as spaces for governmental communication, is unclear.

Meanwhile established newspapers are closing or facing bankruptcy at an alarming rate. In a single week in February 2009, Philadelphia's two local newspapers, the *Philadelphia Inquirer* and the *Philadelphia Daily News* filed for Chapter 11 protection, and Colorado's *Rocky Mountain News* closed. The UK Trinity Mirror group closed 27 UK regional newspapers in 2008,[84] while in early 2009 UK television companies (ITV, Channel 4, Channel 5) were reported to be considering merger for survival. To the financial threats to the survival of the large parts of the media sector, we must add the damage *already done* within media institutions by an overriding emphasis on financial objectives over news-related objectives. The *Los Angeles Times* is an example. In December 2008 it filed for Chapter 11 protection, but this came at the end of an era when successive editors resigned in protest against relentless newsroom cuts. The first, John Carroll, in a much-quoted speech, saw the problem as a 'post-corporate phase of ownership' that has lost touch with the public role of media completely:

> We have seen a narrowing of the purpose of the newspaper in the eyes of its owner. Under the old local owners, a newspaper's capacity for making money was only part of its value. Today, it is everything. Gone is the notion that a newspaper should lead, that it has an obligation to its community, that it is beholden to the public.[85]

Just as we cannot ultimately expect from government oriented to neoliberal principles a respect for processes of public deliberation, so we cannot expect newspapers or other media outlets run on purely financial principles to allocate resources to the interruption of *anything*, let alone the failures of neoliberal democracy. Some put great hope in the critical role of individual bloggers or blogging portals such as *The Huffington Post*, or the rise of 'citizen journalism' and user-generated content. The dynamics of these developments should not be underestimated, but they are very different, as a critical force, from a fully funded newsroom. The long-term constraints on building effective new forms of investigative journalism outside mainstream media institutions should not be underestimated, even if examples of good campaigns from outside the mainstream can always be cited.[86] Even if this were achieved, we cannot assume, given Thomas Meyer's analysis, that the resulting new media/ politics cycle will be any more effective at stimulating policy deliberation within and beyond government than is the current one.

Suppose, alternatively, the UK government discovers ways of amplifying its message that bypass media. The result may also not be democratically positive: Home Office officials have suggested, for example, that, in response to the collapse of local newspaper reporting of criminal courts, they are considering shaming local criminals directly by distributing neighbourhood leaflets about them and their crimes.[87] A hectoring government and an accelerated, increasingly scandal-driven news cycle sustained by a smaller number of more poorly funded players: this may be part of the context in which the more positive potential of mediated politics considered in Chapter Seven will play out.

So we end the book's first part, then, with a sober realization: that neoliberal rationality is profoundly flawed as a model of economic, let alone wider human, action; that politics in neoliberal democracies such as the UK has been thoroughly corroded, with negative consequences for social life and for people's belief in the transformative possibilities of democracy; and that, as argued in this chapter, one great domain of popular voice – media – operates today in ways that reinforce explicit neoliberal values and their wider corrosion of political life, while market conditions in the media sector undermine many sources for critical alternatives.

It cannot simply be enough to point to the current failures of market functioning and hope for a magical transformation. We need *resources* for imagining different models of social organization that move beyond the horizon of neoliberalism, and we cannot assume these resources will emerge from the realm of media. We must look further afield.

Notes

1   Honneth (2004: 474).
2   Foster (2005: 1–2, added emphasis).
3   Bobbitt (2003: 234).
4   Gilbert (2008: 96).
5   Crozier, Huntington and Watanaki (1975: 34, 36, added emphasis).
6   Crozier, Huntington and Watanaki (1975: 115).
7   Posner (2003), cf. much earlier Lippman (1925).

8   Crozier, Huntington and Watanaki (1975: 36–37).
9   Borrowing John Gray's term (1998) for the impacts of market-based economic globalization.
10 Andrejevic (2004), Palmer (2002), Couldry (2003: chapter 6).
11 Bunting (2004).
12 For an important treatment of reality TV on a comparative basis, see Kraidy (2009).
13 Cui and Lee (2010).
14 See especially Hochschild (1997).
15 Quoted Bunting (2004: 71–72).
16 Butler (1990).
17 Bunting (2004: 69, added emphasis).
18 Bunting (2004: 102).
19 Bunting (2004: 103, added emphasis).
20 Bauman (1999: 2).
21 Heelas (2002: 83, original emphasis).
22 Heelas (2002: 89).
23 Ehrenreich (2002: 210).
24 For reality TV as a 'theatre', see Couldry (2006) and McCarthy (2007).
25 Ouellette and Hay (2008), cf. Miller (2008); Hearne (2008).
26 BBC voiceover, 25 January 2000.
27 Alex Patterson on Serious Jungle, quoted in *Observer*, 31 March 2002.
28 BBC (2004).
29 Quoted in *The Guardian*, 28 April 2008.
30 On this point (but not others), I disagree with Sparks (2007).
31 Skeggs, Thumim and Wood (2008).
32 Hill (2004 and 2007).
33 Corner (2002); A. McCarthy (2007).
34 See Leys (2001: chapter 5).
35 Corner (2002: 257).
36 Ytreberg (2009).
37 Channel 4, 16 January 2008.
38 BBC2, 15 January 2008 (my transcript).
39 Couldry and Littler (forthcoming).
40 Andrejevic (2004); Bell and Hollows (2006); Palmer (2002); Ouellette and Hay (2008); Tasker and Negra (2007).
41 McRobbie (2005: 144–150); Phillips (2005).
42 89% in an ICM poll reported by *The Guardian*, 20 October 2007.
43 Wood and Skeggs (2008).
44 Gill (2009); Ringrose and Walkerdine (2008); McRobbie (2009); Press (forthcoming).
45 Coleman (2003).
46 Boltanski and Thévenot (2006: esp. 98–107 and 178–185).
47 Butler (2004).
48 Knorr-Cetina (2001: 527).
49 Knorr-Cetina (2001: 527–529).
50 Honneth (2004).
51 Honneth (2004: 474).
52 On 'survivor' discourse in media and its connections to neoliberalism, see Orgad (2009).
53 Boltanski and Chiapello (2005: 471).
54 Boltanski and Chiapello (2005: 464).
55 Goody (2006: 276–277).
56 Miller (2008); Curran and Seaton (2003).
57 See recently Stiegler (2006).
58 Quotes respectively from Stiegler (2006: 30), Meyer (2002: 57).
59 See, for example, Boorstin (1961), Scammell (1996).
60 Meyer (2002: 40–43).
61 Meyer (2002: 44).
62 See Rosanvallon (2006) on the multiple temporalities of politics.

63 Foster (2005: 185).
64 Meyer (2002: 53), cf. Williams and Delli Carpini (2001 and forthcoming 2010).
65 Skocpol (2003).
66 Elmer and Opel (2008).
67 Foster (2005).
68 Foster (2005: 163–4).
69 Foster (2005: 173).
70 Foster (2005: 115, 116).
71 Foster (2005: 199–200).
72 Sennett (2005).
73 Foster (2005: 221).
74 Foster (2005: 204–205).
75 The Primary Review (2009).
76 Report by Lord Laming, quoted in *The Guardian*, 13 March 2009.
77 Healthcare Commission report, quoted in *The Guardian*, 9 April 2008.
78 *The Guardian*, 27 June 2009.
79 Rosanvallon (2008).
80 Thévenot (2009).
81 Davies (2007); Fenton (2009).
82 Liam Byrne, quoted in *The Guardian*, 27 February 2009.
83 Department for Culture, Media and Sport (2009).
84 Trinity Mirror Group 2008 report, page 14: www.trinitymirror.com.
85 Quoted Baker (2007: 8).
86 Fenton (2009); Witschge, Fenton and Freedman (2010).
87 Reported in *The Guardian*, 25 February 2009. For the decline of local crime reporting, see Davies (2007: 74–84).

Chapter 5

Philosophies of Voice

Back in Chapter One, I set out the aspects of voice as a process to which voice, as a value, is attentive. What matters is less the sonic aspect of voice (deaf people's language of signing is just as much voice, in our sense, as spoken language);[1] more important is voice's role as the means whereby people give an account of the world in which they act. As such, voice is socially grounded, performed through exchange, reflexive, embodied, and dependent upon a material form.

I only hinted then at the philosophical underpinnings of this notion of voice, and its basis in an appreciation of narrative's role in human experience. I went on in later chapters to link voice to other philosophically informed approaches, first, to economic organization (Amartya Sen's theory of freedom and development) and, second, to political and social organization (Axel Honneth's theory of recognition). At that stage I did not bring out the detailed connections between voice and those separate attempts to rethink the ends of economics and democratic politics, but now those connections need to be made.

Readers less interested in philosophical background can safely skip much of this chapter, but should note that the section on 'Philosophical underpinnings of voice' adds important detail to the account of voice given in Chapter One.

Preliminaries

A starting-point for clarifying what is philosophically distinctive about 'voice' does indeed come from reflecting on voice's regular connection with sound. As phenomenologist Don Ihde argued in his pathbreaking 1970s book *Listening and Voice* (recently republished), 'voice is, for us humans, a very central phenomenon. It bears our language without which we would perceive differently'.[2]

Voice and sound

The possibility that voice is often (although not necessarily) sound opens up philosophy to the implications of sound's distinctive working in our lives. First, acknowledging the importance of sound challenges the dominance of visual metaphors of knowledge.[3] Second, because 'sound permeates and penetrates' the person who is listening, the act of listening makes no sense at all except as an experience of *a body* that is itself extended in space.[4] Third, sound extends as much *in time* as in space; 'in the case of the auditory field, [the] horizon [of perception] appears most strikingly as temporal [not spatial]. Sound reveals time.'[5] Voice must therefore be understood from the beginning as a process extended in time. Fourth, the experience of language as sound is inseparable from a process of exchange between self and others:

> The voices of others whom I hear immerse me in a language that has already penetrated my innermost being in that I 'hear' the speech that I stand within. The other and myself are co-implicated in the presence of sounding word ... [my] experience is always already 'intersubjective'.[6]

So there are plenty of reasons why (even if the phrase 'innermost being' might be challenged: see below) a philosophical framework that gives weight to sound's role in human life rejects from the outset the Cartesian tradition – derived from the seventeenth-century philosopher René Descartes – that assumes thought is disembodied.[7] (Descartes wrote, 'I am a substance whose whole essence or nature is only that of thinking, and which, in order to exist, has no need of any place, nor depends on any material thing', but also believed that there was a 'substantial union' between soul and body; he had great difficulty reconciling these two positions!)[8]

This anti-Cartesian starting-point is shared with a great deal of contemporary philosophy, whether in the Continental or Anglo-American traditions. As formulated by Ihde, however, it involves two related appeals – to the *individual subject* and to the *intersubjective* – which are potentially more controversial. The defence of, indeed the necessity in the context of voice for, each of these claims will emerge later in the chapter, but first it is important to emphasize that no assumption is made here of an 'authentic' self without contradictions. Indeed, Ihde (the first edition of whose book came out in 1976 before the huge influence of Jacques Derrida's attack on the 'metaphysics of presence' within the English-speaking world) comments critically that:

> philosophy has often resisted recognizing polyphony as primary. Philosophy's desire and aim has been for a *single voice*, identical 'within' and 'without,' which harbours no hidden side of unsaying or of countersaying. ... but the single 'authentic' voice occurs only in certain privileged moments ... every 'expression' also hides something that remains hidden and thus cannot be made 'pure'.[9]

Indeed, this is what the rejection of the Cartesian notion of disembodied thought implies: there *is* no coherent way of understanding thought as involving anything other than *exchanges* between *embodied* subjects, what Ihde more musically calls 'polyphony'. So it is important to realize that this understanding is *already* built into an account of voice; it follows that post-structuralism's attack on the very notion of an 'authentic self' (most notably Jacques Derrida's deconstruction of the 'metaphysics of presence' formulated in his opposition between 'voice' and 'writing')[10] does not undermine the value of voice from the outset. Nonetheless, there are issues in relation to post-structuralist philosophy that are worth discussing here.

Beyond the 'problem of experience'

In the 1980s and 1990s any account of something like 'voice' would have had to start with a section on the 'problem of experience': the problem of relying on coherent, authentic 'experience' as the ground for any normative, political, indeed philosophical position. But it makes more sense now to foreground as problematic a time when the following statement seemed to represent an analytical and political advance:

> All the effects of psychological interiority, together with a whole range of other capacities and relations, are constituted through the linkage of humans into other objects and practices, multiplicities and forces. It is these various relations and linkages which assemble subjects; they themselves give rise to *all the phenomena*[11] through which, in our own times, human beings relate to themselves in terms of a psychological interior: as desiring selves, sexed selves, labouring selves, thinking selves, intending selves capable of acting as subjects.[12]

Nikolas Rose here abandons not only the notion of interiority, but also that of an individual subject: 'the very idea ... of *the* subject, *the* soul, *the* individual, *the* person is part of what is to be explained, the very horizon of thought that one can hope to see beyond'.[13] If such claims are taken seriously, then the continuous embodied process of giving an account of the world that we imagined to be or value in 'voice' evaporates. Voice, at best, would be 'distributed' (a possibility discussed more later) while neoliberalism's insouciance towards the individual or collective voice would be harmless, even insightful, on this view. The unwitting affinity of such views with radical market liberalism is, as Boltanski and Chiapello note, disturbing: 'if it is no longer acceptable to believe in the possibility of a more "authentic" life at a remove from capitalism ... then what is there to halt the process of commodification?'[14]

Yet we need not go far to find writers, influenced to varying degrees by post-structuralism, who give a very different weighting to individual perspectives on the world: Angela McRobbie, Elspeth Probyn, Valerie Walkerdine, Carolyn Steedman, Cornel West.[15] An early skirmish over the term 'experience' – between Raymond Williams and three interlocutors from the journal *New Left Review* (Perry Anderson, Anthony Barnett, Tom Nairn) – is also revealing. Williams was challenged on the concept of 'lived experience' that his interlocutors found lurking behind his older notion of 'structures of feeling'.[16] Williams' defence of how articulation and silence work together in people's lives is eloquent and hardly simple-minded:

> The peculiar location of a structure of feeling is the endless comparison that must occur in the process of consciousness between

>the articulated and the lived. The lived is only another word ...
>for experience; *but we have to find a word for that level.* ... great
>blockbuster words like experience ... can have very unfortunate
>effects on the rest of the argument. ... But since I believe that the
>process of comparison occurs often in not particularly articu-
>late ways, yet is a source of much of the change that is eventu-
>ally evident in our articulation, one has to seek a term for that
>which is not fully articulated or not fully comfortable in various
>silences .... I just don't know what that term should be.[17]

So Williams requires us to *not* stop listening out for the level to which the term 'experience' points, however problematic some uses of that term may be. The 'problem of experience' was also intensely debated in 1980s feminist work where the early productiveness of recourse to women's experience in challenging standard narratives of sociology and science was later challenged.[18] Williams' insistence on *the level* to which 'experience' gives a name remains crucial, especially given the prominence more recently of a discourse – neoliberalism – that freely dispenses with the level of 'experience' for ends that are hardly radical.

How can we explain the philosophical short-circuit in Rose's account of the self? One reason is his *slide,* in discussing the self, between fully determining conditions and limiting conditions.[19] 'Languages and norms' are treated by Rose in one context as entirely determining of the processes we identify with the 'self',[20] and entirely exterior to the space we label as 'self': 'all the *effects* of psychological interiority ... are *constituted* through the linkage of humans into other objects and practices, multiplicities and forces'.[21] However, room is made for Rose's own critique by allowing that 'the vocabularies that we utilize to think ourselves arise out of our history, but do not always bear upon them the marks of their birth':[22] here external forces suddenly become merely limiting. This concession disrupts Rose's wider claims, yet the contradiction goes unacknowledged.

Meanwhile Rose's reductive account of experience is disabling for personal reflection, 'leav[ing] the subject merely decentered and dispersed' (Jessica Benjamin), and disabling for any transformative politics, as Achille Mbembe notes in his analysis of the African 'post-colony' that rejects accounts of 'the death of "the subject" ... [that] reduce individuals to mere flows of drives and networks of "desires"'.[23] Traces of the same reduction, and similar contradictions, emerge in writers whose aim was to enable spaces of agency. So in a well-known essay on 'Experience', Joan Scott argued for the importance of agency, while insisting we examine 'the historical processes that, through discourse, position subjects and produce their experiences' and shift from thinking about 'individuals' who have experience to 'subjects who are constituted through experience'.[24] The very language of 'subject-positions' which became fashionable in the 1990s is also problematic because it takes no account of the flow and process of experience.[25]

However, the issue goes deeper than description. Behind this reductive approach to experience lie philosophical priorities that were formed as answers to what Gregory Seigworth calls 'the false [philosophical] problem of an interiorized subjectivity [versus] an outside world'.[26] That problem derives from the reductive account of experience that started with Descartes and blocked all effective thinking about how individual and social interrelate. Other approaches to experience are needed, and fortunately the history of philosophy in the twentieth century[27] provides many such approaches, including George Herbert Mead's account of the socially oriented self and Ludwig Wittgenstein's 'private language argument', which showed the *incoherence* of any notion of language as an individual, not social, achievement.[28] Another important reference-point is Charles Taylor's fierce critique of Locke's notion of the '"punctual" or "neutral" self defined in abstraction from any constitutive concerns' in the material world, a notion that Rose's description of experience as mere 'phenomena' unwittingly recalls.[29]

Another useful approach is Gilles Deleuze's insistence on the processes of subjectivity that, in turn, draws on early twentieth-century philosopher Henri Bergson.[30] Bergson offered a fundamental rethinking of perception and consciousness. Consciousness, for Bergson (as for Mead and Wittgenstein), is fundamentally embodied, and inseparable therefore both from 'internal' images of action/perception and an orientation to an 'external' world that is the space for action. Bergson also therefore rejected the Cartesian notion of the 'interior' consciousness, perceiving the world in complete detachment from its bodily engagement with an 'exterior' world: 'perception is ... entirely directed toward action, and not toward pure knowledge'.[31] The problem of solipsism – how can the isolated 'interior' consciousness ever be sure that an 'external' world exists? – is revealed as a non-problem. The consequence is *not* to deny that the flow we refer to as our 'interior' exists, but to insist that it be redescribed in terms not shaped by the misleading opposition between 'interior' and 'exterior'. Bergson *affirms* the body as a site of meaning and worldly experience:

> As for affective sensation, it does not spring spontaneously from the depths of consciousness to extend itself, as it grows weaker, in space; it is one with the necessary modifications to which, in the midst of the surrounding images that influence it, the particular image that each one of us terms his body is subject.[32]

What follows from this? First, the 'level' (to borrow Raymond Williams' term) of bodily experience is inseparable from other embodied *and cumulative* processes of the self, such as memory.[33] Second, once we abandon the language of 'interior' and 'exterior', it becomes unhelpful to talk of 'bodies' as if they somehow lacked the properties that we have previously associated with minds (reflection, memory, feelings). It follows, third, as Brian Massumi argues, that the very notion of bodily experience as 'determined' or 'constructed' by external discourses misses what really matters: 'the nature of the process [of construction]' in everyday practice.[34] Perhaps we should also question talk of 'corporeal *surfaces*', a term which, in the wake of Deleuze's adaptation of Bergson, became fashionable but still carries the metaphorical burden of inside/outside:[35] much within the (no longer strictly 'interior') process of consciousness remains 'personal' to the individual self, unavailable for consultation by other 'bodies' (subjects), so the term 'surface' (which seems designed to suggest unlimited accessibility) misleads.

Fourth, and importantly, Bergson's reorientation of the philosophy of consciousness towards the experience of the individual embodied agent – the person who is conscious *in order to act in the world* – makes irrelevant a recent sceptical strand of post-structuralism that rejects, as starting-points, both the *individuality* of consciousness and the *intersubjective* process by which individual consciousness is mediated.[36] That scepticism can be neutralized in other ways too: for example, via an account of how we use language and what Habermas calls 'the paradoxical achievement of intersubjectivity', which is based on our mutual recognition of each other as subjects who are also separate individuals.[37] It can be neutralized also by an account of the narrative dimension of the self which, as we noted in Chapter One, is always intersubjectively grounded yet individually experienced, what Adriana Cavarero calls 'the familiar sense of every self in the temporal extension of a life-story that is this and not another'.[38]

All these arguments shift the starting-point from which experience is discussed. If we see the 'problems' of interior/exterior, mind/body, and individual/social – that generated both Enlightenment scepticism (Hume) and Kant's attempt to reground knowledge in transcendental forms – as false problems, then we do not need to start out from those problems. There is therefore no need to deny the space of 'the subject' (mistakenly conceived as an interior) or argue that it is wholly occupied by forces conceived as exterior: that is simply to reverse the terms of a redundant debate! Rose's position can now be seen as an inverted transcendentalism that turned the force of transcendental arguments back onto the space of the individual and arbitrarily erased it.

Sidestepping what Cavarero calls the 'superfluous' problem of 'the unsayability of the individual',[39] our account of voice can instead start out from a notion of embodied experience that emerges through an intersubjective process of perception and action, speech and reflection (what Wittgenstein called a 'form of life'),[40] but is no less real, substantial, and important for that.[41] This is the philosophical basis on which we said in Chapter One that voice is the process of giving an account of the world in which we act.

The philosophical underpinnings of voice

Three important questions remained as yet unanswered: first, why exactly is it that giving an account of ourselves and the world in which we act matters to us as human beings? Second, how can we begin to relate this basic human value – if that is what it is – to the more elaborate normative frameworks through which we evaluate complex societies? And third, how can the value of voice be linked to, and put to work within, existing frameworks for interpreting the ends of economics (Sen's account of freedom) and politics (Honneth's account of politics)? I will deal with each of these questions in turn.

Narrative and self-interpretation

'I am a self', Charles Taylor writes, 'only in relation to certain interlocutors ... the nature of our language and the fundamental dependence of our thought on language makes interlocution ... inescapable for us'.[42] But what follows from this immersion in the intersubjective domain of language? Taylor argues that humans do not just experience pain, or sensation, but have a special class of feelings which are 'subject-referring' (for example, a sense of shame) which 'incorporate a sense of what it is to be human ... of what matters to us as human subjects'.[43] This is Taylor's starting-point for arguing that 'man is a self-interpreting animal',[44] because the 'articulations' we make between our own life and a larger moral frame are necessarily interpretations.

While Taylor's point here appears to depend on his specific formulation of our moral universe – which may not be accepted – Taylor's argument is also based more broadly on our capacity for language.[45] We noted back in Chapter One the consequences of denying to people that possibility of self-interpretation: recall Primo Levi's eloquent reflection on Auschwitz that 'nothing belongs to us any more ... if we speak, they will not listen to us, and if they listen, they will not understand'. However, we disagree about the normative framework in which we make detailed sense of self-understanding, the idea that life's status – as something to be interpreted – is what *distinguishes* it as human should broadly be accepted. As Taylor writes: 'the human animal not only finds himself impelled from time to time to interpret himself and his goals, but ... he is always already in some interpretation, constituted as human by this fact'.[46] At this stage, I will deliberately leave the term 'human' unpacked and undefended. We can reach a similar conclusion, without using that term, by arguing from some notion of 'respect', as Taylor does in another essay which draws, by contrast, on Nietzsche: 'to make someone less capable of understanding himself, evaluating and choosing, is to deny totally the injunction that we should respect him as a person'.[47] There is a link here between interpretation and choice that will be important later when we return to Amartya Sen.

You might argue that interpretation need have no connection with a continuous process of narrative, since we are free to offer endlessly new interpretations of the world. But once we drop the Cartesian notion of the thinking self as detached from the process of *persisting* in embodied form in time and space, the connection between interpretation and narrative becomes unavoidable. Since we persist in time, an irreducible dimension of what we must each understand is *how* we persist in time: how 'what I am' is 'what I have become'.[48] This is why narrative is an essential feature of human self-understanding, and why temporality is an essential dimension of human narrative. While a number of writers (in addition to Taylor, the philosophers Hannah Arendt, Judith Butler, Adriana Cavarero, Alisdair MacIntyre and Paul Ricoeur, and psychologist Jerome Bruner)[49] have emphasized the inherent link between being human and making narratives, it is Ricoeur who has brought out best the link between narrative and temporality, and interestingly without relying on the framework of moral comparison that characterizes Taylor's account.[50] Narrative, for Ricoeur, is the linguistic form through which we express the temporal dimension of human life: 'temporality [is] the structure of existence that reaches language in narrativity and narrativity [is] the language structure that has temporality as its ultimate referent'.[51]

Ricoeur is concerned to give a detailed account of how literary and historical narrative convert the 'prefigured time' of items not yet part of a narrative into the 'refigured time' of a narrative, via the act of 'configuration'. We need not be concerned here with the details of Ricoeur's account but his insight – that narrative works by 'grasping things together' and 'extract[ing] a configuration from a succession'[52] – is essential. It suggests, by negative implication, what we must miss in a world that we cannot narrate:

> to follow a story is to move forward in the midst of contingencies ... and under the guidance of an expectation that finds its fulfilment in the 'conclusion' of the story ... [in its] 'end point' which, in turn, furnishes the point of view from which the story can be perceived as a whole.[53]

We sense here why neoliberalism's role in allowing the social world to become unnarratable from certain points of view has major consequences for freedom and why Ken Plummer is right to argue that 'the power to tell a story ... under the conditions of one's own choosing is part of the political process'.[54] Judith Butler, discussing the links between giving an account of oneself and ethics, notes that 'no one can live in a radically non-narratable world or survive a radically non-narratable life',[55] although she does not say why. Ricoeur begins to suggest why, through a link between narrative, time, and the possibility of ethics: 'how can a subject of action give his life an ethical qualification if this life cannot be brought together in the form of a narrative?'[56] This implication of humans' status as 'essentially ... storytelling animal[s]'[57] will be important when we return to Sen's notion of freedom.

Again, nothing so far in my argument assumes that the meaning, or endpoint, of narrative is some simple 'unity' of the self. On the contrary, Paul Ricoeur is at pains to emphasize the unresolved nature of self-narratives, the 'fragility of narrative identity'. For Ricoeur, what distinguishes life histories from literary narratives is that the former can never be grasped as a totality because of narrative's intersubjective basis, the open-ended process of 'entanglement of our stories with the stories of others'.[58] As a result, 'the narrative unity of a life ... must be seen as an unstable mixture of fabulation and actual experience'.[59] But this does not mean that *the need* to narrate our lives is contradictory or incoherent. For narrative's meaningfulness as a process only assumes, minimally, that it is focused on one *particular* embodied consciousness. As Richard Wollheim pointed out, 'it is the [embodied] person himself who provides the terms to the identity-relation' in which a particular narrative is engaged.[60] It is this that makes each human narrative particular, and valuable as such. In this respect, Adriana Cavarero detects a tension between philosophy's will towards generality and the individuated practice of narration, for 'narrations reveals the finite in its fragile uniqueness'.[61]

This point is important, not only to ward off once more the charge that an account of narrative and voice must rely on a naïve notion of 'authenticity', but also to dissociate our argument from any simple claim that, through narrative, we achieve some completion, or coherence, of the self. The work of Adriana Cavarero (who develops aspects of Hannah Arendt's account of action and story) is particularly helpful here. There is something too neat about Alisdair MacIntyre's claim that the reference-point for ethics is 'the *unity* of an embodied narrative in a single life'.[62] Is the aim of life-narrative straightforwardly to achieve a 'coherent plot'? What of painful self-narratives that work, or precisely don't work, in more complex ways? Grasping the obstructions to, and breaks within, narrative may, Butler suggests, be just as important to giving an account of oneself.[63] Cavarero resolves the apparent paradox by showing that the unity that is in question in narrative – and 'everyone looks for that unity of their own identity in the story (narrated by others or by herself)' – 'belongs only to desire'.[64] Cavarero also makes clear that our *sense* of self 'is not the product' of the stories we tell, nor does it 'lie in the construction of the story' but in the 'narrating impulse':[65]

> Not only [is] *who* appears to us ... shown to be unique in cor-
> poral form and sound of voice, but this *who* also already comes
> to us perceptibly as a narratable self with a unique story.[66]

This is important since it undermines any comforting idea that it is our acts of narration or voice that *themselves* sustain the self (as implied by the notion of 'storying the self').[67] Our confrontation with our individual desire to narrate need not be comforting, as Cavarero eloquently brings out in her discussion of the Oedipus myth.[68]

There are at least two other reasons why we must avoid assuming that self-interpretation achieves simple coherence. The first is the importance, for example in twentieth-century Western literature, of reflecting precisely on *the gap* between the act of narrating and any sense of achieved coherence: literary theorist Richard Olney's discussion of what separates Beckett and Kafka from the late eighteenth-century autobiography of Rousseau shows the inadequacy of the cliché that 'a self is created in the stories it talks to and about itself'.[69] Second, we need to take account of huge variation in the forms (religious, cultural, political) through which what counts as a satisfactory narrative of the self has been defined at different times. Olney shapes his whole assessment of 'life-writing' since late antiquity in terms of a shift from 'bios' ('the course of a life-time') to 'autos' ('the self writing and being written'), 'bios' and 'autos' being respectively the Greek words for 'life' and 'self'.[70] The anthropologist Louis Dumont sees an equally fundamental contrast between 'holistic' societies where the only possibility for individual differentiation is to stand outside society versus 'individualistic' societies where differentiation as individuals is available within the everyday.[71] Meanwhile, returning to literature, Richard Freedman has brought out the distinctive concept of 'human will' that in fourth-century North Africa made St Augustine's sense of why narrating his life mattered quite distinctive from anything that had gone before.[72] The historical contingency of what counts as narrative coherence should inform how we think about complex communities formed through difference, a point to which I return. If our account of narrative is to be broad enough to support a general human value relevant to a range of societies, times, ethnicities and classes,[73] it must bracket out any assumptions that authentic identity is simply achieved.

Where is 'voice' in all this? The answer by now should be relatively clear: voice is the process of giving an account of oneself whose distinctive and never simple means (narrative) we have just been exploring, while voice as a value is the second order value that appreciates ways of organizing human life that themselves put value on people's opportunities for voice as a process. This is, I acknowledge, to use 'voice' differently from literary theory, where narrative voice is the consistent perspective that a particular text constructs through various devices.[74] However, when Ricoeur, discussing literature, uses the term 'voice', he captures a sense of potential important for our argument too: 'voice is situated at the point of transition between configuration and refiguration ... the narrative voice is the silent speech that presents the world of the text to the reader'.[75] My usage is also distinct from the concern with narrative and voice in some areas of medicine, particular complimentary healthcare and psychotherapy,[76] because no claim is made here that voice cures or sustains the self in any specific way. Indeed, the value of voice does not derive from any simple celebration of particular voices as such. The value of voice rests instead on the recognition that, as Cavarero puts it, 'every human being, without even wanting to know it, is aware of being a narratable self', a dimension of self which she notes we may perceive in others 'even when we do not know their story at all'.[77] The denial of this aspect of self is a fundamental denial of someone's status as human.

Voice in complex societies

Taken by itself, the general value of voice – relevant to all forms of life and all scales of social organization – is not, however, sufficient for thinking about what satisfying that value would mean for the organization of particular, complex societies. If the value of voice has as its distinctive reference-point a process of exchange we recognize as effective voice (compare Chapter One), we need to distinguish between how that process can be enacted on different scales:

1   the scale on which individuals interact directly with each other (exchanging narratives, and so on);

2   large families, small groups or organizations, and small, not yet institutionalized communities where moments of direct interaction need never long be deferred;

3   a large 'community' that involves many groups, organizations and institutions, and provides multiple roles for individuals;

4   a polity comprising many large communities and a formal representative structure that links them together, where important types of narrative exchange may never occur at all;

5   a federation of such political units in a larger state;

until we finally reach:

6   the scale of those political organizations that have emerged, and will emerge, on a global stage.

The organizational challenges of giving weight to voice on these various scales differ considerably; larger scales must take account of how voice has been taken into account on the smaller scales that they encompass. At some point, then, giving weight to voice flips over from 'first order' acts – acts of speaking with, and listening to, each other – to a combination of first order and second order acts (the latter involving mechanisms for taking account of first order acts of voice).

The shift occurs between scale (2) and scale (3), when we start to need mechanisms of representation that defer and reorganize the matching of speaking and listening that was sufficient on scales (1)–(2). (Note that this deferral has nothing to do with the general issue of deferral (of 'presence') – *différance* – that Derrida famously saw as inherent to all self-awareness.[78] General arguments about the illusion of 'self-presence' get us nowhere in addressing what is distinctive about larger scales of organization.) Those scales raise quite distinct philosophical questions about how we evaluate representative mechanisms' adequacy to processes of voice at other levels. What might 'being adequate' mean here?

The start of our answer was given in Chapter One when we said that all voice requires a form and there is no effective voice unless I recognize my act of producing voice in a specific output. Leaving aside cases where this is problematic even for an individual form of voice, the requirement of 'recognition'[79] arises automatically at any level beyond the individual. For me to feel that a group of which I am a member speaks for me, I must be able to recognize my inputs in what that group says and does: if I do not, I must have satisfactory opportunities to correct that mismatch. Often I do: in a small group, this is a matter of challenging, asking questions; in larger groups, the match will not always be obvious, but can be satisfactorily achieved if I trust in the mechanisms that have led from my input to a particular output: a mechanism for individual voting in collective decisions, a mechanism for tracing organizational action back to the collective voices of the smaller component groups within that organization. Democratic politics are based on the possibility of such acts of recognition of individual voice in collective voice: I need to recognize my individual voice (at least the voice I would have had if I had exercised my opportunity to vote) in an election or referendum's outcome, even if it is in the defeated party/position that match occurs.

But distributed forms of voice (where we have no direct way of linking our particular inputs to particular outputs) raise distinctive issues. We need criteria for whether a particular distribution of inputs and outputs counts as 'voice'. This issue becomes urgent for forms of social and political production where many argue it is the distributed networking that is important. Many recent forms of political activism reject as their starting-point the representative processes of formal and organizational politics, arguing that today's capacities for networked action online enable new types of political action across multiple scales, at unprecedented speed, and in ways that better respect diversity of participants rather than requiring 'members' to conform to party lines. No doubt decentralized networks bring significant assets for mobilization and coordination, a point to whose implications I return in Chapter Seven. But if the distributed form of networks cannot, in principle, count as voice, our argument would have nothing to say about a notable feature of much political practice today, one which claims through the idea of a 'self-generating network' to offer a model for 'reorganizing society based on horizontal collaboration, participatory democracy, and coordination through autonomy and diversity'.[80]

Particularly valuable here is Jeffrey Juris's ethnography of anti-corporate globalization movements since, through its clear-eyed analysis, it exposes the tensions and difficulties of networked politics in practice. There are basically two problems that emerge from Juris's account: what is it that networks articulate their participants *to*? And what are those networks articulations *of*? On the first question, Juris brings out the increasing debates within particular activist networks about whether they need an agreed political statement which can in turn be put to use in actions that articulate directly with wider political processes.[81] On the second question, Juris brings out that there are continuing struggles within networks about whether this or that group or collective is adequately represented in how that network is managed, its communications filtered, and so on – unsurprisingly, because most activists acknowledge that some degree of centralization and hierarchization will inevitably emerge.[82] These problems are, in effect, *problems of voice*, although Juris does not use this term: the first is the issue of whether voice is effective, the second is the issue of fit, or whether participants in a network can recognize their inputs in any specific outcome. The idea of 'self-organization'[83] is often proposed as the answer to the second problem but it works only by assuming that no questions of voice arise any more at the level of the component collectives (oddly referred to here as a 'self') and turns away from the continuing issues of fit across the wider network. If these *are* issues of voice, then, as Juris notes, debating them constitutes much of what activist networks do:

> much of the network communication explored throughout this book has revolved around network structure and process. In this sense, debates *about* social movement networks largely *constitute* social movement networks themselves.[84]

The importance of networks for new forms of political production derives not from their avoidance of the issue of voice. Indeed, network struggles can largely be understood in terms of such issues.

So how might we think more precisely about the means by which distributed voice qualifies as effective. A clue comes from Leon Mayhew's book *The New Public*, which considers how complex political processes can generate normative legitimacy. He starts from the problem of declining trust in political institutions that increasingly rely on generalized mediated communication.[85] His key idea is that deliberation and representation in large societies cannot operate without 'abridged token arguments' which stand in for more explicit direct debate. Crucially, however, to carry legitimacy those rhetorical tokens must be capable at some point of being 'redeemed'.[86] Redeeming means an act of translation (from general to particular) which involves 'respond[ing] to demands for clarification, specification, and evidence to the satisfaction of an audience' that shares enough tacit knowledge with the speaker sufficient 'to fill in the blanks'.[87] An example would be when a politician under challenge comes to a face-to-face meeting to answer criticisms of her conduct. While Mayhew applies this notion to public statements by politicians, it can equally be applied to the 'bottom-up' process of voice: a distribution of inputs and outputs cannot qualify as voice unless the expression-tokens which emerge from it can be translated at some point into specific processes of speaking and listening that plausibly stand in for the countless individual acts of speaking and listening that underlie them.

How can that process of 'standing in' work, when, by definition, it must be different from what it stands in for? The acts of translation involved, to be successful, must operate within a wider framework of distinctions and principles. A hint of those principles is already expressed in the manifesto of one network discussed by Juris, the Movement for Global Resistance:

> We understand freedom as our ability to think critically and intervene in the activities that most affect us. It is therefore necessary to rediscover the importance of democracy in politics.[88]

This is based on an implicit affirmation (a collective recognition) of each other's capacities for voice. To make this link and its normative basis clearer, we need to supplement the value of voice with *bridging concepts*, and the two on which we will draw are 'recognition' (in Axel Honneth's specific sense) and 'freedom' (Sen). Each is a complex norm that applies at any scale. But, unlike 'voice', each comes attached to wider frameworks for thinking about the ends, respectively, of political and economic organization. If we can articulate the value of voice to these two bridging concepts, then voice will be shown to be a value robust enough to evaluate any scale of political or economic organization. This will complete our account of voice as a value.

Voice, freedom and recognition

There is no point pretending that these three concepts are, or can be made to be, fully integrated into a larger conceptual system. They have diverse origins. 'Voice' is the overarching term that, for particular purposes, I have developed to refer to the normative domain that neoliberal doctrine casts into shadow; 'freedom' is the term which Amartya Sen uses to focus his critique of contemporary economics, that nonetheless still draws in many ways on the traditions of liberalism and utilitarianism; 'recognition' is the term which Axel Honneth adapts from the very different philosophical tradition of Critical Theory to reconnect to contemporary social conditions.

My aim is to set these concepts in conversation with each other, bringing out voice's particular role as a connecting concept, and so grounding voice more securely in wider debates about economic and political ends. This is, in part, to follow a path left by Ricoeur in one of his last books, *The Course of Recognition*.[89] Note also that my argument will involve shaking both Honneth's and Sen's concepts slightly loose from their distinctive, and not fully compatible, foundations: in Honneth, a Kantian concept of moral autonomy directed at the fulfilment of a distinctive conception of rational freedom; in Sen, a broadly liberal account of human freedom concerned not with self-fulfilment, but with the ability to choose from a given range of human capacities in pursuing one's priorities, whatever they are. The advantage of this eclecticism, however, is to enable us to see the commonalities and interactions between these two approaches which, together with the concept of voice, can combine in a rich and broadly-based counter-rationality to neoliberalism.

Let me start with Sen's notion of freedom, drawing not on his critique of economics discussed in Chapter Two, but on his positive model of economic development in *Development as Freedom*.[90] Here Sen continues his project of rethinking the ends of economics beyond standard measurements of income or GDP, defining development broadly as 'an integrated process of expansion of substantive freedoms'.[91] Those freedoms of course include economic opportunities, but also 'political freedoms', 'social facilities' (including literacy), 'transparency guarantees' and 'protective security'. Sen's sensitivity to the social conditions (literacy and also gender, class and cultural inequality) for effective political freedom fits well with our concern (see Chapter Six) with the sociology of voice. This account of development is not aimed narrowly at 'developing' countries: it encompasses also, for example, the poverty of US Afro-Americans[92] and is relevant to the UK social deficit discussed in Chapters Two and Three.

We have to go deeper into Sen's account to appreciate its detailed resonance with voice. Sen shows that freedom is not incidental, but essential, to development for two reasons: first, because certain key freedoms (political freedoms, freedom of economic exchange) are partly 'constitutive' of development; and, second, because political freedoms in particular enable other aspects of development to be achieved, allowing people to express what they think about government and their detailed economic needs.[93] Sen's approach to freedom is, as we saw in Chapter Two, much richer than that of neoliberal doctrine, since it is concerned not with negative freedom from interference but with 'substantive freedoms – the capabilities to choose a life one *has reason to value*'.[94] Freedom is therefore more than the maximization of utility in standard economic reasoning; it involves necessarily a process of *individual* reflection.[95] Sen defines capabilities so as to allow scope not only for individual choice about what particular capacities they draw upon in life, but also individuals' varying needs (so a disabled person will require a different basket of goods to exercise effectively a particular capacity).[96] Underlying all this is Sen's understanding of agency as a basic good – 'greater freedom enhances the ability of people to help themselves and also to influence the world' [97] – which in turn is always potentially oriented beyond the self:

> Once the straitjacket of self-interested motivation is removed, it becomes possible to give recognition to the indisputable fact that the person's agency can well be geared to considerations not covered – or at least not *fully* covered – by his or her own well-being.[98]

Like voice, therefore, Sen's notion of freedom is open to multiple forms of fulfilment.

However, there are two respects in which Sen's theory needs to be supplemented. First, although his argument operates in terms wide enough to cover 'developed' as well as 'developing' countries, his primary concern is with the establishment of basic political rights in countries, many of which fail to meet basic human needs (for food, water, and so on). So while he acknowledges in passing the possibility of existing democratic freedoms not being fully used, the main burden of Sen's argument lies elsewhere in how basic democratic rights are first stabilized: given the analysis of Chapters Three and Four, we may be less sanguine than Sen about whether 'in a democracy people tend to get what they demand, and more crucially do not typically get what they do not demand'.[99]

Second, Sen does not fill out in detail the conditions under which substantive freedoms become and remain effective. If freedom means having the 'capability to choose a life that one has *reason* to value', how beyond the basic mechanism of voting are one's reasoned choices to be heard, and one's capacity to formulate reasons sustained? Sen discusses 'political freedom' in terms of 'the opportunities that people have to determine who should govern and on what principles',[100] but says less about how this might be satisfied when a well-established system of representative politics generates policy that systematically ignores the value of voice. But, if choice is inseparable from *interpretation* and if the very possibility of ethical reflection depends on the act of *narrating* our life, then it is the value of voice that underlies Sen's approach to development, as suggested also by the inclusion of 'political voice' as one of the dimensions of wellbeing by the recent French Commission of which Sen was a leading member (see Chapter Two).[101] Sen prioritizes not freedom in the abstract, but freedom oriented towards 'capabilities to choose a life one has reason to value'. The narrative act of giving reasons about our life (our actual life, our possible lives) is therefore a crucial part of what gives substance to Sen's understanding of freedom. Freedom, for Sen, depends on the process of giving an account of our lives and therefore on the value of voice which defends that process from forces that, even in established democracies, undermine it. In this way, voice makes explicit a vital aspect of Sen's notion of political freedom, while fitting well into his wider model of the goods at which economic development, indeed economics itself, should be aimed. If at the root of Sen's normative framework is his concept of 'rights to capabilities',[102] then one of those central capabilities *is*, I propose, the capability of voice.

Turning to recognition, Honneth's theory, like Sen's for economics, aims to reframe entirely our understanding of the ends of political practice. Moving beyond a narrow view (such as in public choice theory) of government as aimed at maximizing the aggregate of private ends, Honneth analyses democracy as a way of living together organized by the end of 'social cooperation' based on mutual recognition.[103] As does Sen, Honneth avoids prioritizing political involvement as an end in itself (republicanism) but, in contrast with Sen, prioritizes social over economic needs. At the same time, Honneth is more sensitive than Sen to the way in which certain outcomes of economic development (for example, the psychic impacts of the inequalities built into the division of labour) can undermine wider political ends.[104]

The tool for reforming the human organization of human life on which Honneth relies is 'recognition'. When Honneth defines recognition (see discussion in Chapter Three), his account is, except in relation to moral accountability, surprisingly unspecific on the role of voice. While the possibility of narrative exchange is implied in the general notion of recognition, at no point is the capacity and need to *narrate* our lives made an explicit theme of recognition;[105] still less does Honneth state that we must recognize in each other an ability through voice to contribute to concrete decision-making. When discussing the social dimension of recognition, Honneth only writes of recognizing others as having 'capabilities that are of constitutive value to a concrete community'.[106] What are those capabilities? Prima facie, Honneth's definition might have been compatible even with the unequal division of political labour that obtained before women were given voting rights, since it does not specify that the capabilities in question include the capacity *for all* to contribute to shared decision-making. Here Honneth's account can be supplemented by Sen's concept of agency where the possibility of reflective *choice about life conditions* is fundamental, a concept which itself, as we have just seen, can be supplemented by voice. Indeed, it is difficult to see how, in recognizing others as having 'capabilities that are of constitutive value to a concrete community', we could not include their capability for voice. Recognition can, via the value of voice, be linked more effectively to Sen's 'basic value that the people must be allowed to decide freely what traditions they wish or might not wish to follow'.[107]

A particular advantage of Honneth's emphasis on recognition, however, is its sensitivity to the role that acknowledging others' accounts of themselves must play in a just social and political life. Recall our earlier discussion of the need in complex societies for acknowledging on one level the outcomes of the exercise of voice on another: the concept of recognition is particularly useful here as a potential principle for regulating the complexities of voice's operations as a value across multiple levels. I return to this topic briefly in Chapter Seven.

But what, you might ask, does Honneth mean by 'concrete community'? Presumably, this means at least those groupings in which people stably cooperate, but does the term 'community' bring with it any implicit boundaries that mark 'them' off from 'us'? Honneth's essay on 'Post-Traditional Communities' clarifies that the dimension of recognition relating to social esteem must be understood in a radically pluralist way,[108] whereby 'all members of society are placed, through a radical opening up of the horizon of ethical value, in the position of being recognized for their own achievements and abilities in such a way that they learn to esteem and value themselves'.[109] Voice as a value underpins this move too, since it is only via the intersubjective exchange of narratives that such a transformative process of mutual esteem can occur.

Voice is not only compatible with Sen's and Honneth's concepts of freedom and recognition, but can usefully supplement those two important approaches to contemporary economics and politics. In this way, the value of voice can be put to work in contesting neoliberal practice, and connected further with John

Dewey's account of democracy as social cooperation between mutually recognizing individuals and groups, already discussed in Chapter Three.

Social/political misrecognition

It is, Ricoeur writes, 'the possibility of *misrecognition* that gives recognition its full autonomy' as a philosophical term, while Honneth acknowledges that an impetus behind his work was 'the social causes responsible for the systematic *violation* of the conditions of recognition'.[110] This is to install disruption – the disruption that must come from unmasking and then challenging a long process of misrecognition – into the heart of political life and, we might argue, economic life too (the classical world after all was based on the misrecognition of slaves as political, economic, even moral agents).[111] But how can this be done with the concepts we have used so far? Leaving voice to one side for the moment, Sen's concept of freedom starts out from certain recognized and universal capabilities and so does not address disruption in those terms, even though he devotes a whole chapter to women's long misrecognized rights in development.[112] Meanwhile, Honneth, in an essay ('Decentered autonomy') on the consequences of psychoanalysis and the linguistic basis of the self for moral autonomy, concludes that 'only a person who is in a position ... to present his or her entire life in an ethical reflected way ... can be regarded as an autonomous person';[113] but this is to pursue 'disruption' into the realm of personal psychology, a long way from questions of politics. Instead, we must pursue the theme of misrecognition right into the heart of the social and the political.

The most helpful guide here is the political theorist Aletta Norval, who, in an account of democratic politics that draws both on post-structuralism (Derrida, Laclau and Mouffe) and on late Wittgenstein, insists that, in politics, we cannot take the concept of voice as simple: 'the place opened for "the human voice" is not one of a pre-constituted mode of political subjectification'.[114] We must avoid, Norval argues, 'assum[ing] the existence of a framework of politics in which in principle every voice could be heard, without giving attention to the very structuring of those frameworks and the ways in which the visibility of subjects is structured'.[115] The status of voice as achieved in politics depends, then, on becoming '*visible*', not in the sense of being physically seen – any more than voice itself, as we noted earlier, depends necessarily on being physically heard – but in the sense of being *regarded as* relevant to the distribution of speaking opportunities. (The clash of metaphors – visibility and voice – is, I assume, deliberate on Norval's part, and intended to indicate that there is no seamless continuity between the process of voice and the heterogeneous processes that are its preconditions: see Chapter Six on 'materialization'.) Discussing the historical process whereby, in Britain from the late eighteenth century onwards, women, in order to acquire political voice, had first to be regarded as humans for whom 'voice' was a relevant attribute, Norval foregrounds the disruption that is required for such a transformation, the 'interruptive moment in which new [political] subjects come into existence'.[116]

Norval asks a crucial question: 'what occurs in this moment when something or someone that was neither visible nor audible becomes visible and finds a voice?'[117] As Norval explains, post-structuralist writers (such as Jacques Rancière) have been particularly good in grasping this moment of disruption, and its implications for the everyday world of political norms that generally ignores it. Indeed, 'for post-structuralists, "voice" is thematized precisely from the perspective of those excluded from the polity'.[118] But the result, as Norval acutely points out, is a problem in theorizing political community in any aspect other than its exclusionary dimension (as we must do if we are to defend the possibility of democracy against neoliberalism).

A key issue which Norval rightly raises is how we can think through the relation of the disruption to political structures (that the emergence of new subjects requires) to processes of political continuity. One way forward she offers is through Wittgenstein's account of language as a practical activity in which we are deeply immersed, yet which we can from time to time *do differently*, because 'language is not fixed and unalterable, but inherently open to the future'.[119] From time to time we come to see things and words under a new aspect, yet that does not stop us going on using those terms or referring to those things. The result is to acknowledge a possibility of rupture within our political and social language that does not prevent, indeed is entangled with, the possibility of continuity.[120]

Another way of re-imagining the space of politics in the light of the disruptive emergence of new political subjects is the concept, drawn by Norval from Stanley Cavell, of 'exemplarity' that in turn derives from Cavell's reading of Nietzsche. Under certain conditions, I can come to see someone's difference from me as not irrelevant, but as providing me with an exemplar that transforms my sense of who *I* could become. Exemplarity works through a feeling of shame, when I come to recognize through an exemplar that I am falling short of my own sense of my possibilities.[121] This introduces a vivid model for understanding democratic transformation which Norval then applies to analysing South Africa's Truth and Reconciliation Commission (TRC), offering an important insight into how voice can work to extend the space of political representation but without – a point Norval emphasizes – needing to assume that some coherent or bounded notion of 'community' is affirmed in the process.

Two points, however, seem missing from Norval's account, and identifying them may clarify how her analysis relates to our wider argument on voice. First, Norval does not explain the underlying term which focuses 'exemplarity': when I recognize someone, or a claim they make, as exemplary for me, it must be by reference to some frame of comparison, some common property or status which I am assumed to share with that other person. The obvious common term is *humanity*: perhaps Norval regards this as too obvious to state, or perhaps she shares the general suspicion towards 'humanism' within post-structuralism. We might reasonably ask, however, what is lost by not making our reliance on a notion of humanity explicit here, and what is gained by leaving the implied aspect of exemplarity unspecified. Second, and particularly if we have made this first move, we can address another question that Norval leaves unanswered, which is *why* the act of narrative is expected, and accepted, as having a transformative role in politics. Norval quotes one survivor, blinded by police brutality in the Apartheid era, who said at the TRC that 'what has been making me sick all the time is the fact that I couldn't tell my story. But now ... it feels like I got my sight back by coming here'.[122] Shortly afterwards, Norval endorses a view that the telling of stories in public at the TRC amounted to a 'form of recognition'.[123] But recognition *as what*? As a political subject in a particular legal system and state? As a political subject of any state? As a human being? The multiplicity of possible identifications is not the point. The interesting question is why the act of *telling* one's story in public (so that it can be heard, and this fact in turn be registered) should be the act that constitutes recognition. The answer cannot be that a particular state (or states in general) require it, since the TRC was a political innovation of global significance. The answer must be that giving an account of oneself for exchange in the world in which one acts *is* a basic feature of what we do as humans, and so a *possible* starting-point for recognizing someone as a political subject.[124]

Conclusion

What Norval's important work on democratic subjectivity also offers, once we have supplemented it with an account of narrative's role in human practice, is a bridge from our account of writers such as Sen and Honneth to the largely independent philosophical terrain of post-structuralism. Norval seeks to develop a post-structuralist rethinking of the democratic tradition, but relies in part on philosophical tools (the work of Wittgenstein) that come from outside it. Norval therefore helps us also to see more clearly what in an account of voice we must, and what we need not, take from versions of post-structuralism (to return to the discussion at the start of this chapter). What we must take is a rejection of the notion that with voice comes the automatic possibility of reading its content and conditions of possibility transparently; and an insistence on the role of power in shaping what subjects can emerge as having voice under particular conditions. These are issues which we take up sociologically in the next chapter.

What we need not and, I would argue, should not take from some versions of post-structuralism is the notion that the practice of politics is forever split between moments of disruptive emergence and contradictory rhetorical claims for consensual 'politics-as-usual'. The starting-point instead for articulating the substantive content of politics can, more modestly, be the forms of life in which we engage when we do politics. The practice of giving, receiving and expecting accounts of ourselves is a form of life in Wittgenstein's sense in which, as human beings required to live together on some terms, we are already involved. It is this form of life that is the practical basis for the value of voice.

It is worth noting, finally, that this is not a foundationalist view of politics and ethics, in the sense that it does not seek a basis in an ultimate foundational value beyond such a form of life; no such values are available in what Habermas calls the age of 'post-metaphysical thinking'.[125] Yet it has 'foundations' of a sort, for this form of life is already a secure basis for thinking about how we conduct our lives, being part of that conduct. Admittedly, some post-structuralist versions of the deconstruction of the myths of Western philosophy (there are other versions of that deconstruction, as we saw) may block us from seeing this basis. For if we are committed to the view that to recognize consciousness as inherently intersubjective, embodied and temporal is always to incur a loss – to suffer the 'break-up of presence' for which we must in some way 'make up' [126] – then we will always find in the concept of 'voice' a compensation for this supposed 'loss'. But if all that has been 'lost' is the habit of thinking and acting on the basis of a particular illusion, then it may be more productive to start from the shape of what we have, from the forms of life such as voice in which we are already engaged.[127] This point becomes important if, as I suggest in the next two chapters, we need to look clear-sightedly at the constraints and political limitations under which this form of life operates today.

Notes

1   Sacks (2000).
2   Ihde (2007: 189).
3   Ihde (2007: 7–15), cf. Levin (1989).
4   Ihde (2007: 44–45).
5   Ihde (2007: 102).
6   Ihde (2007: 118).
7   Ihde (2007: 134).
8   Williams (2005: chapter 10). The Descartes quote is at Williams (2005: 94).
9   Ihde (2007: 178–179).
10 Derrida (1973 and 1976).
11 For the significance of this term, see comment on Taylor and Locke below.
12 Rose (1996: 172, added emphasis).
13 Rose (1996c: 171–172, original emphases).
14 Boltanski and Chiapello (2005: 455, 466).
15 McRobbie (1997), Probyn (1993), Steedman (1986), Walkerdine (1997), West (1992).
16 See also the critique of Williams in Hall (1990 [1980]).
17 Williams (1979: 168) emphasis added. Seigworth (2008) also discusses this passage.
18 Contrast Smith (1987) with Scott (1992).
19 Couldry (2000: 50–51, 118–119).
20 Rose (1996c: 96).
21 Rose (1996c: 172, added emphasis).
22 Rose (1996c: 39).
23 Benjamin (1998: 86), Mbembe (2001: 14).
24 Scott (1992: 34, 25, 26).
25 Couldry (1996: 327), Massumi (2002: 7–8).
26 Seigworth (2008: 113, added emphasis).
27 Charles Taylor goes back to the early nineteenth-century philosopher von Humboldt (1989: 525 n12).
28 Mead (1967) [1934], Wittgenstein (1958).
29 Taylor (1989), Rose (1996c: 172).
30 Deleuze and Guattari (1988), Massumi (2002), cf. Bergson (1991 [1908]).
31 Bergson (1991 [1908]: 28).
32 Bergson (1991 [1908]: 64–65).
33 Bergson (1991 [1908]: 65).

34 Massumi (2002: 12).
35 Grosz (1994).
36 For critique, see Dews (1987: 224–242).
37 Habermas, quoted in Dews (1987: 240). See Ricoeur on intersubjectivity in ethics (1992: 193–194).
38 Cavarero (2000: 34, original emphasis).
39 Cavarero (2000: 89).
40 Wittgenstein (1958), and see final section of this chapter.
41 Inspiring here is David Harvey's defence of the body (2000: chapters 6 and 7).
42 Taylor (1989: 36, 38).
43 Taylor (1986: 60).
44 Taylor (1986: 63).
45 Taylor (1986: 72).
46 Taylor (1986: 75).
47 Taylor (1986: 103).
48 Taylor (1989: 47).
49 MacIntyre (1981), Ricoeur (1984a and 1984b), Bruner (1986), Arendt (1958), Butler (2005), Cavarero (2000).
50 See Background Note.
51 Ricoeur (1980: 165).
52 Ricoeur (1984a: 66).
53 Ricoeur (1984a: 67).
54 Plummer (1995: 26).
55 Butler (2005: 59).
56 Ricoeur (2005: 103), cf. Ricoeur (1992: 160–161).
57 MacIntyre (1981: 201).
58 Ricoeur (2005: 104), (1995: 10). The metaphor of entanglement here goes back to Arendt (1958: 184).
59 Ricoeur (1992: 162).
60 Wollheim (1984: 19).
61 Cavarero (2000: 3).
62 MacIntyre (1981: 243, emphasis added), discussed in Cavarero (2000: 40), Honneth (2007: 190).
63 Butler (2005).
64 Cavarero (2000: 41).
65 Cavarero (2000: 35).
66 Cavarero (2000: 34).
67 Finnegan (1997).
68 Cavarero (2000: chapters 1 and 4).
69 Olney (1998: 283).
70 Olney (1998: xv).
71 Dumont (1985: 95).
72 Friedman (2001).
73 On class's role in shaping possible narratives of self, see Gagnier (1991), Skeggs (1997).
74 Genette (1980: 213).
75 Ricoeur (1984b: 99).
76 Frank (1991), White and Epston (1990).
77 Cavarero (2000: 33–34).
78 Derrida (1973).
79 For 'recognition' in this general sense, see Ricoeur (2005).
80 Juris (2008: 17).
81 Juris (2008: 264–265).
82 Juris (2008: 17, 207, 212–213, 230 emphasis in original).
83 Juris (2008: 16).
84 Juris (2008: 298).
85 See especially Mayhew (1997: 236–238).

86 Mayhew (1997: 6).
87 Mayhew (1997: 13).
88 Quoted in Juris (2008: 93).
89 Ricoeur (2005).
90 Sen (1999).
91 Sen (1999: 8).
92 Sen (1999: 21–24).
93 Sen (1999: 148).
94 Sen (1999: 74, added emphasis).
95 Sen (1999: 56–66).
96 Sen (1999: 74).
97 Sen (1999: 18).
98 Sen (1987: 41, discussed by Ricoeur (2005: 142–146 emphasis in original).
99 Sen (1999: 156).
100 Sen (1999: 38, added emphasis).
101 Commission on the Measurement of Economic Performance and Social Progress (2009: 11).
102 Ricoeur (2005: 143), discussing Sen's *Commodities and Capabilities* (1985).
103 Honneth (2007: 232).
104 Honneth (2007: 235).
105 Cf. Ferrara (1998: 17).
106 Honneth (2007: 137).
107 Sen (1999: 32).
108 Ricoeur (2005: 201-216, esp. 202, 209), linking to Boltanski and Thévenot (2006) (see Chapter Four above).
109 Honneth (2007: 261).
110 Ricoeur (2005: 36), Honneth (2007: 72).
111 Finley (1966: esp. 148–150).
112 Sen (1999: chapter 8).
113 Honneth (2007: 191).
114 Norval (2007: 129).
115 Norval (2007: 102).
116 Norval (2007: 79).
117 Norval (2007: 76).
118 Norval (2007: 141); McNay's (2008) important critique of recognition (particularly Charles Taylor's concept) covers similar ground.
119 Norval (2007: 116).
120 Norval (2007: 117).
121 Norval (2007: 187–196). For 'exemplarity' and narrative, see Ferrara (1998: chapters 1 and 2).
122 Norval (2007: 1999), quoting source.
123 Norval (2007: 203), quoting Jonathan Allen (no direct source given).
124 Norval mentions 'the role of stories, narratives' in politics but without emphasis (2007: 139–140).
125 Habermas (1992).
126 Derrida (1973: 104)
127 It is striking that Katherine Hayles (1999: 285) makes a similar point in developing her account of the 'post human' that rejects the humanism of liberal individualism. There is no space to discuss the relation between the version of humanism offered above and Hayles' 'posthumanism', except to suggest that they are less opposed than first appears.

Chapter 6

Sociologies of Voice

What would a sociology look like that paid attention to voice – that is to the conditions under which we can give accounts of our lives and to how those accounts are valued, or perhaps not valued at all?

This neglected aspect of sociological inquiry has potential for detailed application in any area of life (work, family, consumption, politics), and clearly, in one brief chapter, we cannot apply this approach across all those specific domains. Just as important, in any case, are the connections, or missing connections, between different areas of life. When workers interviewed by *Guardian* journalist Madeleine Bunting found that their values counted for little in influencing their working conditions, even though those same conditions invaded their home and family life and undermined those very values, they bore witness to a sociological problem not just about work or family but about the broader conditions under which people's lives become, or cease to be, *narratable* in a satisfactory way. A sociology of voice would seek to register the lived relations and dislocations between domains that, as we saw in earlier chapters, come with the implementation of neoliberalism.

There might still seem something paradoxical in arguing that there is a crisis of voice today and we need a sociology *of* voice to address it. Don't we see everywhere a huge explosion of voice – in reality TV, magazine confessions, blogs, social networking sites – and the therapeutic industries that incite and manage this process? Hasn't sociology long since registered this in Nikolas Rose's account of therapeutic discourse and Anthony Giddens' theory of 'reflexive modernity' in which more and more aspects of life are increasingly detraditionalized, requiring individuals to reinterpret and reinvent the reference-points by which they live?[1] And didn't Ulrich Beck capture a key dynamic of late modernity when he argued that increasingly we are required to develop 'biographical solutions to structural problems'?[2]

But, as Beck's resonant phrase already suggests, it is not enough to register the growth of particular types of personal narrative, important though these are. For 'voice' is about more than just speaking and the growing incitements to speak. An attention to voice means paying attention, as importantly, to the conditions for effective voice, that is, the conditions under which people's practices of voice are *sustained* and the outcomes of those practices *validated*. This is one implication of voice's duality as a concept, its reference to both process *and* value,[3] which in turn requires a sociological attention to the processes of valuing voice. These operate, necessarily, on and across multiple scales. A sociology of voice, or perhaps better sociologies of voice, have, as its/ their reference-points, not just individuals but also the 'landscape' in which they speak and are, or are not, heard.[4]

There is no short-cut to understanding neoliberalism's consequences for people's daily conditions of voice without listening to the stories people tell us about their lives. As Zygmunt Bauman notes, 'articulation of life stories *is* the activity through which meaning and purpose are inserted into life'.[5] So sociology must think carefully about the listening that it does. We will get nowhere, however, through a simplified view of the 'identities' enunciated through voice. As the Lebanese writer Amin Maalouf writes, to assume that 'there is just one affiliation that really matters, a kind of "fundamental truth" about each individual' is to write as if 'a person's whole journey through time, the beliefs he acquires in the course of that journey; his own individual tastes, sensibilities and affinities; in short his life itself counted for nothing'.[6]

We start this chapter, then, from complexity, from unfinished processes of telling, but also with a sensitivity, informed by the preceding chapters, to the multiple factors which today are constraining or overriding voice, even as voices appear to multiply. It may be that through the quality of its attention to these processes, sociological research and education have something distinctive to contribute to sustaining the value of voice more widely, a contribution which should be defended in the face of the neoliberal reforms that are currently sweeping the university sector in the UK, the USA and elsewhere.[7]

'The individual'

Let me start with the possibility that individual variations in resources for voice, and in the practice of self-narrative, might be particularly important for a sociology of voice. Already, by foregrounding the possibility that individual accounts of the world *might* be sociologically interesting, we have distanced ourselves from mainstream sociology that has, historically, put more emphasis on processes of socialization than individuation, let alone on the trajectories of particular individuals.[8] Indeed, a number of anthropologists and sociologists have insisted that holistic accounts of culture or society ignore the limits to the effectiveness of cultural and social frameworks over individual agency.[9]

Perhaps the most vocal challenges to conventional understandings of the individual's relationship to society have come from the French sociologist Alain Touraine and his followers. A quarter of a century ago, Touraine announced that sociology should drop the notion of 'society' entirely, for a world where individuals no longer had clear social roles or frameworks to guide them, and concentrate instead on how individuals 'act upon themselves', with the help of whatever resources and models come to hand, to *acquire* a sense of individual and common purpose.[10] François Dubet developed a less apocalyptic version of Touraine's position, insisting only that sociology should study actors' distance from social categories, and their critical capacities as manifested in their self-knowledge.[11] Even if 'social integration' has not completely disappeared, Dubet argued, 'social action' was no longer of a pure type but irreducibly complex: an uncertain intersection between (1) individuals' internalizations of available models of behaviour, (2) the strategic rationality of action, and (3) what Touraine and Dubet call 'subjectivation', that is, the subject's active interpretation of the situations in which she finds herself.[12]

It is on this basis that Danilo Martuccelli has recently developed a highly sophisticated model of 'the individual'. In doing so, Martuccelli starts out from Beck's idea that the late modern individual must find 'biographical solutions to systemic contradictions', but insists that such 'solutions' do not always emerge in a single way, but (following Dubet) operate on multiple dimensions.[13] The result is a 'sociological grammar of the individual' with five 'axes': *support, role, respect, identity* and *subjectivity*. While Martuccelli would not necessarily accept a single term such as 'voice', it is clear that a sociology of voice can learn a great deal from his analysis of each of these axes, which in turn are based on a complex account of individuation as covering dimensions as different as legal autonomy, attachment, functional control and self-expression.[14]

'Support' covers 'the ensemble of elements, material and immaterial, tying [the individual] to his context'.[15] While 'support' is different from the individual's own narrative work or voice, it is of considerable importance to whether an individual's voice is sustainable. Supports are varied, from formal networks to individuals' degree of acknowledged legitimacy, to the invisible supports (the PA, the travel assistant, the analyst) which, for those with high status, sustain their possibility of acting.[16] We touched on this topic in Chapter Two when, discussing Boltanski and Chiapello, we noted that flexible labour markets increasingly push the cost of maintaining labour capacity back on to individual workers, except the privileged who are, by definition, those who are more mobile.

'Role' is a term familiar from mainstream sociology, but Martuccelli insists on destabilizing our assumption that all roles are fixed and to an equal degree. Roles instead refer to the '*degree* of codification and constraint which characterizes contexts of action',[17] and again can be of many sorts, some relating not to individual functions but, like cogs in wheels, to the 'gearing' between different domains of action: so the 'role' of celebrity (my example) enables individual actors to cross multiple domains of action, 'gearing' their practice as, say, a musician or actor to possible political interventions. Roles, as traditionally understood, provide contexts in which the individual can act, but for Martuccelli this context can vary in 'consistency'.[18] Martuccelli's metaphor is that of an elastic bond ('le liant') which connects individuals and contexts but with varying degrees of flexibility.[19] And individuals too inhabit roles with varying degrees of freedom or rigidity. If we consider the analysis of neoliberal democracies in earlier chapters, we can express aspects of it in terms of the *breakdown* of the gearings that so far have linked, say, work roles and family roles and so underpinned the possibility of a life-narrative that links the two domains.

'Respect' relates to the broader political and cultural narratives which shape individuals' sense of their scope for action and competitive interaction: in the course of a historical account of the shift from 'hierarchical' regimes of interaction and those based on equality and/or 'difference', Martuccelli acknowledges the importance of Axel Honneth's theory of recognition, but notes plausibly that we cannot assume that every form of disrespect is connected with a sense of injustice that resonates politically.[20] What is less clear is Martuccelli's own perspective on the shifts between regimes of interaction, especially the recent 'compartmentalization' (characteristic of neoliberalism) between economic, cultural and social domains, and the problems that arise in each.[21] 'Identity' and 'subjectivity' relate more directly to the terrain we have called 'voice'; 'identity' to the process of 'express[ing] oneself ... through essential identities and stable oppositions' and 'subjectivity', by contrast, to the less socially oriented struggle to defend an autonomous space of individual action.[22] It is clear that the process of 'voice' crosses both: it is both an attempt to achieve a satisfying narrative that fills in the gaps social narratives leave unfulfilled[23] *and* the carving out of an exclusive space of personal reflection.

What is most useful about Martuccelli's analysis is its separation of different strands of resource which surround and sustain the possibility and practice of voice, while insisting that the outcome is not a simple or unified process. Martuccelli is sensitive to the contradictory feelings that characterize the space of contemporary voice: the demand, on the one hand, for recognition as uniquely different and, on the other, the insistence on the protection afforded by a universalized formality.[24] Less helpful is Martuccelli's seeming lack of interest in media's role in the work of the individual, media being dismissed merely as a universal mass message, rather than a contributor to individual perspectives on the world.[25] Nor need we follow Martuccelli's suggestion that the theory of the individual should become a separate discipline from the rest of sociology.[26] On the contrary, we need to connect Martuccelli's subtle analysis more closely than he does to underlying differentials of class and power, 'race' and gender, as well as to macro-contexts such as neoliberalism.

In spite of these limitations, Martuccelli's suspicion of accounts of identity developed from general analyses of 'socialization' resonates strongly with other recent work in sociology, cultural studies and critical psychology, even if those other approaches give class a more important role. As Bev Skeggs points out, we cannot take for granted the desire to produce an individual narrative, since the forms of self-narrative that we recognize as 'individual' are themselves marked by class in countries such as Britain:

> 'Individuals' are the product of privilege, who can occupy the economic and cultural conditions which enable them to do the work on the self. The 'individual' is part of a very different class project to the one these women [her book's subjects] are involved in.[27]

Skeggs interviewed working-class women in subordinate class positions who avoided a self-narrative in terms of class in favour of acts of 'passing', that is, acting as if they occupied other class positions. These narrative acts, which fell short of explicit narratives, were formed out of a 'desire not to be shamed, but to be legitimated'.[28] What Skeggs brings out – it is missing in Martuccelli's account – is an understanding of how, given conditions of uneven recognition, individuals do not have control of many of the narrative resources on which a self-narrative might be built. We cannot judge in advance what narrative forms are appropriate to particular people. Both Valerie Walkerdine and Julie Swindells, in their studies, respectively, of young girls' identities and Victorian women's autobiographies,[29] bring out the role of popular cultural sources in providing working-class subjects with narrative materials for use in ways at odds with conventional assumptions about what constitutes a 'good' life-narrative. As Carol Gilligan insisted, we need to be sensitive to the very different landscapes of speaking and listening in which particular individuals speak.[30]

Martuccelli's account must also be supplemented by more serious attention to the impacts of traumas or major losses that block off narrative completely. Angela McRobbie's recent account of young British women's 'illegible rage' and its basis in their loss of access to a feminist narrative offers one example.[31] W. G. Sebald's reflections on how 'the experience of terror dislocates time' offer another.[32] Recall Ricoeur's insight that 'temporality [is] the structure of existence that reaches language in narrativity': to be unable to narrate is, in a sense, to fall out of time, which may well make life intolerable, but is no less real a possibility for that.

Where does this deepened individual perspective on voice leave us, and leave sociology? Certainly with a healthy scepticism towards general narratives of social change or social force that take too little account of the complexity of the individual point of view;[33] certainly also with a scepticism towards Dubet's claim that freedom and domination is now '*defined* by the ability to master and construct [one's] experience',[34] which is perhaps to give *too much* prominence to individual voice in the overall set of goods to which we need access; and finally, with an unanswered question about how relations of power are involved in shaping the space of individual narratives.

Hidden injuries

Sociologies of voice must listen carefully to accounts not just of recognition, but also of misrecognition. This follows once we understand the space in which individual voices are recognized as the result of continuous struggles of recognition and battles over symbolic power.

Surprisingly, however, this is an area to which sociology has given relatively little explicit attention. And while the distinguished tradition of oral history has celebrated the role of individual narratives as new forms of historical evidence or testimony, it is not (as the French sociologist turned oral historian Daniel Bertaux makes clear) concerned directly with the conditions that regulate the availability of voice for individuals.[35]

Class and contemporary conditions of work

Our starting-point here is research that, although it operates with some of the same materials as oral history (both Bertaux and Richard Sennett have interviewed bakers, in France and the USA respectively), offers a broader account of the conditions of voice as such. Important here is work that foregrounded the symbolic dimensions of power relations in class-based societies such as the USA. Richard Sennett and Jonathan Cobb's 1972 book, *The Hidden Injuries of Class*, examined the damage that class inequality, embedded through the education system and division of labour, did to individual members of the American working class. They discuss a manual labourer, 'Rissarro', who 'believes people of a higher class have a power to judge him because they seem internally more developed human beings. ... He feels compelled to justify his own position [in relation to them]'.[36] Their analysis has resonances with accounts of peasants' 'self-depreciation' in highly unequal agrarian economies.[37] Yet it is difficult to believe, nearly four decades since that fieldwork, that the point of comparison and difference would today be expressed in quite these terms ('formal education' versus 'manual labour').

Sennett, however, in his later study *The Corrosion of Character*, tracks new forms of symbolic dislocation which reproduce power in no less important ways in today's 'flexible' labour markets; strikingly, these new dislocations all derive from the way that people have, or do not have, available to them narratives that can make sense of their work experience. First, there is the business consultant son of a Boston cleaner that Sennett had interviewed for his earlier book, whose life is a constant battle to manage time and survive uncertainty. Sennett sees in his story a loss of the experience of commitment, at least in the form of a story of a consistent working self that can be passed on to his children. It is a problem that 'Rico cannot offer the substance of his work life as an example to his children of how they should conduct themselves ethically'.[38] While the experience of less than meaningful work is hardly new, what Sennett is trying to capture are the ethical consequences of a shift in the status of work narratives (remember Ricoeur's comment on the link between being able to gather one's life into a narrative and having an ethical stance: see Chapter Five). Sennett's point is not that people cannot live with the constant disruption of contract switching, or bidding for new business (they can because they have to), but that the internalization of this instability is at best a repeated, forced acceptance that does not involve, maybe even undermines, the possibility of a *narrative that explains* such insecurity.[39]

A number of other factors intersect in Sennett's account. The operation of power in contemporary decentralized organizations operates behind the screen of a certain 'disorder' and informality which does not undermine the ultimate distribution of power over who gets employed (this remains centralized), but creates a gap between the actual dynamics of power and workers' ability *to say* what is going on.[40] Meanwhile the increasingly fast, computerized, multi-tasked work environment has changed the stories that workers can tell about themselves and their skills: 'now in the flexible regime, the personal qualities of being a good worker [seem] harder to define'.[41] A wider craft-based story of collective struggle is unavailable.[42] Finally, and most worryingly, the need of employers to implement continual 'change' has led to an increasing devaluation of loyalty and experience with consequences for workers' relationships *to time* (and so, following Ricoeur, to narrative). Sennett states this with great clarity: 'the passage of years seems to hollow us out. Our experience seems a shameful citation. Such convictions put our sense of self-worth at risk.'[43]

On multiple levels, routes to narrative about work are blocked, cut short. The result is a form of 'alienation',[44] which we cannot register unless we attend to questions of voice and narrative. Indeed, the power of Sennett's analysis is inseparable from his unusual sensitivity to people's need to find a place, or form, for their narratives.[45] Sennett shares this sensitivity with Axel Honneth, who argues that traditional class analysis must be supplemented by an awareness of the very uneven distribution of individual opportunities to 'find intersubjective recognition' and the resulting processes of 'desymbolization' which Honneth, referring directly to Sennett and Cobb, saw in German work cultures of the 1980s and 1990s.[46]

For the most powerful extension of Sennett's insights into narrative and voice, however, we must turn to research on gender and 'race', sexuality and age.

Gender and morality

Psychologist Carol Gilligan's interest 'in the way we listen to ourselves and to others, in the stories we tell about our lives' uncovered major differences in how highly educated Harvard students and graduates talked about their lives and sense of moral responsibility, depending on whether they were female or male.[47] The difference was in part a positive one: an 'ethics of care' among women that emphasized 'a central insight that self and other are interdependent'.[48] On the negative side, the difference lay in a frequent difficulty of women in finding a voice or recognizing themselves as having moral agency, and (Gilligan's wider thesis) the inability of mainstream psychology at the time to recognize the female view of moral responsibility as suggesting an equally valid model of human development alongside the more instrumental male model. Gilligan's attention to voice thus led her to a major critique of her own discipline, and the language of educational development, for its 'difficulty in hearing what [women] say when they speak'.[49]

Carol Gilligan's more recent work addresses the intersection of race, class and gender in the disempowering of poor black or Latina girls and young women. Here the sense of lacking a voice was not, as with the Harvard students, subtle or understated, but a direct fact of experience, as adolescent girls in their first relationships encountered the pressures against speaking openly on the morality of what they saw around them:

> Girls in [this] study live in a territory between voice and
> silence: if they continue to speak from their experience, they
> may find that their voice is out of relationship, too loud, off
> key. If they remain silent, they are in immediate danger of
> disappearing.[50]

In these difficult circumstances, being able to speak out becomes either an
abnormality or a distant dream:

> My aunt ... she's the type that, she's crazy ... You know, she
> listens. (Ana, Latina American, tenth grade)

> I'm kind of like quiet about my business, you know what
> I mean? If I want people to know, I'd probably put it on the
> news. (Mary, Irish American, tenth grade)[51]

What Gilligan's work brings out is the intense and local forces which, for some
people, close down their opportunities for speaking and being recognized
positively for what they say, within a wider social distribution of voice that is
highly gendered.

The consequences of gender norms for the stories women can tell have, of
course, been long debated more widely in feminism in the 1970s and 1980s,
particularly because, under cover of natural boundaries between 'the sexes',
they represented centuries, indeed millennia, of power and domination.[52] But
they acquire particular complexity when, in what many writers call a 'post-
feminist era',[53] apparently emancipatory discourses (and invocations of female
voice) are combined with deeply retrogressive models of what counts as
success for a woman.[54]

Sexuality and the materiality of voice

A good way of exploring such contradictions further is through the parallel debate
developed in the 1980s and 1990s on the intersection of gender norms with the
regulation of sexuality. Whereas under current conditions the types of closure of
voice identified by Gilligan seemed relatively open to articulation and potentially
to long-term unravelling, those around sexual regulation, and the framework of
'heteronormativity' that assigns particular sexual roles and desires to each gendered body, may appear difficult even to formulate in sociological terms. Here the
crucial reference-point is the work of philosopher Judith Butler.

Butler argues that, to be understood, acknowledged and recognized *as* a
subject, 'I' have to satisfy certain 'norms of intelligibility'.[55] Gender and sexuality are inseparably interwoven with those norms; gender is regulated in
a way that is linked to the regulation of sexuality. Not only is gender constructed as a relation between two mutually exclusive genders, but particular (heterosexual) sexual inclinations are mapped on to those genders. As a
result, the 'sexed nature' of women and men is produced as '*predi*scursive',[56]

so that sex can appear as the 'natural' grounding of gender difference. Subjects that do not correspond to this preconditioned grid of gender and sexuality are, Butler argues, simply not recognizable as full subjects; they remain deficient voices, automatically excluded from the possibility of full speech and subject-recognition.

Butler was not the first to argue for the non-natural status of cultural norms, but her version is radical because it moves beyond earlier arguments that all social and cultural terms are, by definition, 'constructed'. Conventional notions of social construction imply that concepts and categories are fully open to renegotiation. Butler, however, argues that various important categories and norms are embedded into *material* practice – 'below' the level of dialogue and discussion.[57] Certain embodiments of sexuality and gender are, Butler argues, simply not recognized as *possible* forms of embodiment and individuation. The regulation of sexual difference is therefore not simply an 'effect' of discourse, nor is it open to adjustment simply through new forms of discourse. The regulation in question works already through a process of *value* – 'the constitutive force of exclusion, erasure, violent foreclosure, abjection'[58] – that regulates 'bodies that matter' and distinguishes them from those that do not.

Many different readings of Butler are possible, and some, emphasizing her reliance on arguments from psychoanalysis and philosophy of language, would not place her work within a sociology of voice at all. But that, I suggest, would be to miss the interesting ways in which Butler criticizes philosophical arguments for their detachment from historical and social conditions and even makes sociological claims herself.

On the first point, in *Bodies That Matter*, Butler rejects, as unhelpful to her arguments, abstract psychoanalytic accounts of meaning which leave no room for cultural contestation; Zizek and Lacan provide insufficiently historical accounts of the supposedly absolute constraints attached to any individual's entering 'the symbolic' at all.[59] Instead, Butler draws on philosophy of language and Jacques Derrida's notion of 'citationality'.[60] Derrida had argued that any linguistic expression has meaning only on condition that the context which classifies its meaning and reference is never fully specifiable (otherwise that expression would be unable to function in relation to an infinitely variable range of contexts). As a result, each term, according to Derrida, must be 'cited' in a specific context every time it is used, in order to secure its meaning: this 'citing' introduces what we might call a *non-negotiable negotiability* into each term's meaning. This enables Butler to argue that only by being cited (as a law) can a norm function as a norm, which means that every norm requires what Butler calls 'temporalization',[61] a never-to-be-completed sequence of moments when it is cited, re-cited and potentially therefore 'imperfectly' cited. But in *Excitable Speech*, Butler seeks to distance herself from the a-historical implications of Derrida's concept of citationality, which, as Butler now remarks, appears to 'paralyz[e] the social analysis of forceful utterance'[62] because it is concerned with the properties of all linguistic terms whatsoever.

Turning to the sociological claims implicit in Butler's writings, in *Precarious Life* Butler shifted her focus from the specific context of gender and sexuality to issues of 'humanity' and the global political question of '*human intelligibility*'.[63] How, Butler asks, can we 'establish modes of public seeing and hearing that might well respond to the cry of the human within the sphere of appearance'?[64] The question is how best to understand the forces that work to constrain voice, how best to understand voice's material conditions in a media-saturated age. As Butler makes clear, these conditions are not all available to be read off from a culture's explicit signals. Some can only be traced by reading back from the landscape they have formed to an underlying process of *materialization*, the process whereby value emerges in the possible orders of the social world.[65] Butler raises difficult questions for a possible sociology of voice to which we must return.

Double consciousness: 'race' and age

Questions of 'race' are equally crucial to a sociology of voice. W. B. Du Bois' analysis of 'double consciousness' – the 'sense of always looking at one's self through the eyes of others'[66] – provided, at the beginning of the twentieth century, a powerful deconstruction of any simple notion of voice as natural or immediate. For under important and prevalent conditions of racial conflict, the very language and imagery of self-narrative was poisoned by category distinctions that directly undermined the dignity of black people.

Frantz Fanon went further and argued against the possibility of an authentic 'black soul' (a 'white man's artefact').[67] Instead, even a basic account of how self-narratives are constructed must take account of how white narratives are entangled with the voices of those who are not white:

> I am given no chance. I am overdetermined from without. I am the slave not of the 'idea' that others have of me but of my own appearance.[68]

Fanon's point is not to deny that at some level ideas matter, but rather, like Butler, to insist that categorical differences have already been naturalized in the material form of white bodies' automatic reactions to black bodies.

Laid over these fundamental conditions of voice's relations to 'race' are the consequences of different countries' histories of race-based oppression. Cornel West analysed these for the US case in a controversial essay on 'Nihilism in Black America': such nihilism, he argued, is not a considered rejection of the world, but 'far more, [the result of] the lived experience of coping with a life of horrifying meaninglessness, hopelessness, and (most important) lovelessness'.[69] 'Race' is a fundamental dimension of how the material conditions of voice are shaped.

An important, but less often considered, category affecting voice, where the notion of double consciousness may also be relevant, is *age*. There are age-related factors relating to the flexibilization of labour markets in neoliberal democracies that we touched on earlier. Less often noted is how everyday dealings with the aged involve a violent distortion of their conditions of voice. Ronald Blythe, in a pioneering oral history, noted that 'constantly, as one talked to the aged, one felt this struggle to say who they *are*, not just who and what they have been'.[70] This derives not just from a rejection of the aged body, but a moral rejection, based in the decline, in Britain at least, of shared narratives in which both the aged and the young could equally be subjects: 'such a situation can only alter', Blythe argues, when the narratives change, 'when it becomes natural to say that the old *are* us – and to believe it'.[71]

As Haim Hazan notes in an insightful study, whose critique of academic and official language has some parallels with Gilligan's, the constraining of the voice of the aged leads to some powerful blocks in older people's ability to narrate their lives. As the body declines, and older people do what they can to maintain *control* over their declining opportunities for independent action, these same people are stigmatized as a social *problem*.[72] The result is narrative dislocation: a gulf develops between others' descriptions of the aged (as a group who share a final and *unchanging* status close to death) and the aged's own perception of themselves as experiencing rapid and difficult *change* in their physical and social conditions.[73] Older people's diminished voice stems quite directly from no longer having a socially valued place from which to speak. Indeed, the imposition of others' discourse on the aged (what Jean Améry calls a 'total social determination')[74] is violent and consistent enough, perhaps, to merit Du Bois' term 'double consciousness'.

Injuries beyond categories

The landscape in which each individual acquires a voice is shaped in advance in these pervasive ways (about which, of course, much more could be said) that can only with the greatest difficulty be challenged by individuals.

Indeed, once we acknowledge, following Sennett, the possibility of 'hidden injuries' to people's sense of self-worth, we can quickly see other aspects of contemporary life that have general consequences for voice. If, for example, we interpret media not as open systems for representing our world back to us but as highly particular *concentrations* of narrative and other resources, then it becomes plausible to see this concentration as generating hidden injuries for those who are less well placed in the distribution of symbolic power. Whether we see media such as reality TV as providing a solution to, or as just one further part of, such problems of exclusion is perhaps unanswerable:[75] it may be better to leave open the question I have posed elsewhere of the 'hidden injuries of media power'.[76]

We cannot simply assume that popular culture is empowering here, as we know very little about the degree to which popular culture does *or does not* supply narrative resources that sustain people's ability to given accounts of their own lives in terms that are satisfactory to them. As Carolyn Steedman put it for the case of class, 'accounts of working class life are told by tension and ambiguity, out on the borderlands. The [particular] story ... cannot be absorbed into the central one: it is both its disruption and its essential component'.[77] So, too, we might add, for gender and sexuality, ethnicity and age. As political theorist Iris Marion Young notes, norms of speech have major consequences since they often operate to exclude whole social groups, such as women, from the 'central' conversations of their time.[78]

It is this divided territory which sociologies of voice must reflect. We need to think about how constraints on voice, initially based on direct acts of exclusion, become reinforced and naturalized. As Charles Tilly noted in his important book *Durable Inequality*, inequality becomes particularly durable when two major categories (for example, gender and 'race', or gender and class) are overlaid in everyday interactions, so that the operations of one category are normalized and naturalized under cover of the other.[79] Implicit here is a connection between discourse *and space* with which, in basic form, we are familiar from the idea that boundaries can express category differences, whether in ritual performance or in the segregation of living or other spaces.[80] What if the *articulation of space* – the spatial connections that are possible, even encouraged, versus those that are difficult, even impossible – may affect the *articulation of narrative*, that is, what narratives can be told in what context. One of the very few writers to notice this is again Richard Sennett who, as early as *The Fall of Public Man*, commented on the loss of public space as a space for narrative exchange; instead it has become, he argued, 'dead space', a mere 'means of passage to the interior'.[81] This broadens our understanding of how space and voice are linked. The articulation of space must be understood in relation to the connections that are inherent to, or blocked within, the process of narration.

So consideration of the conditions for voice takes us into broader questions about the organization of culture and space. What of historical conditions which might now be shaping possibilities of voice?

Wider conditions for voice

We should not expect a simple causal process whereby a change in dominant discourses directly changes the narrative forms that individuals or groups use. Even in conditions of poverty and deprivation, most people may remain actively reflexive in adapting to, and making sense of, their living conditions, *however constrained*.[82] To assume otherwise would be to deny the first principle of a sociological approach to voice, that narrative is a fundamental capacity of human beings, and its exercise crucial to living, *whatever* the conditions. This also throws into question Walter Benjamin's often quoted thesis from 1930s Europe that the saturation of life with information (particularly media news) has automatically undermined the practice of individual storytelling: 'by now almost nothing that happens benefits storytelling; almost everything benefits information'.[83] While the contexts of individual and collective narratives have clearly changed, for reasons linked to the growth of media technologies, what if practices of narrative have adapted to these new circumstances? We need to reframe our question by looking at the wider organization of narrative resources in social and economic life: in this way, we will be able to return at the end of the section to Butler's concept of materialization.

Narrative resources

We might start from the recent explosion of online opportunities for giving an account of oneself from *YouTube* to digital storytelling that potentially provide important forms of self-validation, public recognition and narrative exchange.[84]

Sometimes *YouTube* videos generate huge attention (for example, the *YouTube* make-up tutorials that gave Lauren Luke a sudden celebrity in the UK in early 2009)[85] but that is not the same thing as a broader recognition of the person involved: how often is a genuine exchange of recognition the outcome? A sociology of voice needs to look critically at these practices, which are often standardized and asymmetrical, and consider the degree to which they meet Axel Honneth's criteria for recognition.

However, other online spaces clearly open up new possibilities for voice. When we consider ethnicity and contemporary complex forms of diasporic identity at a time of intensified migration, recent work by Ananda Mitra and others has noted the scope for diasporic voice that online fora now provide.[86] But there, too, the broader issue of how such spaces are articulated to wider discursive and cultural domains must be asked.[87]

There are other complicating conditions which a sociological approach to voice should not neglect. First, there is the issue of social opacity. A number of writers have argued that the social world has become increasingly opaque;[88] as a result, older narratives that explained the social world's dynamics (for example, in terms of class struggle or the struggle between rich and poor) are no longer plausible, with impacts on the types of story that individuals and groups can tell about their role and place in the social world. We can approach this topic from various angles.

The increasing opacity of 'society' puts a premium on narratives that explain social happenings in non-social ways, for example in terms of individual failings or initiatives. Individual stories of distress or triumph may, paradoxically, be encouraged as a result of a wider collapse of explanatory narrative. This is French sociologist Alain Ehrenberg's account of the rise of the talk show in 1980s and early 1990s France,[89] a displacement of politics that does not, however, meet the same needs as political narratives since its logic is entirely individualized: 'reality spectacles ... do not replace politics in its function of representation, because they respect [people] by giving form to a solidarity which operates from individual to individual'.[90] There was no space in such talk shows for narratives that validate group action or collective mobilization: the qualification for being able to speak is having some *particular* story to tell, or being an accredited expert about the types of *individual* narrative under discussion.

Eva Illouz's analysis of the *Oprah Winfrey* show is potentially more positive. Examining the language of moral commitments that guests, audience, Oprah herself, and programme marketers use, Illouz finds evidence of a moral language which foregrounds 'moral dilemmas that pertain to the definition of the good life and good selves',[91] while expanding our grasp of the moral range of everyday life and deconstructing simple moral distinctions.[92] The programmes are more than texts because they include the willed narratives of people engaged in describing their lives.[93]

Oprah Winfrey is, however, a privileged site at which to examine the intersection between media narratives and processes of moral recognition. Other writers are more pessimistic about whether media provide narratives that compensate for the opacity of the social world. Henry Giroux's concern is with the absence (and thereby implicit devaluation) of all narratives of self-transformation aimed at US children which do not privilege market logics: 'where can children find narratives of hope, semiautonomous cultural spheres, discussions of meaningful differences, and non market-based democratic identities?'[94] An important part of Giroux's argument is that this deficit is not confined to media, too often a convenient scapegoat, but is a wider feature of everyday life in the USA, for example in the increasingly corporate language in US schools. For Giroux, silence about the possible 'civic function' of public education, by contrast to much talk and imagery that affirms the role of corporations in supplying children's needs, contributes not so much to the opacity of the social world, as to a new and strong reading of that world as a place where children associate democracy with the unfettered right to consume.[95] Meanwhile, alternative narratives which confirm the authority of teachers as educators and young people as potential citizens fall away as reference-points, with long-term consequences for how the social futures with which educational institutions remain entrusted get defined.[96] So the issue is not just social opacity, but the loss of quite specific narratives that make meaningful specific types of agency.

Carl Nightingale's concern in an important study of black youth in Philadelphia is different once again: plenty of media-sourced narratives are available to them, but the narratives of consumption that capture their imaginations risk holding out a promise of material success that will never be delivered. Nightingale's account is poignant: 'already at five and six, many kids in the neighbourhood can recite the whole canon of adult luxury – from Gucci ... and Pierre Cardin, to Mercedes and BMW ... to Eddie Murphy's mansion with two pools, to Donald Trump's massive casino'.[97] The consequences of such narrative promises for family solidarity are devastating:

> For kids the experience of living in a poor family amid a mass culture of abundance quickly sours their attitudes towards cooperation. ... Parents' inability to provide the basic needs of childhood 'as seen on TV' ... help forge a set of cynical assumptions about other people's motives in general.[98]

For Nightingale, then, the wider reference-points of media culture pull the space of everyday narrative out of alignment. This is an example of the conflict that, in the 1930s at the height of structural functionalism, Robert Merton expressed as existing between 'cultural goals' and 'institutional norms' of behaviour.[99] Today, in the context of a sociology of voice, we might express it in terms of a conflict between widely available media narratives of high legitimacy and the impossibility of fitting them with the actual conditions of life, which leads to a breakdown at the level of both action *and narrative*.

Narrative strategies

How might we connect our map of the questions posed by sociologies of voice to the argument developed earlier in the book about the consequences of neoliberal discourse? Bear in mind that we are now looking at things from the opposite direction: no longer starting out from neoliberal doctrine's ambition to change the social terrain, we are looking for changes 'on the ground', as it were, in the pattern and organization of people's practices of voice.

Is it true, for example, as Zygmunt Bauman argues, that 'the stories we tell nowadays and are willing to listen to rarely, if ever, reach beyond the narrow and painstakingly fenced-off enclosure of the private and the "subjective" self'?[100] Or is the problem, just as much, that the stories that *do* reach beyond the private self do so in particular ways – for example, through accounts of famous selves (celebrity) or collective narratives in a sphere distant from most individuals' life conditions (large-scale sporting narratives) – and not others (accounts of community or organizational action and change)? Perhaps general diagnosis of this sort is impossible, and we can only make progress by asking, for specific sites and practices: what narratives are possible here or required? What links to other sites and practices do such narratives make? What links are not made?

What matters, then, is how we apply very general theoretical insights to particular locations. Take Georg Simmel's early twentieth-century insights in *The Philosophy of Money* into the impacts of a money economy on everyday action. Simmel offered an important general insight, that money extends the actions we can perform by linking together multiple series of actions, and so multiple scales and temporalities of action (so that 'the goal of the moment more usually lies beyond that moment, or even beyond the horizon of the individual').[101] The result, Simmel argues, is that:

> The conceivable elements of action become objectively and subjectively calculable rational relationships and on so doing progressively eliminate the emotional reactions and decisions which only attach themselves to the turning points of life, to the final purposes.[102]

But this insight gets its real bite when we apply it, for example, to a situation where governments are seeking to encourage the monetization of activities (such as care) that have not previously been monetized in detail, or to impose controls on time use that have their basis in large-scale targets about monetary resources (compare Chapter Three). What narratives about resources and action become prioritized in these circumstances and what narratives become difficult? How do people's accounts of what they do, and aim for, *change* under these circumstances? What previous narratives are blocked off – and with what consequences for the coherence of people's larger account of themselves as agents worthy of emotional, moral and social recognition (Honneth's three levels of recognition)? And what, in turn, are the wider consequences for the life-narratives of those who work in the management of such service providers or in government? We saw one indirect consequence in Chapter Three when we noted that in a UK government White Paper about empowering local citizens, no mention was made of citizens influencing the larger framework that determines how local government deals with central government: amid talk of 'democratization', a crucial (and older) narrative of empowerment ceases to be heard and our account of democracy's potential is weakened.

Or take Simone Weil's insights in the 1930s about the importance of time and rhythm in work, and the consequences when workers, say on an assembly line, lack the time to think freely about the flow and sequence of their work. Weil's concern derived from her belief that 'our thought is intended to master time',[103] and so the loss of time for thought has major consequences for our general ability to manage our life. At a general level, perhaps the implications are ambiguous: don't flexible work contracts and home and mobile allow us to manage our life better? But we must ask more specific questions: what possibilities for control or 'mastery' of their time are available to particular home-workers, and which are not? Under what conditions can a freelance worker, contracted to multiple clients or buyers, manage his or her time, to fit his or her own needs for rest, caring responsibilities or time to think? And what larger narrative about that worker's control of her time and tasks can be sustained under these circumstances? These questions, although about the conditions of work, are always also about narrative, as Weil herself saw: 'many indispensable truths ... go unspoken ... those who could utter them cannot formulate them and those who could formulate them cannot utter them'.[104] But why cannot certain 'truths' that have been formulated not be uttered? What are the implications for opportunities for voice (or the lack of them) in contemporary flexible work cultures under the new spirit of capitalism?

This takes us to the question of what larger collective narratives are available to articulate social change and, indeed, political change at particular times. A sociology that stays at the level of *individual* narrative resources cannot be adequate. This is true, above all, when certain types of collective narrative (for example, of workers' organizing for extra-institutional goals) have been devalued and other collective narratives (expressing passionate commitment to particular institutions or around corporate transformation, for example) have been highly valued. The US legal sociologist Robert Cover offered here a crucial insight:

Narratives are models through which we study and experience transformations that result when a given simplified state of affairs is made to pass through the force field of a similarly simplified set of norms.[105]

While Cover was concerned with the 'normative universe'[106] that underlies particular sovereign states at a general level, in this book we are concerned with the possibility that under particular historical circumstances a specific discourse (neoliberalism) has operated to *change* the normative universe which underpins what states and other actors can do, reframing what actions are possible and desirable on various levels.

How do collective narratives change on this large scale? The interesting issue for a sociology of voice is not so much what stimulates change: clearly major events that are successfully presented as 'exemplars' (to use Norval's term), such as the fall of the Berlin Wall or 9/11, are major stimuli to change in collective narratives. The most interesting question for us is: through what mechanisms is *change enacted*? Older narratives do not simply disappear from thought or imagination; instead, as Sennett puts it, they cease to 'have [a] home'.[107] How does this happen? At a certain point, I suggest, the larger narrative frames in which smaller narratives inhere lose their legitimacy and power as exemplars or explanations, leaving smaller narratives which depended on them to wither, unsupported. Crucial to our understanding of this process are *the larger frameworks that contextualize detailed narrative practice*. As Zygmunt Bauman puts it:

> The distinctive feature of the stories told in our times is that they articulate individual lives in a way that excludes or suppresses (prevents from articulation) that possibility of tracking down the links concerning individual fate to the ways and means by which society as a whole operates ... [so social factors become] 'brute facts' which the storytellers can neither challenge nor negotiate whether singly, severally, or collectively.[108]

This helps us understand why the closing down of voice in contemporary working conditions is not necessarily a process that itself can be accessed in narrative. Key aspects of work experience may be a domain of silence.

How then might alternative, more supportive connecting narratives be tracked down? One type of narrative is associated with the networked cultures of protest that Jeffrey Juris has analysed and that we considered in Chapter Five. As Juris brings out, these can be understood as attempts, in part, to enact new narratives and models of social change, what he calls 'informational utopics'.[109] These are important new possibilities for voice that must be traced into the circumstances of everyday life.

Here we reach a difficult issue for sociological approaches to voice: the organization of narrative and action *in space and time*. Just as collective memory needs a material form if it is to survive[110] – a particular organization of time and place whereby the acts of remembering can be performed – so too with narrative and voice generally. Voice as a practice is embodied, and its context is often, although not always, the presence of other bodies: an occasion to speak or remember, an opportunity to exchange stories, a shared act of interpretation. We must not lose hold of this insight if we are serious about developing a counter-rationality to neoliberalism. For neoliberal rationality very well appreciated this connection between voice and practice, when in place of older narratives for thinking about the social world it installed a different narrative on every scale down to the most local: the narrative of market functioning. At this point, we must return to Judith Butler's concept of materialization.

Spaces for voice?

We cannot simply take voices, and the spaces in which they appear, as given. As Axel Honneth notes, we are all engaged in *struggles* for recognition. Admittedly, recognition is not what economists call a 'rival good' (like an orange, a unit of electricity) that literally is used up once a first person has consumed it – it is always possible that more people start recognizing each other, expanding the sum total of recognition – but our practices of recognition (and so our practices of voice) are limited by the histories of the spaces where we find ourselves: the histories of others' struggles of recognition before us, the history of our own struggle to be recognized by contrast to particular others. Spaces for voice are therefore *inherently* spaces of power; their link to power does not just derive from institutions such as government seeking to manage them. So a sociological approach to voice can never just be based on a celebration of people speaking or telling stories: it must be placed in a sociological context which is always, in part, a political context (lack of this is a problem, I suggest, with David Gauntlett's otherwise useful account of narrative and creativity).[111] We need to grasp the long history of materialization (the hidden evaluations) that has gone on before someone speaks or falls silent.

People's voices only count if their bodies 'matter'. This book's title deliberately echoes Judith Butler's crucial insight into materialization. Butler expresses this in terms of 'bodies' because it is through direct discriminations between possible and impossible bodies that the regulation of sexuality is performed. But her fundamental insight applies to forms of regulation other than sexuality and to discriminations made not directly through judgements on bodies as such. As Aletta Norval notes (see Chapter Five), people need first to be *visible* before they can be recognized as having voice; they must first be regarded as part of the landscape in which struggles for voice go on. Geographer David Sibley analyses the energy spent in 'purifying' spaces so that certain types of people are not there to be counted (the long-term exclusion of women from places of political decision-making, the continuing exclusion of migrant populations from narratives of national politics or culture).[112] Such purifications aim to leave no mark of their operations; they aim precisely to create a 'pure' space for voice. Those acts of purification, when grasped by those at whom they have all along been directed, hurt a great deal.[113]

A more subtle type of purification occurs when a particular framing of the conditions for voice – the appropriate topics for the exercise of voice – becomes dominant. It is much too early to say how the new spaces of self-display, whether of a quasi-broadcast nature (*YouTube*) or semi-private (social networking sites), will develop. But, as we saw in Chapter Two, Sarah Banet-Weiser's and Alison Hearn's work points to a disturbing possibility: that the apparently free space for new voices that these sites offer may be dominated by norms and strategies that replay, in performance mode, the values and logic of neoliberalism. A logic of 'self-branding'[114] prima facie offers a route to voice and recognition, but each is on offer *only* on the terms that govern a competitive market of appearances. In that respect, the language of self-branding is honest, but in another respect it is not, when it forces those spaces of possible reflection, play and sociality into becoming domains for realizing entrepreneurial benefit.

It is here we need to remind ourselves (see Chapter One) that voice – the full social process of voice, listening and exchange that sociologies of voice seek to register – is an *externality* of market functioning. We can believe otherwise by fusing the space of the self with the path of a commodity, by fusing the process of voice with the projection of a reliable brand image, but in doing so we lose touch with the reflexive complexity that is a distinctive capacity of human beings. If sociologies of voice have a point, it is to register this price and explain why it is a price too high to pay.

Conclusion

In spite of the urgency of this task, a consistent attention to voice is missing from much mainstream sociology devoted to broad theory or quantitative data: as Les Back argues, the 'art of listening' is in danger of become a lost art.[115] Yet such listening – and the example of 'narrative hospitality'[116] it sets – matters a great deal at a time when other large-scale forces, within and far beyond the academy, are working to devalue voice.

In learning of the complexities of others' voices, we may learn something about the complexities of our own. In reverse, many writers have asked whether, by grasping the uncertainties of my own voice, I am better placed to accept the complexities of others' voices. Some (Julia Kristeva, Jessica Benjamin, Judith Butler) have approached this from the perspective of psychoanalysis, others (Ricoeur and Elspeth Probyn) more from the perspective of history.[117] The underlying point is an ethical one and it is Paul Ricoeur who states it most clearly: a 'recourse to a narrative identity' is 'perverse', Ricoeur writes, without both self-reflexivity and the recognition of 'the entanglement of our stories with the stories of others'.[118]

Sociologies of voice, then, involve both a practice of recognition (listening to others' voices, registering them as important) and a realistic analysis of the obstructions to recognition, even at times when we are told we *have* voice, we *can* reinvent ourselves, we *can* be heard. Only in this way can we generate the evidence on which a wider politics that challenges neoliberalism can build. The nature of such a politics is the topic of the final chapter.

Notes

1   Rose (1990), Giddens (1991), Illouz (2007).
2   Beck (1992: 137).
3   See Chapter One.
4   For 'landscapes' of voice, see Steedman (1986) and Taylor, Gilligan and Sullivan (1995: 1).
5   Bauman (2001: 13, added emphasis).
6   Maalouf (2000: 4).
7   Giroux (2007).
8   Martuccelli (2002: 11–14).
9   In anthropology, see Moore (1994: chapter 3), Cohen (1994); in sociology, see Craib (1998), Touraine (1988).
10   Touraine (1984: xxiv, 8, 11, 17).
11   Dubet (1995: 103).
12   Dubet (1995: 111–112, 116), cf. (1994).
13   Martuccelli (2002: 31–35).
14   Martuccelli (2002: 46–50).
15   Martuccelli (2002: 77).
16   Martuccelli (2002: 92).
17   Martuccelli (2002: 143, added emphasis).
18   Martuccelli (2002: 175–176).
19   Martuccelli (2002: 178ff.).
20   Martuccelli (2002: 261).
21   Martuccelli (2002: 262).
22   Martuccelli (2002: 407, 468–469).
23   Martuccelli (2002: 370).
24   Martuccelli (2002: 298).
25   Martuccelli (2002: 360–361).
26   Martuccelli (2002: 557).
27   Skeggs (1997: 163).
28   Skeggs (1997: 87).
29   Walkerdine (1997), Swindells (1985).
30   Gilligan (1982: 173).
31   McRobbie (2009).
32   Sebald (2004: 154).
33   For similar conclusions from different starting-points, see Boltanski and Thévenot (2006: chapter 1); Bourdieu (1999).
34   Dubet (1995: 11, added emphasis).
35   See, for example, Thompson (1982: 17–19), Bertaux (1982: 102).
36   Sennett and Cobb (1972: 25).
37   Freire (1972: 38–39).
38   Sennett (1998: 21).
39   Sennett (1998: 31).
40   Sennett (1998: chapter 3), cf. Boltanski and Chiapello (2005), Ross (2004).
41   Sennett (1998: 71).
42   Sennett (1998: 74).
43   Sennett (1998: 97).
44   Sennett (1998: 146, cf. 117).

45 Sennett (1998: 74).
46 Honneth (1995a: 229, 217).
47 Gilligan (1982: 2).
48 Gilligan (1982: 74).
49 Gilligan (1982: 173).
50 Taylor, Gilligan and Sullivan (1995: 202).
51 Taylor, Gilligan and Sullivan (1995: 116, 101, layout of attributions changed).
52 Riley (1988).
53 McRobbie (2009), Gill (2009), Tasker and Negra (2007).
54 For an earlier discussion of 'voice' in relation to gender and communication, see Rakow and Wackwitz (2004).
55 Butler (1990: 17).
56 Butler (1990: 7).
57 Cf. Bourdieu (1990: 73) on patterning that works 'below the level of consciousness'.
58 Butler (1993: 8)
59 Butler (1993: 206–207)
60 Derrida (1991 [1972]).
61 Butler (1993: 90).
62 Butler (1997: 150).
63 Butler (2004: 35).
64 Butler (2004: 147).
65 Butler (1993: 1).
66 Du Bois (1989: 3 [1903]).
67 Fanon (1986: 16).
68 Fanon (1986: 116).
69 West (1992: 42).
70 Blythe (1979: 15).
71 Blythe (1979: 19).
72 Hazan (1994: 76, 81).
73 Hazan (1994: 74).
74 Améry (1994: 67).
75 Cf.Walkerdine (1997: chapter 7) on the older notion of 'going on the stage'.
76 Couldry (2001).
77 Steedman (1986: 22).
78 Young (2000: 55–56).
79 Tilly (1998).
80 Sibley (1996). For a more complex account, see Moore (1986).
81 Sennett (1977: 12–16), cf. (1994: introduction).
82 Bertaux (2001).
83 Benjamin (1968: 89).
84 Burgess and Green (2009); Fyfe et al. (2009), Lambert (2007), Lundby (2008). See also http://storiesforchange.net.
85 See www.youtube.com/view_play_list?p=DA17880307AB6B95&search_query=make+up+tutorial+lauren+luke.
86 Mitra (2001), Mitra and Watts (2002), Mainsah (2009).
87 Byrne (2008).
88 Ehrenberg (1995: 22), Touraine (1984), McDonald (1999).
89 Ehrenberg (1998: 283–240).
90 Ehrenberg (1995: 298).
91 Illouz (2003: 49).
92 Illouz (2003: 67–68, 74).
93 Illouz (2003: 84).
94 Giroux (2000: 11).
95 Giroux (2000: 90, 95).
96 Cf. Grossberg (2005).
97 Nightingale (1993: 153–154).

98 Nightingale (1993: 160).
99 Merton (1938).
100 Bauman (2001: 12).
101 Simmel (1978: 431).
102 Simmel (1978: 431).
103 Quoted in Blum and Seidler (1989: 161).
104 Quoted in Blum and Seidler (1989: 192).
105 Cover (1992: 102).
106 Cover (1992: 103).
107 Sennett (1998: 74).
108 Bauman (2001: 9).
109 Juris (2008: 267–286).
110 Halbwachs (1992).
111 Gauntlett (2007: esp. 186–192).
112 Sibley (1996).
113 For a moving autobiographical account of just such a process, see Dunbar (1997: 85).
114 Banet-Weiser (forthcoming), Hearn (2008).
115 Back (2007).
116 Ricoeur (1995: 8).
117 Kristeva (1991), Benjamin (1998), Butler (2005), Probyn (1993), Ricoeur (1995).
118 Ricoeur (1995: 9–10).

Chapter 7

Towards a Post-Neoliberal Politics

Neoliberalism is a rationality that denies voice and operates with a view of human life that is incoherent. As a culture within the economy, it is unsustainable and, as a template for politics, it produces a democratic process that is self-harming; little within the processes of mainstream media interrupts, and much reinforces, this self-harm. This is the neoliberal crisis of voice analysed in Chapters One to Four. But we still have to ask: is a 'post-neoliberal' politics,[1] which challenges the 'rationality' of neoliberalism, possible? How can we begin to formulate it? The neoliberal crisis of voice presents us with a decision-point (the original meaning of the word 'crisis')[2] that is both normative and practical.

Neoliberalism, after all, started with a decision, somewhere: perhaps it was the moment when von Hayek argued that the only source for our moral sense was the *individual*'s sense of control over his or her own life, the 'freedom to order our own conduct in the sphere where material circumstances force a choice upon us'. On this view, cooperation, though often desirable, is purely a matter of individual will.[3] Driven by his fear of 'collectivism' in the USA and the UK, and his revulsion against Soviet socialism and German national socialism, von Hayek turned his back on John Dewey's broader view of freedom, based in the social grounding of human experience and the communicative (not merely economic) exchange through which individuals orient themselves to the world.[4] There is no need for us to repeat von Hayek's mistake now. Recent developments in brain science insist that the human brain is *always and from the start* oriented towards registering the experiences of others alongside its own.[5] Can we go further and find starting-points for a new politics in a view of human life as inherently oriented both to social exchange and the form of life we have called voice?

The issue is perhaps best stated the other way round: can we afford to think of politics in a way that *neglects* this grounding for our possibilities of social and political cooperation? As John Dewey put it, 'democracy is more than a form of government'.[6] Admittedly, Dewey reflected on political cooperation at a time (the 1920s and 1930s) when this meant building hierarchical organizations (parties, unions, national leagues) and when the place of work was unequivocally central to establishing practices of mutual recognition between people whose relations were face to face much more than today. Now many work and social relationships are established and coordinated at a distance and new models of political action have developed that avoid formal organization, downplay the face to face and even sometimes the reference-point of work, finding new inspiration in computer-mediated networking at a distance.[7] Those new models discussed by Jeffrey Juris involve utopian visions of a workless society and economy, casting their imagination far into the future. But, unless, with Hardt and Negri, we 'black-box' modernity and insist arbitrarily that its earlier visions have no relevance for us now,[8] we should allow for the possibility that Dewey's vision of democracy as social cooperation can orient us to democratic possibilities *precisely* in a networked age when social cooperation takes important new forms. Even approaches to democracy (such as John Keane's)[9] that reject *any* attempt to relate democratic practice to positive principles, insisting only on the negative principle of 'no body rules', rely on *some* understanding of human capacities that justifies interrupting the rule of particular elites in the name of excluded others, the demand 'that the ability of citizens equally to grasp the world around them' is acknowledged.[10] Underlying all such approaches is the value of voice, expressed in a political form: the value denied by neoliberalism.

A starting-point for a post-neoliberal politics may, then, be alarmingly simple: to insist that no form of social or economic organization on any scale (from corporation to group, from transnational network to national government) has legitimacy if it prioritizes other values over the value of voice. By 'legitimacy' here I mean something more than formal legitimacy, since the crisis of voice under neoliberalism derives precisely from the fact that voice-denying rationalities take forms (in government, in management) that have formal legitimacy yet fail to be based on the values on which democratic life is generally assumed to be based: it is value-based legitimacy in which I am interested here. To those who insist on the overriding necessity of economic goals or needs for security, Amartya Sen's answer – that economic development and the provision of basic goods is poorly directed without citizens' contribution of their knowledge[11]– already serves as a starting-point for formulating post-neoliberal politics. A 'democratic' politics that seeks to deliver economic or other forms of security without voice is both illegitimate and blind. We might imagine a group or people delegating to a particular leadership, perhaps at times of great danger, the right to act on their behalf without referral, but that is not what we are confronting in neoliberalism. Neoliberalism is not based on voluntary delegation, but rather on an absence of voice or (at best) a renunciation of voice in one domain in order, supposedly, to retain voice in another. But given the interdependence of all sectors and scales of life (social, economic, political), such renunciation is not coherent. To renounce 'voice', for example, over the conditions of one's work and economic security, and delegate it permanently to 'market forces' – let alone, to treat the self as if it were only a commodity – is to lack voice on some crucial level. A counter-neoliberal rationality cannot get under way without asserting the value of voice and challenging the legitimacy of forms of institutional organization and self-discipline which deny that value.

Whatever else has happened since his election, Barack Obama's words in Grant Park Chicago just an hour after his victory in the 2008 US Presidential election can still be seen as signalling what it would be to value voice:

> If there is anyone out there who ... still doubts the power of democracy, tonight is your answer ... It's the answer told by lines that stretched around schools and churches in numbers this nation has never seen by people who waited three hours and four hours, many for the first time in their lives, because they believed that this time must be different, that their voices could *be* that difference.

In these words, Obama faced down the neoliberal insistence that nothing matters more than markets, and declared that at least one thing mattered more: a vision of democracy as acting together through voice. And he went further, choosing to focus the election's significance for a national global media audience through its impact on the narrative of a single life, that of a black woman, Ann Nixon Cooper, who had voted, for the first time, that day in Atlanta at the age of 106. Some might dismiss this as the personalization of politics. But in this gesture Obama showed he understood that this is *exactly* the level of personal significance that grounds why democracy matters, recognizing the capacity of all of us to participate in decision-making by acting on our interpretations of the world around us. And this acknowledgement was not sudden: during his campaign, Obama supporters were asked by email to encourage new voters to register 'and help bring new voices into the political process while there's still time',[12] echoing Obama's expressed belief that 'in the joining of voices ... what binds us together might somehow ultimately prevail'.[13] Obama's speech was an example of the affirmation of voice that sometimes – as after three decades of neoliberal discourse – needs, quite simply, to be made.

A post-neoliberal politics will, however, fail at first base if it reduces to simply calling for more voices. Nine months on in US politics, and during bitter battles over President Obama's proposals for a more socially inclusive healthcare system, it is failed Vice-Presidential candidate Sarah Palin who is using *Facebook* pages to tell her half a million 'friends' 'to make [their] voices heard'.[14] If our only principle was 'more voices', we should be celebrating Palin's call unequivocally; and whether we celebrate it or not, we must assume that new voices can come from anywhere in the political spectrum. The issue instead is what *values* are articulated through such voices: a post-neoliberal politics only gets moving if it articulates ways of organizing society, the economy and politics that *enable* voice *to matter*. Although we can perhaps now imagine a post-neoliberal politics, we do not live in a post-neoliberal age. On what resources can such a politics draw, knowing that it will face fierce resistance?

We have already reviewed some philosophical and sociological resources. In Chapter Five we saw human experience as inherently intersubjective, self-interpreting and entangled in an open-ended social process of narrative. The value of voice, which is grounded in this view of human life, works well with other principles – Axel Honneth's principle of recognition, Amartya Sen's understanding of freedom – to generate a broad philosophical foundation for a counter-rationality to neoliberalism. An important feature of that counter-rationality, however, is regular reassessment of the hidden exclusions on which any particular form of social or political organization is based. In Chapter Six, we explored some of those prior processes from the perspective of an emerging sociology of voice that listens out for how well voice is valued under particular social and historical circumstances. But all this still leaves undeveloped how such values might relate to the difficult processes of getting things done on large scales and amid profound conflicts over ends and means – in short, to 'politics'.[15]

I want tentatively, in concluding, to explore some starting-points for linking the value of voice to how we might think about, indeed rethink, political practice.

The challenge of imagination

What, French political sociologist Pierre Rosanvallon argues, if we now lack 'a way of gaining practical experience of the general will'?[16] The problem was identified two centuries ago when Benjamin Constant commented that, by contrast with the citizen of classical democracy, modern citizens lack 'tangible evidence of [their] cooperation' and 'have lost in imagination what [they] have gained in knowledge'.[17] This is normally considered a reflection on the possibility of democratic politics on a *large* scale. But, because of the growing interdependence of economic, social and political actions across *every* scale, the problem of imagining the 'general will' also applies on every scale: think of a small community organization, all of whose parameters of action are constrained by external economic forces, government regulations and media-enforced norms. As Chapters One to Four argued, neoliberal discourse has aggravated this problem by erasing many of the sites of political voice entirely.

It is unhelpful, however, to start by assuming neoliberalism's victory! Rather, let's ask: what would it be to rebuild ways of organizing life that instead act on the basis that voice matters? To help us imagine a starting-point, we can turn to Colombia's Andean region, a state where relentless violence and injustice have taken a huge toll on the mechanisms of democracy. The words of Alirio González, the founder of community station Radio Andaquí, quoted in Clemencia Rodriguez's wonderful new fieldwork seem, in their directness, strangely appropriate for other places too:

> What we need is for this territory to re-think itself as a subject, as an actor. The people here need to re-think their identities, their goals, and who they want to be.[18]

Nothing less, perhaps, is at stake in the many countries where recovery from the neoliberal experiment is needed.

A post-neoliberal politics, whatever detailed form it takes, must face at least four types of challenge. First, it must deal with the overhang of a different understanding of democracy (neoliberalism) which implicitly devalues voice and undermines the conditions that sustain voice. John Dewey foresaw the problem back in 1918: 'The attempt to identify democracy with economic individualism as the essence of free action has done harm to the reality of democracy and is capable of doing even greater injury than it has already done'.[19] But he could not have foreseen how dominant neoliberal discourse would become, and how deeply embedded in everyday understandings of the self and its capabilities.

Then there are three formidable political challenges. There is the need to reverse the exclusions of voice that neoliberalism endorsed: to reintegrate back into democratic processes the voices of workers whose political recognition through trade unions or other organizations has been eroded by comparison with the continuous ever-present voice of management and capital, or, as in India, never developed sufficiently (which India's New Trade Union Initiative aims to challenge).[20] This is part of a broader problem of developing new critiques of capitalism (it is for this task that Boltanski and Chiapello, borrowing Hirschman, reserve the word 'voice'),[21] and recognizing the economy once more, in J. K. Gibson-Graham's words, 'as *a site of decision* ... instead of as the ultimate reality/container/constraint'.[22] But it is also, as Steven Greenhouse notes at the end of his eloquent book on the unjust treatment of US workers over the past three decades, a matter of restoring 'respect'.[23] Then there is the need to include new voices: to allow space in democratic mechanisms for the agency of those, such as migrant workers, whose trajectories across space don't fit – or don't yet fit – with the inherited scale of national citizenship,[24] but who contribute greatly to the life of the citizenry that currently decides on their life-conditions.[25] This means building new scales of connection and comparison in political argument. And finally, there is the need, on all political scales and for all political actors, to address certain fundamental policy problems (such as declining oil resources and global warming) that cannot, on most views, be addressed without major changes in how all of us live our lives and manage our resources.[26]

Fortunately, a post-neoliberal politics can also draw on some important new resources, even if we need to be cautious in assessing them.

New technologies of voice ...

In his great book, *The Public and its Problems*, John Dewey sought to acknowledge the force of pessimistic arguments about democracy's workings (such as Walter Lippman's) that later informed US neoliberalism. He asked:

> What, after all, is the public under present conditions? ... What hinders it from finding and identifying itself?[27]

But there are strong arguments today for interrupting that pessimism. The growth of the internet and the world wide web – the advanced networking of so-called Web 2.0 (*Facebook, YouTube* and Twitter), the vastly increased opportunities enabled by digitalization for exchanging images, narratives, information and ways of managing data – suggest many ways in which a new public 'is finding and identifying itself'. Has one building-block of neoliberal thinking about the limits of democracy fallen away?

We can distinguish five new possibilities that recent technologies and software innovations have enabled.[28] First, *new voices*: not just more voices than before, but voice in public for a vastly increased range of people. Sitting in London, I can now sample at least in fragments the texture of people's daily accounts of their lives in many countries around the world (*GlobalVoices*), their experience of immediate events (via Twitter) and their commentary on media's representations of those events (on *YouTube*). The blog is now a familiar tool of expression both outside and within institutions (from media producers like the BBC to Microsoft to the US super-union AFL-CIO). Second, greatly increased *mutual awareness* of these new voices, as a result of the distributive capacities of the web itself: not only can someone in Iran take a photo at a street protest with their phone and upload it to a website or on to Twitter, but many others can re-circulate that photo, or incorporate it in their own public reflections. The potential impacts are clear for transforming our experience of politics in distant countries – no longer just government statements and pictures of protesters, but words and images circulated by those protesters themselves – but also our experience of politics closer to hand. Third, *new scales of organization*: the internet's capacities for circulating digital material enable organized political action of a scale and complexity previously impossible, unfolding in direct response to events: the worldwide anti-Iraq war protests in 2003, Burmese people's recruiting of international support for their anti-government protests in 2007. The boundaries around sovereign territories and powerful institutions are potentially reconfigured.

Fourth, our understanding of *what spaces are required* for political organization is now changed: no longer just the closed room, public meeting or party mailing list, but networks of people who have never met, with or without formal leadership, within or across local and national boundaries, with multiple institutional supports or none at all. Decentred political networks (for example, around opposition to corporate globalization) have emerged;[29] new types of political portal (Moveon.org in the USA and its transnational and multilingual counterpart, Avaaz.org;[30] in the UK, Tescopoly, which campaigns against the economic power of the UK's largest supermarket chain)[31] are gathering resources for political mobilization online and at the same time building narratives of common or parallel action out of the specific practices of scattered and diverse communities. The US political scientist Lance Bennett argues as a result that 'the dynamic network becomes *the unit* of analysis in which all other levels (organizational, individual, political) can be analysed more coherently'.[32] Finally, the combined result of all these changes is to generate potential *new intensities of listening*: each of us as citizens can, and public bodies including governments arguably must, take account of a vastly increased range of public voices. Governments cannot any longer say they don't hear.

Communication technologies themselves are not automatically political (the uses of *YouTube*, for example, are generally 'underdetermined', not just in relation to politics).[33] But many initiatives are under way for expanding political voice. Some are concerned with developing new mechanisms of consultation and awareness online (in the USA, the National Institute for Democracy and Healthy Democracy; in the UK, MySociety).[34] Others, such as the Transition Initiative, which advocates planning for global warning and declining oil supplies, mix new media technology with attempts to help people in towns across the UK and elsewhere combine more effectively and develop ideas face to face. New types of campaign are developing involving both mainstream media and web interfaces, such as the *Guardian*-sponsored 1010 campaign to encourage individuals and organizations to reduce their carbon emissions 10% by 2010.[35] The Obama campaign in 2008 afforded clear evidence of the effectiveness of Web 2.0 interfaces for political mobilization.[36] It is the strength of Manuel Castells' recent analysis of 'communication power'[37] that it recognizes the potential of communication networks to enable political action on new scales.

We *seem*, then, to live in an era when, in technological form, we can imagine with John Dewey how to turn 'the Great Society into the Great Community',[38] or with Pierre Balibar how to 'set the idea of a "community of citizens" back into motion'.[39] Is this the start of the answer to neoliberalism? But we must go more slowly.

First, we must ask: how much do important events such as Obama's victory or the last-minute turning of the Spanish general election in March 2004 against the incumbent Prime Minister Aznar (another key case for Castells) tell us about more lasting transformations in political organization, and the possibilities for a post-neoliberal politics? Is a different type of *everyday* politics emerging that can generate new types of political intervention? Or indeed – turning again to the case of Obama's mid 2009 difficulties over healthcare reform – an everyday *governmental* politics that can effectively promote political reforms with a vast but poorly financed constituency of support and facing a better financed popular opposition? To build a post-neoliberal politics, new '*social* practices' of politics are needed, as Castells acknowledges,[40] that operate within the conditions and constraints of everyday life. We must beware of celebrating as a source of political advantage what is now a given for *all* political actors, whether their goal is the defence of neoliberal politics or its defeat. It is a given that, where there is already a level of political mobilization or organization, coordinated action can be quickly developed on larger scales online: local groups that once operated separately can be combined in vast tactical alliances, while the template of such appliances offers new groups the instant legitimation of a 'brand', a network, a space of validation and potential voice. What is *not* a given is whether these new means for rescaling political action provide resources for *generating* new political mobilization or the means for those already mobilized to get *heard against* political opponents who themselves use the very same resources of online organization. Of the examples of networked political expression in Castells' latest book, two relate to election campaigns (times of authorized change) and two relate to broad campaigns on global environmental issues and opposition to globalization. He provides no examples relating to what we might call 'everyday neoliberalism': workers' challenging worsened conditions of, or loss of, employment, wider groups of citizens blocking or reversing the marketization of public services.[41] Yet these are areas where neoliberal politics has drastic impacts on living conditions.

Something, then, appears to be missing from accounts of politics' rescaling. The late Charles Tilly argued that processes of democratization are fragile and can equally well go into reverse; indeed, *de-democratization* usually happens quicker than democratization.[42] It is vital, therefore, to introduce both historical and *social specificity* into our analysis. Theda Skocpol's analysis of the seachange in US civic life during the twentieth century finds that, while levels of civic activity (on crude measures of organizational activity) may not have declined, the quality and social representativeness of civic participation is now very different from before 1960. From national, multi-branch civic organizations with local members recruited across classes (but not yet, admittedly, bringing genders or ethnicities together), US civic life switched around the 1970s to a professionalized, upper middle-class, largely Washington-focused, form of organization that does not mobilize locally:

> No longer do civic entrepreneurs think of constructing vast federations and recruiting interactive citizen-members ... even a group aiming to speak for large numbers of Americans does not absolutely need 'members' in any meaningful sense of the word.[43]

The class profile of US civic life as a result, Skocpol argues, dramatically changed. The counter-argument, presumably, would be that even radical politics would show the same features, because the practical basis of all political activism has changed in societies that have been profoundly individualized.[44] But Skocpol's underlying point is to ask in relation to any form of networked action: *who exactly* are we talking about? Sociologically unspecific claims about the political potential of new technologies, for example Henry Jenkins' much-discussed analysis of 'convergence culture', tell us less than first appears.[45] Was the Obama campaign's successful mobilization across age and ethnic barriers (discussed by Castells)[46] a short-term exception to Skocpol's pessimistic diagnosis or the first sign of a new rule? We cannot possibly know yet, but everything will depend on the sociological detail.

Another point of difficulty (acknowledged by Jeffrey Juris in his account of anti-corporate globalization movements)[47] is how particular practices of voice get *articulated or not* to practices of government. As Skocpol points out, a strength of older US civic organizations was that they could connect their varied, highly dispersed membership to conversations, and confrontations, with representatives of the political elite.[48] More generally, Andrew

Chadwick, reviewing 'e-democracy' projects in 2006, concluded that there is always a 'missing link [to] policy making that takes place in formal institutional spheres'.[49] From another perspective, Pierre Rosanvallon argues that what contemporary democracies lack – at least on a large scale – is not opportunities for citizens to express their dissatisfaction with government (through forms of vigilance, denunciation and evaluation),[50] but the means by which those voices can be valued within a wider process of policy development. Without such means, he suggests, the outcome is a form of *'counter-policy'* that generates an 'unpolitical democracy' and undermines faith in the principles and practice of democracy.[51]

Some might argue in response that a post-neoliberal politics requires much deeper long-term transformations of social and economic organization, indeed perhaps the replacement of capitalism itself. Yet it is not actions over the long term with which we are concerned here: the neoliberal crisis of voice is *now*, the need to develop a counter-rationality to neoliberalism is *now*. While we may doubt whether Obama is a post-neoliberal politician in many or most respects, the absence now of a politics in the USA that can develop effective alliances in support of Obama's healthcare reform is worrying.[52] Given Tilly's argument that one dimension of democratization is the way that the large-scale networks of trust on which people rely for insuring their social and economic needs become oriented towards institutional providers associated with the state and political institutions,[53] Obama's defeat would represent a concrete defeat for potential *new* processes of democratization. More broadly, we might ask: leaving aside the biases built into particular political systems and what Rosanvallon calls the 'obvious' sociological fact that 'negative coalitions are easier to organize than positive majorities',[54] what if new forms of networked politics, with their accelerated mobilization and coordination, are more effective in *opposing* governments and *blocking* change than in *proposing* fundamental policy shifts? And what if large-scale media work most of the time to reinforce, not challenge, such a tendency?

We cannot, then, grasp the significance of new forms of voice without knowing the larger processes in which they are *articulated*.[55] We are, in a sense, back to the issue raised in Chapter One, about the need for voice to have a material form that fits with its features, but now on the largest political and social scale. A failed democracy, Dewey reflected on the eve of World War II, 'limits the interactions by which experience is steadied while it is also enlarged and enriched'.[56] It is the interactive dimension of voice that is crucial: technological forms enable, but cannot guarantee, this. Voices may multiply, but democracy still fail.

... and value deficits?

If that possibility seems depressing, it is a necessary consequence of appreciating that 'voice' is not just the process of giving an account of oneself, but also the value given to that process, the process *of valuing* voice appropriately.

Yet many writers agree with Rosanvallon that citizens lack a sense of their place 'in a legible, visible totality' in the sense of a *common* world in which they and their governments act.[57] Whether those writers see a 'crisis of responsibility' in a world of excessive information, or the need to establish an 'orientation to wider civil solidarity' or produce a new sense of 'the common', they agree that *meaningful* political cooperation has become difficult to imagine:[58] narratives of political involvement fail. This narrative deficit seems to have inspired the organizational model of the UK Transition Initiative, which replaces top-down instruction with locally-based processes of collective thinking, learning and imagination: 'we can only move toward something', its founder Rob Hopkins writes, 'if we can imagine what it will be like when we get there'.[59] But part of what has to be imagined *is* the connection from particular actions to a wider frame of political relevance. That link is problematic if it comprises nothing more than the right to complain about, or limit, government power.[60] Democracy can only work as 'a cooperative process'[61] if we start seeing what citizens and governments do as part of a continuous space of action.

But what *is* this shared space of action? Hardt and Negri, in their celebrated book *Multitude,* suspend the context of the nation-state and invoke the global conditions of labour exploitation, but the relationship between 'the social' (life/being/world) that Hardt and Negri imagine emerging from the common conditions of labour in a globalized world[62] and particular historical contexts of interaction remains obscure: the concept of networks is at best an alibi that occludes the difficulty of finding everyday social spaces that are also spaces of politics. As Boltanski and Chiapello remind us (see Chapter Two), network logics cross space very effectively but *do not* necessarily sustain the local resources that cooperation in any one place still requires; in addition, other forces may undermine our sense that politics is possible, whether centuries of hegemonic domination by others or a quasi-social value that 'we don't talk politics here'.[63]

The difficulty is not of Hardt and Negri's making, since neoliberal governments have hardly helped us imagine new ways in which relations between government and citizen might be understood. What if governments themselves have *not yet imagined* – and perhaps have no plans to imagine – what it would be to acknowledge citizens' role in rethinking, or refashioning, government policy and strategic objectives? No 'duty to inform, consult and involve' (imposed by the UK government in 2009 on 'best-value organizations') or Open Government Directive (issue by President Obama in January 2009)[64] can compensate for that lack of imagination. As we saw in Chapters Three and Four, neoliberal government practices, however well disguised, are poorly suited to give weight to citizens' ability to reflect on strategic choices: government as 'management' and 'delivery' converts positive processes of political engagement into mere externalities to be discounted or controlled.

The fundamental deficit in neoliberal democracies is, then, not one of voice but of ways of valuing voice, of putting voice to work within processes of social cooperation. Unless we delegate the task of a post-neoliberal politics to completely new forms of economic and social organization (the work of many decades, for sure), we have no choice but to give renewed attention to how existing democratic processes might work better to value voice. This requires considering the uneven distribution of effective voice even in an environment where voice generally is stimulated. One crucial factor is what Bruce Williams and Michael Delli Carpini call the overall 'media regime', that is the 'historically specific, relatively stable set of institutions, norms, processes and actors that ... determine ... the gates through which information about culture, politics and economics passes, thus shaping the discursive environment in which such topics are discussed, understood and acted on'.[65] Another factor is the broader institutional structures available to contest or support particular forms of change and political innovation. Such institutional structures cannot, of course, be changed overnight by will or imagination. But this should not discourage us from considering the 'small acts'[66] and new 'habits'[67] from which, even within those structures, a different form of political life might be built. Recalling Dewey, we need to consider new acts of cooperation and a new story that can motivate cooperation among those who have not worked together before.

New acts

As European social democrats John Cruddas and Andrea Nahles have recently argued, 'the market state and its agencies need to be transformed into a civic state that is democratised and made more responsive'.[68] But remembering John Dewey's insistence that democracy as a *social* ideal must, to be meaningful, extend to 'all modes of human association',[69] more thought needs to be given to the implications for corporations, civil society actors, public bodies, educational institutions and trade unions.[70] That means confronting, of course, the degree to which neoliberal discourse has become already embedded in many of those institutions: how difficult now, for example, while teaching in a UK school or university, to reconnect with John Dewey's vision of educational institutions as democratic spheres for the exercise of voice,[71] against the grain of the recent managerialism in educational culture?

It may help to think modestly: grand mechanisms of formal deliberation may be less important than what Pierre Rosanvallon calls 'an authentic rediscovery of ordinary politics'.[72] The formal actions of a civic code may be less important than what Engin Isin calls the informal 'acts of citizenship' that 'transform ... modes ... of being political by bringing into being new actors [and] creating new sites and scales of struggle'.[73] We may need, quite simply, to do new things.

One would be acts of political *greeting*. When new voices, or voices that have long grown silent, need to be heard, they must be welcomed by an act of 'greeting'. The late Iris Marion Young saw the act of greeting as essential to democratic exchange, those 'communicative ... gestures' by which people 'recognize others as included in the discussion, especially those with whom they differ in opinion, interest or social location'.[74] Such acts challenge the definition of who is a candidate for political voice or action, *seeing* new people *as* parties to debate about common issues.[75] The great strength of the networked politics praised by Castells and Juris is that it allows disparate groups of activists to amass a presence at key sites of traditional political power that gets them recognized, if not yet warmly greeted, as political actors, although we have already noted that networked politics is equally available to those who would oppose a post-neoliberal politics.[76] But the act of greeting can be as simple as letting migrant workers attend, speak at, and have their views taken into account at a council or town hall meeting. Acts of greeting address the forms of *invisibility* that exclude people from the range of possible political actors: media are crucial to this, a point to which I return.

Vital, too, are acts of *exchange*. One way of thinking about new acts of political exchange is in terms of *listening*. The occasions for governments to listen to the range of citizen opinions have increased hugely. There are blogs on any number of topics from political gossip to the working life of doctors, police officers and school teachers (none yet by a university teacher so far as I know!).[77] But surprisingly little attention has been given to what listening involves: what would it mean both for governments to listen better to citizens and for citizens to listen better to each other?

A network of researchers in Australia has recently come together to explore these very questions,[78] while practical techniques for listening more effectively to voice – such as the 'Open Space Meetings' that the Transition Initiative uses –[79] are emerging. But the context required for acts of listening to be effective is a complex one. By listening, we acknowledge each other's status as beings capable of giving an account of ourselves and the world we share. A single act of listening can therefore be undermined by a wider pattern of action where reciprocity between the same parties is missing. Government attempts to 'listen' to citizens often fail doubly: because face-to-face there is no actual *exchange* of narratives (no initial reciprocity), and because *actions* taken by government do not subsequently register the fact that listening has taken place (a second lack of reciprocity). Democratic government as social coop-eration means taking seriously such moments of exchange. James Bohman is one of the few political theorists to have considered how, as the scale and subject of politics changes, so the interrelations between democratic institu-tions and citizens must change too. The relationship must, Bohman argues, become 'fully reciprocal and *co-constitutive*': 'publics [must] be able to shape the very institutions that in turn shape their freedoms and powers'.[80] Put less abstractly, the issue is what governments *do with* voice, once expressed: are they prepared to change the way they make policy? Governments so far are a long way off acknowledging this.

We need also to think more about the background acts that prepare the spaces of political exchange. For it is not enough that networks link people across new scales, or that more opportunities for exchanging narratives occur in absolute terms. It is important also that spaces are created that enable the exchange between narratives normally regarded as *irrelevant* to each other; that means challenging the blocks that prevent certain types of narrative being heard. Seeing new people as relevant to political exchange requires *seeing new spaces of narrative exchange as possible*: this requires a pragmatic understanding of political space whose concern is more with 'seeing connections' than with reproducing existing boundaries.[81] Why accept as legitimate any claim, for example, that management goals, government targets or market forces make irrelevant the hearing of affected workers' accounts of what it is like to operate under those same conditions? Yet Boltanski and Chiapello's analysis of 'the new spirit of capitalism' and its injustices – or, indeed, Barbara Ehrenreich or Madeleine Bunting's research on 'overwork culture' in the USA and the UK – show us that few narratives of everyday suffering are given a place in contemporary politics and contemporary media. Such a huge deficit in actual voices can only be interrupted by challenging the framework which casts as politically irrelevant large categories of social experience. Neoliberalism can be understood as a historic attempt – largely successful so far – to recast the sites of social experience and political conflict as spaces of market functioning where individuals and market-oriented corporations operate, subject only to the limited external constraints of government. A counter-rationality to neoliberalism must change our everyday map of politics' topics, subjects and values.

This takes us to wider acts of *retelling*. We need frames within which new acts of political exchange can make sense. The facts of cooperation – new types of exchange, new terms of mutual recognition – between governments, individuals and groups must be registered in new narratives. What would otherwise be regarded as a failure of government – as delays in 'delivery' – must be made sense of through a different understanding of how governments 'deliver' on their commitments, and show competence. The relentless drive towards government in 'the immediate moment' (discussed in Chapter Four) can only be challenged if another narrative is developed that values the 'public time'[82] of consultation and policy testing, as not obstructing but extending and enriching the process of government.

Note that the retelling of the democratic process proposed here is very different from the neoliberal principle of limiting the spheres of legitimate government intervention (whether in the ongoing US culture wars against 'big government' or in the UK Conservative leader David Cameron's recent proposals to reduce 'big state power').[83] The root of the neoliberal view, as we saw at the start of the chapter, was von Hayek's account of human beings' potential for cooperation, which was so limited that it condemned the individual to be perpetually at odds with a wholly 'external' process called 'government'. It is vital for a post-neoliberal politics to recall that in autumn 2008 the nation-state (in the USA, the UK, Germany, China and elsewhere) played the central role in halting the most serious financial crisis the global system has yet seen;[84] neoliberal accounts are ready to efface or misrecognize this, as indeed they must if neoliberal politics' coherence is to be restored. The challenge for a post-neoliberal politics, then, is not to neglect government, or reduce the scope of its decision-making, but to offer ways of rethinking how government can use more effectively its populations' resources for cooperation, including the enhanced resources that now exist online for social production.[85] This is one reason why recent calls led by Joseph Stiglitz and Amartya Sen to change what economic statistics measure and to reoriente economic and development policy towards a broader notion of 'wellbeing' that takes account of voice (see Chapter Two) are encouraging, although there is no reason yet to think they will be heeded.[86]

I have listed some acts that are necessary preconditions for a post-neoliberal politics. Rethinking what we mean by democratic cooperation is a large task. The types of act I have listed will need to become embedded in the fabric of everyday life: it is not enough just to identify them! Each such act – of greeting and listening, of constructing new spaces of relevance and new frames for making sense of collaborative action – will require struggle: struggles oriented to the value of voice that challenge the legitimacy of existing voice-denying ways of doing things and build different ways of doing things in their place. But the acts just discussed are not, in themselves, sufficient for a post-neoliberal politics: they must take their place alongside other acts of contention in formal and symbolic politics and distributed acts of voice in markets (coordinated boycotts are a very effective way for citizens to influence corporations with whom they have no wider contractual relationship and who prove impervious to political intervention on their labour or other practices).[87]

Media will be vital to these struggles: media are crucially involved in almost all contemporary contests to be visible and to be heard, while at the same time being organizations embedded in networks of commercial and political power. No amount of large-scale online networking by enthusiastic activists will in itself correct for the *breaks* in communication that result when particular types of political actor are invisible in the political domain. New political acts (not just moments of spectacle) will need to be *recognized* in the news coverage of mainstream large-scale media; any expansion of the cooperative process within democratic politics must be represented in media coverage. Media institutions are very good at voicing 'counter-democracy', but it is unclear whether they are good at reflecting new forms of political cooperation or 'ordinary democracy' (using Rosanvallon's terms). Perhaps media's role in politics needs to be reframed as part of this process. Media institutions, unlike political institutions are not directly subject to tests of legitimacy, unless perhaps they are publicly funded. But at a time of uncertainty about the economic basis of media (see Chapter Four), market signals are not completely divorced from issues of legitimacy and trust: media will need to compete for attention and 'loyalty'.[88] It is possible that if processes of politics are transformed, media institutions themselves, as James Bohman insists, will need to interact more closely with their public over 'both the ways in which [that] public is addressed and how its opinion is represented'.[89] Given that, as we saw in Chapter Four, media operations have complicated the embedding of neoliberal rationality, we would expect them to complicate the development of a counter-rationality to neoliberalism too, in ways that as yet are unpredictable.

Taken together, these transformations are the task of a generation, but it is a task that, act by act, can be imagined and started now.

A new story

None of this is to forget that the problems of scale that contemporary democracy faces are acute in what Ulrich Beck called global 'risk society'.[90] The recent financial crisis, even as it shone a brief light on these problems, exposing, for example, the necessity in Europe of transnational institutions of banking regulation, only intensified them on a national scale by mortgaging future resources to stem immediate market failures. We don't yet know how to build processes of decision-making that can take more satisfactory account of the destructive local consequences of distant economic decisions or market collapse or address the consequences for workers' lives of dependency on multiple short-term employers and unceasing insecurity.[91] At most we know how social production, using new technologies of online mobilization, can interrupt *some* market-based decisions.[92] But that is a long way from knowing what it would be for current decision-structures – including processes behind closed corporate doors *not yet seen as* spaces for cooperative decision-making – to 'take seriously', and on a regular basis, more 'kinds of speech'.[93]

Neoliberalism 'solves' the problem of democratic scale by rationalizing democracy's failures. It is neoliberalism that rests ultimately on fantasy (von Hayek's self-reliant individual who may occasionally feel moved to cooperate with his neighbours), when what is needed is clear-eyed commitment to new, uncertain, inevitably conflicted, long-term processes of cooperation that can take better account of people's capacities for collaborative reflection on every scale. For this, the structures of the market-state are inadequate: no clear answers have evolved as to what must replace them. The only starting-point is a more basic act of retelling that calls today's democratic outcomes what they are: a collective *failure* to sustain forms of organization that would take satisfactory account of voice.

Meanwhile, elsewhere, other acts of retelling are under way. For some, the weight of the global financial crisis of late 2008 is lifting, like a bad dream. The contradictory signs of economic revival (in the USA, France, Germany and Japan, but less convincingly so in the UK) will no doubt tempt many to forget the short period in late 2008 and early 2009 when it seemed possible to raise political, even moral, questions about the equity of how the immediate banking crisis was resolved, let alone the long-term distribution of wealth and risk between financial industries and wider populations. Mike Duke, CEO of Walmart, the world's largest retailer well-known for its aggressive stance on workers' wages and conditions,[94] told the company's celebrity-adorned annual meeting in June 2009 that 'never has there been a time when the strengths of our company were more aligned with what the world needs than right now'.[95]

The challenges left by neoliberalism remain: reorienting government away from the assumption that market functioning trumps all, rethinking the space of politics so that its narratives bear some credible relation to the lives of most of those it purports to represent; articulating more specific policies that give weight to voice in everyday social and political organization; supplanting the view that markets are the only reference-point for social, political and individual organization. Those challenges do not straightforwardly converge. Meanwhile, the market-state's circular logic, uncomfortably exposed for a while, will continue unless a broader political process chooses to interrupt it; indeed, neoliberalism may acquire new disguises, perhaps a version of social Darwinism that offers even more reductive understandings of human life than neoliberalism proper.

The questions, then, remain: can a post-neoliberal future be envisaged? Do we accept the consequences, if it cannot? Or will we simply retreat into blaming government and its representatives for all our ills while abstaining, as Pierre Rosanvallon suggests in his disturbing vision of 'counter-democracy', from the long task of building a politics that tells a more satisfactory story of what we have and do in common? The forces of inertia and silence lie, largely, on neoliberalism's side. Making voices *matter* is hard; it is even harder, amid a proliferation of new voices, to challenge the hidden forces and dislocations that prevent them mattering when it counts. But remember the Danish philosopher Søren Kierkegaard's warning: 'the fact of having kept silent ... this is the most dangerous thing of all. For by keeping silent one is relegated to oneself'.[96] Keeping silent is neoliberalism's way with democracy. For now at least, another story can be told.

Notes

1 Fraser (2009: 116).
2 From the Greek words for decision and judgement, 'krisis' and 'krinein'.
3 Von Hayek (1944: 157, 156).
4 Von Hayek saw Dewey's positive notion of freedom as confusing freedom with questions of power (von Hayek 1944: 19; 1960: 16–17).
5 Rizzolatti and Sinigaglia (2008).
6 Honneth (2007: 232), Dewey (1993: 110).
7 Juris (2008: chapter 1).
8 See Hardt and Negri (2006: 198–200) on Dewey.
9 Keane (2009).
10 Keane (2009: 862).
11 Sen (1999).
12 Campaign email issued by Pennsylvania@barackobama.com, 29 September 2008.
13 Obama (2007: 438).
14 See Sarah Palin's 'notes' at www.facebook.com/notes.php?id=24718773587, 7 August 2009.
15 I follow here broadly David Easton's definition of 'politics' as 'the authoritative allocation of goods, services and values': Easton (1965), quoted in Delli Carpini and Keater (1996: 12).
16 Rosanvallon (2008: 312).
17 Quoted in Rosanvallon (2008: 310).
18 Quoted in Rodriguez (forthcoming).

19 Dewey (1993: 209).
20 www.ntui.org.in.
21 Boltanski and Chiapello (2005: 489).
22 Gibson-Graham (2006: 87, added emphasis).
23 Greenhouse (2009: 302–303).
24 Benhabib (2004).
25 Fraser (2007), Nyers (2008). On the scale of politics, see Beck (2000b), Sassen (2006), Bohman (2007).
26 Hopkins (2008).
27 Dewey (1946: 125).
28 For extended discussion of technology's relation to narrative, see Bassett (2007).
29 Juris (2008), Smith (2008: chapter 6).
30 On Avaaz.org, see Kavada (2009).
31 www.tescopoly.org.
32 Bennett (2003: 164, added emphasis), quoted in Castells (2009: 343).
33 Burgess and Green (2009: 103).
34 www.ni4d.us; www.healthydemocracy.org; www.mysociety.org.
35 www.guardian.co.uk/environment/10–10.
36 Clark and Aufderheide (2009), Castells (2009: esp. pp. 364–372).
37 Castells (2009).
38 Dewey (1946: 142).
39 Balibar (2004: 50).
40 Castells (2009: 346, added emphasis).
41 However, Castells' example of the 'People Power II' protests in the Phillipines in January 2001, and coordinated by mobile phone is striking: Castells et al. (2007: 186–192).
42 Tilly (2007: xi, 195).
43 Skocpol (2003: 210).
44 Bennett (1998), Turner (2001).
45 Jenkins (2006).
46 Castells (2009: 369–372).
47 Juris (2008: 9, 286).
48 Skocpol (2003: 124).
49 Chadwick (2006: 113).
50 Rosanvallon (2008: 13).
51 Rosanvallon (2008: 23, 257 n4).
52 See www.moveon.org petition on US healthcare reform, 7 September 2009.
53 Tilly (2007: 59).
54 Rosanvallon (2006: 242).
55 On 'articulated', see Background Note.
56 Dewey (1993: 245 [passage originally published 1939]).
57 Rosanvallon (2008: 308).
58 Terranova (2004: 35), Alexander (2006: 99), Hardt and Negri (2006). On imagination in politics, see Dahlgren (1995), Plummer (2003), Rosanvallon (2008: 306).
59 Hopkins (2008: 141). See Chapter One for a different perspective via the concept of 'radical hope'.
60 Rosanvallon (2008: 258).
61 Honneth (2007: 234).
62 Hardt and Negri (2006: 188, 192, 318), cf. (2005: 100, 219) on the multitude as 'social subject'.
63 Freire (1972), Eliasoph (1998).
64 www.communities.gov.uk/localgovernment/performanceframeworkpartnerships/bestvalue/; www.whitehouse.gov/the_press_office/TransparencyandOpenGovernment/
65 Williams and Delli Carpini (forthcoming).
66 Gilroy (1996).
67 Compare Hardt and Negri (2004: 197).
68 Cruddas and Nahles (2009: 7).
69 Dewey (1946: 143).

70 For an interesting discussion, see Howard (2007).
71 Giroux (1986). For the corporatization of the US university, see Giroux (2007).
72 Rosanvallon (2006: 250).
73 Isin (2008: 39). See also Background Note.
74 Young (2000: 61).
75 Norval (2007) on 'seeing as'.
76 See McCurdy (2009).
77 Coleman (2008).
78 O'Donnell, Lloyd and Dreher (2009); special issue of journal *Continuum* 23(4) 2009.
79 Hopkins (2008: 162–163); see also the 'Listening Guide' of Taylor, Gilligan and Sullivan (1995: 28–36).
80 Bohman (2007: 91), cf. Bohman (2000).
81 Tully (1995: 110), quoting Wittgenstein (1958: para 122).
82 Giroux (2004b: 160).
83 Cameron (2009).
84 Krugman (2009).
85 Benkler (2006), Leadbeater (2008a).
86 See the *Financial Times* editorial (15 September 2009) in response to the French Commission report.
87 Tilly (2006), Tarrow (1998), Klein (2000).
88 Hirschman (1969).
89 Bohman (2000: 56).
90 Beck (1992).
91 For some important proposals, see Boltanski and Chiapello (2005).
92 Benkler (2006) provides good examples of this.
93 Adapting Bickford (1996: 149).
94 Greenhouse (2009: 49–55, 98–103, 134–157).
95 Quoted in *Financial Times*, 6 June 2009.
96 Kierkegaard (1954: 167 [1849]).

Background Note

Chapter endnotes give bibliographical references only. A few longer background comments are collected here.

Chapter 1

In introducing 'voice' in this chapter, I defer until Chapter 5 to the philosophical debates that the term automatically raises from post-structuralist perspectives, including my defence of using the term notwithstanding Derrida's (1976) association of it with a discredited 'metaphysics of self-presence'. Thanks to my colleague Les Back for alerting me to the wider relevance of Jonathan Lear's work. Charles Taylor's review (2007: 8) of Lear also takes up the invitation of considering applications of Lear's argument beyond the exceptional circumstances of Native Americans.

This book's argument to some extent runs in parallel with work on voice around development and poverty (Deane 2004; Lister 2004; Appadurai 2004), from which some interesting connections have been made to voice in politics in 'developed' countries by Cornwall (2008).

With regard to the issue of the underlying complex variations of the policy frameworks that, for strategic purposes, I am simply calling 'neoliberal', see generally Harvey (2005: chapter 3) and specifically Stephen Ball's study of the transition from Thatcherite 'neoliberal' to Blairite 'post-neoliberal' or 'Third Way' policy in the UK education sector (Ball 2007: especially chapter 9). It is the degree of continuity implied by Ball's term '*post*-neoliberal' that is my focus in this book. My own use of that term in Chapter 7 will be different.

Chapter 2

For literature debating explanations of the current financial crisis, see Blackburn (2008), Wade (2008), Madrick (2009), Panitch and Konings (2009). A rare insight into arguments behind the scenes on issues of global banking regulation came when *The Guardian* on 17 January 2009 reported on its front page that in response to Presidents Merkel and Sarkozy, the UK Chancellor Alistair Darling had written to G20 finance ministers saying 'any clampdown had to start from the belief that markets were a force for good'. The UK government's subsequent weakness in dealing with the issue of banking regulation has confirmed the tight grip that neoliberal thinking has on it.

Note that, while I find Thomas Frank's account of US market populism and its surprising links to UK New Labour illuminating, I would distance myself from other aspects of his account (for example, his discussion of the supposed politics of 'cultural studies').

The terms 'ideology' and 'hegemony' require much longer discussion than I can give here. Boltanski and Chiapello retain the term 'ideology' but in a sense far from Marx's original sense and closer to the term hegemony (see also Chapter One above). My suggestion – that neoliberalism is both broad hegemonic discourse yet generates offshoots that work more straightforwardly as ideology for specific ends – is, I believe, compatible with their account.

Behind this chapter's discussion of work lies a major debate on shifts towards 'immaterial' and 'affective' labour, influenced particularly by Italian theory. While aspects of such debates (the argument that all wage labour is now 'flexible' (Virno 2004: 101) and increasingly 'precarious') capture an important dimension of neoliberal work cultures, other aspects (the emphasis on 'affective', even 'immaterial' labour) seem to ignore crucial distinctions between different types of work and work-based power/status (see Hesmondhalgh and Baker (2008), Ross (2008) for critical discussion). Still wider debates about the revolutionary potential of 'precarity' as a general identity-category, or of refusing work entirely, lie outside the scope of my argument here; while I accept the importance of the task of finding new ways of producing 'the common' (Hardt and Negri 2006: xv; Neilson and Rossiter 2008), I am not convinced that recent accounts of the changing conditions of contemporary labour yet offer a convincing route towards cross-class, cross-continental social organization (see Gill and Pratt 2008: 9–13, 15–17 for useful discussion).

Chapter 3

A recent OFCOM survey of civic-related Internet use (OFCOM 2009) provides a more upbeat assessment of the state of UK democracy than I do, but in my view exaggerates the degree of citizen action online in the UK through its broad definitions and insufficient attention to questions of frequency. The decline of trust in UK politics is, however, part of a long historical trend in Western democracies (Pharr, Putnam and Dalton 2000).

The chapter's argument about the 'cultural' implementation of neoliberal discourse and policy priorities on the ground takes account of important debates in economic sociology on what are the processes that enable the boundaries of 'the economy' and practical economic reasoning to be constructed, normalized and occasionally shifted (Barry and Slater 2002).

In relation to the socioeconomic statistics quoted in the chapter, for the rise in income inequality in the UK, see www.statistics.gov.uk, search under 'income inequality' (last accessed 29 April 2008); on the geographical distribution of suicide rates, see www.statistics.gov.uk/statbase/Product.asp?vlnk=13618, and go to link on Corrected Geographical suicide rates (last accessed 22 January 2009). For international comparative purposes, a useful collation of statistics can be found on the excellent Worldmapper site run by University of Sheffield: www.sasi.group.shef.ac.uk/149worldmapper/data_data.xls

The UK government has attempted to appear more responsive by allowing e-petitions to the website of the Prime Minister (http://petitions.number10.gov.uk). At the beginning of September 2009, that site listed 32,000 rejected petitions, 24,000 completed petitions (each with a response) and 4,500 current petitions. The impact of such petitions on UK politics would appear so far to have been negligible.

The account of recognition offered in this chapter follows Axel Honneth's (2007) account, rather than Charles Taylor's (1989) account, partly in light of Lois McNay's (2008) recent critique of the latter.

Chapter 4

Changing Rooms is no longer on air after a long run; *Trinny and Susanna* after five BBC seasons was followed in October 2006 by the ITV series *Trinny and Susanna Undress*. I discuss reality TV in more detail in Couldry (2003, 2004, 2006).

Another link to neoliberalism from reality television not considered in the chapter is the production cultures that underlie such programmes and their harsh labour regimes (see Grindstaff 2002; Hesmondhalgh and Baker 2008). For a brilliant account of the more extreme atrophy of public culture in neoliberal USA, see Giroux (2008).

Chapter 5

While this chapter considers various philosophical approaches to voice, it makes no claim to be comprehensive, focusing on those which fit best into the broadly political focus of this book. I do not discuss, for example, a recent Lacanian treatment of 'voice' which defines it as 'the material element recalcitrant to meaning' (Dolar 2006: 15).

My discussion of the 'subject' in this chapter draws on and develops an earlier treatment which also reviews a range of cultural studies' writing about the self: see Couldry (2000: chapters 3 and 6). My approach here does not represent the mainstream of cultural studies but has parallels in some other writers, for example Probyn (1993: 17–22); Pickering (1997: 43–45). In a helpful recent essay, Gregory Seigworth (2008) makes interesting links between the recent fashion for Deleuze and Raymond Williams' discussion of experience, also quoted here.

In drawing both on Charles Taylor and Pierre Ricoeur on narrative, there is no space here to discuss the difference of emphasis between their two lines of argument. But contrast Taylor ('because we have to determine *our place in relation to the good*, therefore we cannot be without an orientation to it, and hence must see our life in story': 1989: 52) with Ricoeur ('time becomes *human* time to the extent that it is organized after the manner of a narrative': 1984a: 3, emphasis added).

On Sen, we can apply his theory of capabilities to the distribution of media resources: for pioneering accounts see Garnham (1999), Mansell (2002).

In emphasizing the human universality of certain forms of life, I am broaching language that post-structuralism, particularly in its anti- or post-humanist strands, has avoided. But once we make this point explicit, there may be other gains, for example the recognition of certain 'non-relative' ends of humanity with wider relevance for ethics (Nussbaum 1993), leading us back to Sen's account of capabilities (1999: 24).

My use of Wittgenstein in the last section of this chapter could no doubt be developed further, and Norval's work here is particularly helpful. Whether, however, we can talk of the historically specific *institution* of democracy as a 'form of life' (Norval 2007: 185), I am not sure, but my argument does not depend on this. I freely acknowledge the broader difficulty of staying with Wittgenstein's minimal vision of what philosophy knows, on which see McDowell (1998: 60–61), discussing Cavell (1976: 52). That difficulty is the point of the vigilance towards our language and rhetoric on which Derrida's version of post-structuralism rightly insists. But Wittgenstein in important ways enables us to go beyond some of the formulations of post-structuralism.

Chapter 6

For an earlier discussion of some of the approaches to voice discussed in this chapter, see Couldry (2000: chapter 3).

Chapter 7

This chapter reaches rather different conclusions from Henry Jenkins' suggestive account of the political potential of 'convergence culture', an account whose broader sociological relevance is limited in my view by its being based largely (as Jenkins, to his credit, admits) on evidence from what small groups of white, middle-class, young, time-rich fans of particular sorts of popular entertainment do (Jenkins 2006: 23).

My use of the word 'articulated' in this chapter is intended to refer to how practices are combined into larger habits and patterns (cf. Couldry, Livingstone and Markham 2007: chapter 4).

The chapter's discussion of 'new acts' for the building of 'post-neoliberal politics' is meant only to be suggestive, but it is inspired in part by the more concrete attempt recently of Peter Dahlgren to develop a new, more dynamic model of the elements of 'civic culture' (Dahlgren 2003, 2009).

The chapter's concluding call for 'another story' of what democracy is about takes some inspiration from Jacques Derrida's invocation of a 'democracy to come' (1997: 306): see Norval (2007: 145–148) for discussion. A difference, however, is that the horizon of action discussed here takes its shape not from the openness inherent to all language (that rhetoric always works to close down), but from the specific organizational failures of our neoliberal past and the specific challenges of a possible post-neoliberal future.

References

Government and civil society reports

Bank of International Settlements (2009) *Press Release on 79th Annual Report*, 29 June, www.bis.org/press/p090629.htm (last accessed 30 June 2009).

BBC (2004) 'Sir Alan Sugar confirmed for BBC Two's *The Apprentice*', 18 May, www.bbc. co.uk/pressoffice/pressreleases (last accessed 26 April 2008).

Chartered Institute of Personnel Development (2008) *Factsheet*, www.cipd.cp.uk/ subjects/hrpact/hoursandholidays/ukworkhrs (last accessed 7 March 2009).

Commission on the Measurement of Economic Performance and Social Progress (2008) *Issues Paper*, www.stiglitz-sen-fitoussi.fr/documents/Issues_paper.pdf (last accessed 3 February 2009).

Commission on the Measurement of Economic Performance and Social Progress (2009) *Report*, www.stiglitz-sen-fitoussi.fr/documents/rapport_anglais.pdf (last accessed 21 September 2009).

[UK] Department of Communities and Local Government (2008) *Communities in Control: Real People, Real* Power, www.clg.gov.uk (last accessed 18 August 2008).

[UK] Department of Culture Media and Sport (2009) *Digital Britain Final Report*, www.culture.gov.uk/images/publications/digitalbritain-finalreport-jun09.pdf (last accessed 8 August 2009).

[UK] Department of Health (2006a) *A Stronger Local Voice*, www.dh.gov.uk/prod_consum_dh/groups/dh_digitalassets/@dh/@en/documents/digitalasset/ dh_4137041.pdf (last accessed 17 August 2009).

[UK] Department of Health (2006b) *Our Health, Our Choice, Our Say*, www.dh.gov.uk/ prod_consum_dh/groups/dh_digitalassets/@dh/@en/documents/digitalasset/ dh_4127459.pdf (last accessed 17 August 2009).

Electoral Commission (2004) *Political Engagement Among Young People: An Update.* London: Electoral Commission.

Electoral Commission (2005) *Election 2005: Turnout. How Many, Who and Why?* London: Electoral Commission.

Electoral Commission (2007) *An Audit of Political Engagement 4*. London: Electoral Commission.

Hansard Society, The (2008) *An Audit of Political Engagement 5*. London: Hansard Society.

House of Commons Select Committee on the Office of the Deputy Prime Minister (2004) *Ninth Report*, 12 July, www.parliament.the-stationery-office.com/pa/cm200304/ cmselect/cmodpm/402/40204.htm (last accessed 7 March 2009).

House of Lords (2009) *Surveillance: Citizens and the State*. Select Committee on the Constitution, Volume 1. House of Lords Paper 18–I, February.

International Monetary Fund (2009) *The State of Public Finances: Outlook and Medium-term Policies after the 2008 Crisis*, March, www.imf.org/external/np/pp/eng/2009/030609.pdf (last accessed 7 March 2009).

Joseph Rowntree Foundation (2009a) *Ending Child Poverty in a Changing Economy*. York: JRF, www.jrf.org.uk (last accessed 15 February 2009).

Joseph Rowntree Foundation (2009b) *Modern Social Evils*. Bristol: The Policy Press.

Power (2006) *The Report of Power: An Independent Inquiry into Britain's Democracy*, www.powerinquiry.org/report/index.php (last accessed 15 May 2009).

National Centre for Social Research (2006) *British Social Attitudes: The 23rd Report*. Aldershot: Gower.

OFCOM (2009) *Citizens' Digital Participation*, March, www.ofcom.org.uk (last accessed 15 May 2009).

Office for National Statistics (2004) *The Health of Children and Young People*, March. www.statistics.gov.uk/CHILDREN/ (last accessed 15 May 2009).

The Primary Review (2007) *Community Soundings: The Primary Review Regional Witness Sessions*, November, www.primaryreview.org.uk (last accessed 15 May 2009).

The Primary Review (2009) *Towards a New Curriculum*, February, www.primaryreview.org.uk (last accessed 15 February 2009).

UNCTAD (2007) *World Investment Report*, www.unctad.org/Templates/Page.asp?intItemID=3277&lang=1 (last accessed 3 March 2009).

UNDP (2007 and 2008) *Human Development Reports*, www.undp.org (last accessed 3 March 2009).

UNICEF (2007) *Child Poverty in Perspective: An Overview of Child Well-Being in Rich Countries*, www.unicef.org/irc (last accessed 3 March 2009).

World Bank (2009) *Global Economic Turmoil Having Dramatic Effects on Developing Countries* (press release), web.worldbank.org/WBSITE/EXTERNAL/NEWS/0,,contentMDK:22216950~pagePK:64257043~piPK:437376~theSitePK:4607,00.html (last accessed 28 August 2009).

World Health Organization (2008) *World Health Statistics*, www.who.int/whosis/whostat/2008/en/index.html (last accessed 3 March 2009).

Academic and media references

Agamben, G. (1998) *Homo Sacer*. Stanford, CA: Stanford University Press.

Agamben, G. (2005) *State of Exception*. Chicago: Chicago University Press.

Aglietta, M. (1998) 'Capitalism at the turn of the century', *New Left Review* 232: 41–90.

Alexander, J. (2006) *The Civil Sphere*. Oxford: Oxford University Press.

Améry, J. (1994) *On Aging*. Indianapolis, IN: Indiana University Press.

Andrejevic, M. (2004) *Reality TV: The Work of Being Watched*. Boulder, CO: Rowman and Littlefield.

Appadurai, A. (2004) 'The capacity to aspire: culture and the terms of recognition', in V. Rao and M. Walton (eds), *Culture and Public Action*. Stanford, CA: Stanford University Press, pp. 59–84.

Arendt, H. (1958) *The Human Condition*. Chicago: Chicago University Press.

Arendt, H. (2004 [1951]) *The Origins of Totalitarianism*. New York: Schocken Books.

Aristotle (1992) *Politics*. Harmondsworth: Penguin.

Arrow, K. (1963) 'Uncertainty and the welfare economics of medical care', *The American Economic Review* 53(5).

Badiou, A. (2005) *Metapolitics*. London: Verso.

Back, L. (2007) *The Art of Listening*. Oxford: Berg.

Baker, R. (2007) 'Goodbye to newspapers', *New York Review of Books* 16 August: 24–27.

Balibar, E. (2004) *We the People of Europe?* Princeton, NJ: Princeton University Press.

Ball, S. (2007) *Education plc*. London: Routledge.

Banet-Weiser, S. (forthcoming) *Authentic™*. New York: New York University Press.

Barry, A., Osborne, T. and Rose, N. (1996) 'Introduction', in A. Barry, T. Osborne and N. Rose (eds), *Foucault and Political Reason*. London: UCL Press, pp. 1–18.

Barry, A. and Slater, D. (2002) 'Introduction: the technological economy', *Economy and Society* 21(2): 175–193.

Bassett, C. (2007) *The Arc and the Machine*. Manchester: Manchester University Press.

Bauman, Z. (1989) *Modernity and the Holocaust*. Cambridge: Polity.

Bauman, Z. (1999) *In Search of Politics*. Cambridge: Polity.

Bauman, Z. (2001) *The Individualized Society*. Cambridge: Polity.

Beck, U. (1992) *Risk Society*. London: Sage.

Beck, U. (1997) *The Reinvention of Politics*. Cambridge: Polity.

Beck, U. (2000a) *Brave New World of Work*. Cambridge: Polity.

Beck, U. (2000b) 'The cosmopolitan perspective: sociology of the second age of modernity', *British Journal of Sociology* 51(1): 79–105.

Becker, G. (1991) *A Treatise on the Family* (Enlarged edition). Cambridge, MA: Harvard University Press.

Beckett, S. (1975) *The Unnameable*. London: Calder & Boyars.

Bell, D. and Hollows, J. (2006) *Historicising Lifestyle*. Guildford: Ashgate.

Benhabib, S. (2004) *The Rights of Others*. Cambridge: Cambridge University Press.

Beniger, J. (1987) *The Control Revolution*. Cambridge, MA: Harvard University Press.

Benjamin, J. (1998) *The Shadow of the Other*. New York: Routledge.

Benjamin, W. (1968) 'The Storyteller', in *Illuminations*. New York: Schocken Books, pp. 83–110.

Benkler, Y. (2006) *The Wealth of Networks*. Cambridge, MA: Harvard University Press.

Bennett, L. (1998) 'The Uncivic Culture: communication, identity and the rise of lifestyle politics', *PS: Political Science and Politics* 31(4): 740–741.

Bennett, L. (2003) 'Communicating global activism', *Information Communication and Society* 6(2): 143–168.

Bergson, H. (1991 [1908]) *Matter and Memory*. New York: Zone Books.

Berlin, I. (1958) *Two Concepts of Liberty*. Clarendon Press: Oxford.

Bertaux, D. (1982) 'Stories as clues to sociological understanding', in P. Thompson (ed.), *Our Common History*. London: Pluto Press, pp. 94–108.

Bertaux, D. (2001) 'Between Integration and Exclusion: European Households in Situations of Precariousness', Keynote address to biennial conference of the European Sociological Association, Helsinki, 1 September 2001.

Bickford, S. (1996) *The Dissonance of Democracy*. Ithaca, NY: Cornell University Press.

Blackburn, R. (2008) 'The subprime crisis', *New Left Review* (ns) 50: 63–108.

Blanchflower, D. (2009) 'This lays bare the human crisis', *The Guardian* 13 August.

Blum, L. and Seidler, V. (1989) *A Truer Liberty*. New York: Routledge.

Blumenberg, H. (1992) *The Legitimacy of the Modern Age*. Cambridge, MA: MIT Press.

Blythe, R. (1979) *The View in Winter*. London: Allen Lane.

Bobbitt, P. (2003) *The Shield of Achilles*. Harmondsworth: Penguin.

Bohman, J. (2000) 'The division of labour in democratic discourse', in S. Chambers and A. Costain (eds), *Deliberation, Democracy and the Media*. Lanham, MD: Rowman and Littlefield, pp. 47–64.

Bohman, J. (2007) *Democracy across Borders*. Cambridge, MA: MIT Press.

Du Bois, W. (1989 [1903]) *The Souls of Black Folk*. New York: Bantam.

Boltanski, L. and Chiapello, E. (2005) *The New Spirit of Capitalism*. London: Verso.

Boltanski, L. and Thévenot, L. (2006) *On Justification*. Princeton, NJ: Princeton University Press.

Boorstin, D. (1961) *The Image*. London: Weidenfeld and Nicolson.

Bourdieu, P. (1990) *Logic of Practice*. Cambridge: Polity.

Bourdieu, P. (1998) *Acts of Resistance*. New York: New Press.

Bourdieu, P. (1999) *The Weight of the World*. Cambridge: Polity.

Brewer, J. and Porter, R. (eds) (1993) *Consumption and the World of Goods*. London: Routledge.

Brown, W. (2003) 'Neo-liberalism and the end of liberal democracy', *Theory & Event* 7(1): 1–23.

Bruner, J. (1986) *Actual Minds Possible Worlds*. Cambridge, MA: Harvard University Press.

Bruni, L. and Porta, P. (2005) 'Introduction', in L. Bruni and P. Porta (eds), *Economics and Happiness*. Oxford: Oxford University Press, pp. 1–28.

Buckley, S., Duer, K., Mendel, T. and O'Siochru, S., with M. Price and M. Raboy (2008) *Broadcasting, Voice, and Accountability: A Public Interest Approach to Policy, Law, and Regulation*. New York: World Bank Press and the University of Michigan Press.

Bunting, M. (2004) *Willing Slaves*. London: HarperCollins.

Bunting, M. (2008) 'From buses to blogs: a pathological individualism is poisoning public life', *The Guardian* 28 January.

Bunting, M. (2009) 'Again social evils haunt Britain: do we still have the spirit to thwart them?', *The Guardian* 15 June.

Burchell, G. (1996) 'Liberal government and techniques of the self', in A. Barry, T. Osborne and N. Rose (eds), *Foucault and Political Reason*. London: UCL Press, pp. 19–36.

Burgess, J. and Green, R. (2009) *YouTube*. Cambridge: Polity.

Butler, J. (1990) *Gender Trouble*. New York: Routledge.

Butler, J. (1993) *Bodies That Matter*. New York: Routledge.

Butler, J. (1997) *Excitable Speech*. New York: Routledge.

Butler, J. (2004) *Precarious Life*. London: Verso.

Butler, J. (2005) *Giving an Account of Oneself*. New York: Fordham University Press.

Byrne, D. (2008) 'The future of the "race": identity, discourse and the rise of computer-mediated spheres', in A. Everett (ed.), *Learning Race and Ethnicity*. Cambridge, MA: MIT Press, pp. 15–38.

Cameron, D. (2009) 'People now see the state as enemy instead of ally. We need a massive, radical redistribution of power', *The Guardian* 26 May.

Castells, M. (2009) *Communication Power*. Oxford: Oxford University Press.

Castells, M., Fernandez Ardevol, M., Qiu, J. Linchuan and Sey, A. (2007) *Mobile Communications and Society*. Cambridge, MA: MIT Press.

Cavarero, A. (2000) *Relating Narratives*. London: Routledge.

Cavell, S. (1976) *Must We Mean What We Say?* Cambridge, MA: Harvard University Press.

Chadwick, A. (2006) *Internet Politics*. Oxford: Oxford University Press.

Chakrabortty, A. (2009) 'This unexpected radical shows up an abject failure to tame the banks', *The Guardian* 28 August.

Chong, D. (2000) *Rational Lives*. Chicago: University of Chicago Press.

Clarke, J. (2004) *Changing Welfare, Changing States* . London: Sage.

Clark, J. and Aufderheide, P. (2009) *Public Media 2.0: Dynamic Engaged Publics*, www. centerforsocialmedia.org/resources/publications/public_media_2_0_dynamic_ engaged_publics/ (last accessed 14 September 2009).

Cohen, A. (1994) *Self-consciousness*. London: Routledge.

Cohen, E. (2003) *A Consumer's Republic*. New York: Alfred Knopf.

Cole, D. (2005) 'What Bush wants to hear', *New York Review of Books*, 17 November: 8–12.

Cole, D. (2006) 'How to skip the Constitution', *New York Review of Books*, 16 November: 20–22.

Cole, D. (2009) 'What to do about the torturers', *New York Review of Books*, 15 January: 20–24.

Coleman, S. (2003) 'A Tale of Two Houses: the House of Commons, the *Big Brother* house and the people at home', *Parliamentary Affairs* 56(4): 733–758.

Coleman, S. (2005) 'The lonely citizen: indirect representation in an age of networks', *Political Communication* 22(2): 197–214.

Coleman, S. (2008) 'Blogs and the politics of listening', *Political Quarterly* 76(2): 272–280.

Comaroff, J. and Comaroff, J. (2001) 'Milennial capitalism: first thoughts on a second coming', in J. Comaroff and J. Comaroff (eds), *Millennial Capitalism and the Culture of Neoliberalism*. Durham, NC: Duke University Press, pp. 1–56.

Corner, J. (2002) 'Performing the real: documentary diversions', *Television and New Media* 3(3): 255–269.

Cornwall, A. (2008) *Democratising Engagement: What the UK Can Learn from International Experience*. London: Demos.

Couldry, N. (1996) 'Speaking about others and speaking personally', *Cultural Studies* 10(2): 315–333.

Couldry, N. (2000) *Inside Culture*. London: Sage.

Couldry, N. (2001) 'The hidden injuries of media power', *Journal of Consumer Culture* 1(2): 155–179.

Couldry, N. (2003) *Media Rituals: A Critical Approach*. London: Routledge.

Couldry, N. (2004) 'Teaching us to fake it: the ritualised norms of television's "reality" games', in S. Murray and L. Ouellette (eds), *Reality TV: Remaking of Television Culture*. New York: New York University Press, pp. 57–74.

Couldry, N. (2006) 'La téléréalité ou le théatre du néoliberalisme', *Hermès* 44: 121–128.

Couldry, N. and Littler, J. (forthcoming) 'Work, power and performance: analyzing the "reality" game of *The Apprentice*', *Cultural Sociology*.

Couldry, N., Livingstone, S. and Markham, T. (2007) *Media Consumption and Public Engagement*. Basingstoke: Palgrave Macmillan.

Cover, R. (1992) 'Nomos and narrative', in M. Minow, M. Ryan and A. Sarat (eds), *Narrative, Violence and the Law*. Ann Arbor, MI: University of Michigan Press, pp. 95–172.

Craib, I. (1998) *Experiencing Identity*. London: Sage.

Crouch, C. (2000) *Coping with Post-democracy*. London: Fabian Society.

Crozier, M., Huntington, S. and Watanuki, J. (1975) *The Crisis of Democracy*. New York: New York University Press.

Cruddas, J. and Nahles, A. (2009) *Building the Good Society*. London: Compass. Also available at: www.goodsociety.eu/ (last accessed 28 August 2009).

Cui, L. and Lee, F. (forthcoming 2010) 'Becoming extra-ordinary: negotiation of media power in the case of *Super Girls' Voice* in China', *Popular Communication*, 8(4).

Curran, J. and Seaton, J. (2003) *Power without Responsibility* (3rd edition). London: Arnold.

Dahlgren, P. (1995) *Television and the Public Sphere.* London: Routledge.

Dahlgren, P. (2003) 'Reconfiguring civic culture in the New Media Milieu', in J. Corner and D. Pels (eds), *Media and the Restyling of Politics.* London: Sage, pp. 151–170.

Dahlgren, P. (2009) *Media and Political Engagement.* Cambridge: Cambridge University Press.

Davies, N. (2007) *Flat Earth News.* London: Chatto & Windus.

Deane, J. (2004) 'The Context of Communication for Development, 2004', Paper prepared for 9th United Nations Roundtable on Communication for Development, 6–9 September 2004, FAO, Rome, Italy.

Deleuze, G. and Guattari, F. (1988) *A Thousand Plateaus.* London: Athlone Press.

Delli Carpini, M. and Keater, S. (1996) *What Americans Know about Politics and Why It Matters.* New Haven: Yale University Press.

Delli Carpini, M. and Williams, B. (2001) 'Let us infotain you', in L. Bennett and R. Entman (eds), *Mediated Politics.* Cambridge: Cambridge University Press, pp. 160–181.

Derrida, J. (1973) *Speech and Phenomena.* Evanston, IL: Northwestern University Press.

Derrida, J. (1976) *Of Grammatology.* Baltimore, MD: The Johns Hopkins University Press.

Derrida, J. (1991 [1972]) 'Signature event context', in P. Kamuf (ed.), *A Derrida Reader.* New York: Harvester Wheatsheaf.

Derrida, J. (1997) *Politics of Friendship.* London: Verso.

Dewey, J. (1946) *The Public and its Problems.* Chicago: Gateway.

Dewey, J. (1993) *The Political Writings.* Indianapolis: Hackett.

Dews, P. (1987) *Logics of Disintegration.* London: Verso.

Didion, J. (2006) 'Cheney: the fatal touch', *New York Review of Books* 5 October: 51–56.

Dolar, M. (2006) *A Voice and Nothing More.* Cambridge, MA: MIT Press.

Downs, A. (1957) *An Economic Theory of Democracy.* New York: Harper & Row.

Dubet, F. (1994) 'The system, the actor and the social subject', *Thesis Eleven* 38: 16–35.

Dubet, F. (1995) 'Sociologie du sujet et sociologies de l'expérience', in F. Dubet and M. Wieviorka (eds), *Penser le Sujet.* Paris: Fayard, pp. 103–121.

Dumont, L. (1985) 'A modified view of our origins: the Christian beginnings of modern individualism', in M. Carrithers, S. Collins and S. Lukes (eds), *The Category of the Person.* Cambridge: Cambridge University Press, pp. 93–122.

Dunbar, R. (1997) 'Bloody footprints: reflections on growing up poor white', in M. Wray and A. Newitz (eds), *White Trash.* New York: Routledge.

Durkheim, E. (2006 [1897]) *On Suicide.* Penguin: Harmondsworth.

Dyson, M. Eric (2005) *Come Hell or High Water: Hurricane Katrina and the Color of Disaster.* New York: Basic Books.

Easton, D. (1965) *A Systems Analysis of Political Life.* New York: John Wiley.

Easton, M. (2009) 'Map of the week: trust and belonging', www.bbc.co.uk/blogs/thereporters/markeaston/2009/01/map_of_the_week_trust_and_belo.html?page=19 (last accessed 20 June 2009).

Ehrenberg, A. (1995) *L'Individu Incertain.* Paris: Hachette.

Ehrenberg, A. (1998) *La Fatigue d'être soi.* Paris: Odile Jacob.

Ehrenreich, B. (2002) *Nickel and Dimed.* London: Granta.

Eliasoph, N. (1998) *Avoiding Politics.* Cambridge: Cambridge University Press.

Elliott, L. (2009a) 'It's not bankers Labour is watching, it's you', *The Guardian* 11 May.

Elliott, L. (2009b) 'The softly-softly slope', *The Guardian* 18 June.

Elmer, G. and Opel, A. (2008) *Preempting Dissent.* Winnipeg: Arbeiter Ring Publishing.

Elster, J. (1985) *Making Sense of Marx.* Cambridge: Cambridge University Press.

Fanon, F. (1986) *Black Skin White Masks*. London: Pluto Press.

Fenton. N. (ed.) (2009) *New Media, Old News: Journalism and Democracy in the Digital Age*. Sage: London.

Ferrera, A. (1998) *Reflexive Authenticity*. London: Routledge.

Finlayson, A. (forthcoming) 'Financialisation, financial literacy and asset-based welfare', *British Journal of Politics and International Relations* 11(3).

Finley, M. (1966) *The Ancient Greeks*. Harmondsworth: Pelican Books.

Finnegan, R. (1997) 'Storying the self', in H. Mackay (ed.), *Consumption and Everyday Life*. Milton Keynes: Open University Press, pp. 69–102.

Flew, T. (2009) 'The citizen's voice: Albert Hirschman's exit voice and loyalty and its contribution to media citizenship debates', *Media Culture & Society*, 31(4): 978–995.

Foster, C. (2005) *British Government in Crisis*. Oxford: Hart Publishing.

Foucault, M. (2008) *The Birth of Biopolitics*. Basingstoke: Palgrave.

Frank, A. (1991) *The Wounded Storyteller*. Chicago: University of Chicago Press.

Frank, T. (2001) *One Market under God*. London: Secker and Warburg.

Fraser, N. (2000) 'Rethinking recognition', *New Left Review* (ns) 3: 107–120.

Fraser, N. (2005) 'Reframing global justice', *New Left Review* (ns) 36: 69–90.

Fraser, N. (2007) 'Transnationalizing the Public Sphere' *Theory Culture & Society* 24(4): 7–30.

Fraser, N. (2009) 'Feminism co-opted', *New Left Review* (ns) 56: 97–118.

Freire, P. (1972) *Pedagogy of the Oppressed*. Harmondsworth: Penguin.

Friedman, M. (1982) *Capitalism and Freedom* (2nd edition). Chicago: Chicago University Press.

Friedman, R. (2001) *Threads of Life*. Chicago: Chicago University Press.

Fyfe, H., Lewis, K., Pratt, S., Rose, M. and Wilson, M. (2009) *A Public Voice: Access, Digital Story and Interactive Narrative*, www.bbc.co.uk/blogs/knowledgeexchange/glamorgan.pdf (last accessed 4 September 2009).

Gagnier, R. (1991) *Subjectivities: A History of Self-Representation in Britain 1832–1920*. Oxford: Oxford University Press.

Garnham, N. (1999) 'Amartya Sen's "Capabilities" approach to the evaluation of welfare: its application to communications', in A. Calabrese and J.-C. Burgelman (eds), *Communication, Citizenship and Social Policy*. Boulder, CO: Rowman & Littlefield, pp. 113–124.

Gauntlett, D. (2007) *Creative Explorations*. London: Routledge.

Genette, G. (1980) *Narrative Discourse*. Ithaca, NY: Cornell University Press.

Gibson-Graham, J.K. (2006) *A Post-Capitalist Politics*. Minneapolis, MN: University of Minnesota Press.

Giddens, A. (1991) *Modernity and Self-identity*. Cambridge: Polity.

Giddens, A. (1998) *The Third Way*. Cambridge: Polity Press.

Gilbert, J. (2008) *Anticapitalism and Culture*. Oxford: Berg.

Gilbert, J. (2009) 'Postmodernity and the crisis of democracy', 28 May, www.opendemocracy.net (last accessed 28 May 2009).

Giles, C. (2009) 'Record level of inequality hits Labour's image', *Financial Times* 8 May.

Gill, R. (2009) 'Post-feminist Media Culture: elements of a sensibility', *European Journal of Cultural Studies* 10: 147–166.

Gill, R. and Pratt, A. (2008) 'In the social factory? Immaterial labour, precariousness and cultural work', *Theory Culture & Society* 25(7–8): 1–30.

Gilligan, C. (1982) *In a Different Voice*. Cambridge, MA: Harvard University Press.

Gilroy, P. (1996) *Small Acts*. London: Serpent's Tail Press.

Giroux, H. (1986) 'Radical pedagogy and the politics of student voice', *Interchange* 17(1): 48–69.

Giroux, H. (2000) *Stealing Innocence*. New York: St Martin's Press.

Giroux, H. (2004a) *The Terror of Neoliberalism*. Boulder, CO: Paradigm Books.

Giroux, H. (2004b) 'Public time versus emergency time: politics, terrorism and the culture of fear', in *The Abandoned Generation*. Basingstoke: Palgrave Macmillan.

Giroux, H. (2006) *Stormy Weather: Katrina and the Politics of Disposability*. Boulder, CO: Paradigm Books.

Giroux, H. (2007) *The University in Chains*. Boulder, CO: Paradigm Books.

Giroux, H. (2008) 'Beyond the biopolitics of disposability: Rethinking neoliberalism in the New Gilded Age'. *Social Identities* 14(5): 587–620.

Goldthorpe, J. and Jackson, M. (2007) 'Intergenerational class mobility in contemporary Britain: political concerns and empirical findings', *British Journal of Sociology* 58(4): 525–546.

Goody, J. (2006) *Jade: My Autobiography*. London: HarperCollins.

Gramsci, A. (1971) *Selections from the Prison Notebooks*. London: Lawrence & Wishart.

Gray, J. (1998) *False Dawn: The Delusions of Global Capitalism*. London: Granta.

Gray, J. (2007) *Black Mass*. Harmondsworth: Penguin.

Green, D. and Shapiro, I. (1994) *Pathologies of Rational Choice Theory*. New Haven, CT: Yale University Press.

Greenhouse, S. (2009) *The Big Squeeze* (2nd edition). New York: Anchor Books.

Grindstaff, L. (2002) *The Money Shot*. Chicago: Chicago University Press.

Grossberg, L. (2005) *Caught in the Crossfire*. Boulder, CO: Paradigm Books.

Grosz, E. (1994) *Volatile Bodies*. Bloomington, IN: Indiana University Press.

Guerrera, R. (2009) 'A need to connect', *Financial Times* 13 March.

Habermas, J. (1992) *Post-metaphysical Thinking: Philosophical Essays*. Cambridge: Polity.

Haigh, G. (2008) 'Catch-all solution', *The Guardian*, Education, 8 January, p. 4.

Halbwachs, M. (1992) *On Collective Memory*. Chicago: Chicago University Press.

Hall, S. (1990) [1980] 'Politics and letters', in T. Eagleton (ed.), *Raymond Williams: Critical Perspectives*. Cambridge: Polity, pp. 54–66.

Hannerz, U. (1980) *Exploring the City*. New York: Columbia University Press.

Hardt, M. and Negri, T. (2006) *Multitude*. Harmondsworth: Penguin.

Harvey, D. (1990) *The Condition of Postmodernity*. Oxford: Blackwell.

Harvey, D. (2000) *Spaces of Hope*. Edinburgh: Edinburgh University Press.

Harvey, D. (2005) *A Brief History of Neoliberalism*. Oxford: Oxford University Press.

Hay, C. (2007) *Why We Hate Politics*. Cambridge: Polity.

von Hayek, F. (1944) *The Road to Serfdom*. London: George Routledge and Sons.

von Hayek, F. (1949) *Individualism and Economic Order*. London: Routledge and Kegan Paul.

von Hayek, F. (1960) *The Constitution of Liberty*. London: Routledge and Kegan Paul.

Hayles, N.K. (1999) *How We Became Posthuman*. Chicago: University of Chicago Press.

Hazan, Hakim (1994) *Old Age: Decontructions and Constructions*. Cambridge: Cambridge University Press.

Head, S. (2007) 'They're micromanaging your every move', *New York Review of Books*, 16 August: 42–44.

Hearn, A. (2008) 'Variations on the branded self: Theme, invention, improvisation and inventory' in D. Hesmondhalgh and J. Toynbee (eds) *The Media and Social Theory*. London: Routledge, pp. 194–210.

Heelas, P. (2002) 'Work ethics, soft capitalism and the "turn to life"', in P. Du Gay and M. Pryke (eds), *Cultural Economy*. London: Sage, pp. 78–96.

Held, D. (1996) *Models of Democracy* (2nd edition). Cambridge: Polity.

Henley, J. (2008) 'It's a great big toy. Go on, play!', *The Guardian*, G2 section, 31 January.

Hesmondhalgh, D. and Baker, S. (2008) 'Creative work and emotional labour in the television industry', *Theory Culture & Society* 25(7–8): 97–118.

Hilberg, R. (1985) *The Destruction of the European Jews* (volume 3). New York: Holmes and Meier.

Hill, A. (2004) *Reality TV*. London: Routledge.

Hill, A. (2007) *Restyling Factual TV*. London: Routledge.

Hills, J., Sefton, T. and Stewart, K. (2009) 'Conclusions', in J. Hills, T. Sefton and K. Stewart (eds), *Towards a More Equal Society?* Bristol: The Policy Press, pp. 341–360.

Hirschman, A. (1969) *Exit Voice and Loyalty*. Princeton, NJ: Princeton University Press.

Hirst, P. and Thompson, G. (1996) *Globalization in Question*. Cambridge: Polity.

Hochschild, A. (1983) *The Managed Heart*. Berkeley: University of California Press.

Hochschild, A. (1997) *The Time Bind*. New York: Metropolitan.

Holmes, J. (2009) *Katrina: A Play of New Orleans*. London: Methuen Drama.

Honneth, A. (1995a) *The Fragmented World of the Social*. Albany, NY: SUNY Press.

Honneth, A. (1995b) *The Struggle for Recognition*. Cambridge: Polity.

Honneth, A. (2004) 'Organised self-realization: some paradoxes of individualization', *European Journal of Social Theory* 7(4): 463–478.

Honneth, A. (2007) *Disrespect*. Cambridge: Polity.

Hopkins, R. (2008) *The Transition Handbook*. Totnes: Green Books.

Howard, A. (2007) 'The future of global unions: is solidarity still for ever?', *Dissent*, Fall: 62–70.

Hutton, W. (2009a) 'The love of Labour', *The Guardian*, 27 January, p. 31.

Hutton, W. (2009b) 'High stakes, low finance', *The Guardian*, Saturday Review, 2 May.

Ihde, D. (2007) *Listening and Voice* (2nd edition). Albany, NY: SUNY Press.

Illouz, E. (2003) *Oprah Winfrey and the Glamor of Misery*. New York: Columbia University Press.

Illouz, E. (2007) *Cold Intimacies*. Cambridge: Polity.

Isin, E. (2008) 'Theorizing acts of citizenship', in E. Isin and G. Nielsen (eds), *Acts of Citizenship*. London: Zed Books, pp. 15–43.

Jenkins, H. (2006) *Convergence Culture*. New York: New York University Press.

Jenkins, S. (2007) 'The state has only aided our seasonal spates of thuggery', *The Guardian*, 22 August.

Jones, R. (2009) 'In our constipated care culture, thank heavens for the rule benders', *The Guardian* 10 February.

Judt, T. (2005) 'The New World Order', *New York Review of Books*, 14 July: 14–18.

Juris, J. (2008) *Networking Futures: The Movements against Corporate Globalization*. Durham, NC: Duke University Press.

Kaletsky, A. (2009) 'Task no 1 for Barack Obama: reinvent capitalism', *The Times*, 22 January.

Kavada, A. (2009) 'Collective action across multiple platforms: Avaaz on Facebook, MySpace and YouTube'. Paper presented to Transforming Audiences 2 conference, University of Westminster, September.

Kay, J. (2009) 'Labour's affair with bankers is to blame for this sorry state', *Financial Times*, 25/26 April.

Keane, J. (2009) *The Life and Death of Democracy*. New York: Simon & Schuster.

Keater, S., Zukin, C., Andolina, M. and Jenkins, K. (2002) *The Civic and Political Health of the Nation: A Generational Portrait*. Available at: www.pewtrusts.com/pdf/public_policy_youth_civic_poltiical_health.pdf (last accessed 3 April 2006).

Kellner, D. (2003) *From 9/11 to Terror War*. Boulder, CO: Rowman and Littlefield.

Kierkegaard, S. (1954 [1849]) *The Sickness unto Death*. New York: Doubleday.

Klein, N. (2000) *No Logo*. London: Flamingo.

Klein, N. (2007) *The Shock Doctrine*. London: Allen Lane.

Knorr-Cetina, K. (2001) 'Postsocial relations', in G. Ritzer and B. Smart (eds), *The Handbook of Social Theory*. London: Sage.

Kraidy, M. (2009) *Reality Television and Arab Politics*. Cambridge: Cambridge University Press.

Kristeva, J. (1991) *Strangers to Ourselves*. Chicago: Chicago University Press.

Krugman, P. (2006) 'Left behind economics', *New York Times*, 14 July.

Krugman, P. (2009) 'Saved by Big Government', *The Guardian*, 11 August.

Lane, R. (2000) *The Loss of Happiness in Market Democracies*. New Haven, CT: Yale University Press.

Lambert, J. (2007) *Digital Storytelling* (2nd edition). Berkeley, CA: Digital Diner Press.

Lardner, J. (2007) 'The specter haunting your office', *New York Review of Books*, 14 June: 62–65.

Lawson, N. (2007) 'A shameful report card', *The Guardian*, 14 February.

Lawson, N. and Harris, J. (2009) 'No turning back', *New Statesman*, 9 March: 36–39.

Layard, R. (2005) *Happiness: Lessons From a New Science*. Harmondsworth: Penguin.

Layard, R. and Dunn, J. (2009) *A Good Childhood*. Harmondsworth: Penguin.

Leadbeater, C. (2008a) *We-think*. London: Profile Books.

Leadbeater, C. (2008b) 'This time it's personal', *The Guardian*, Society, 16 January.

Leadbeater, C. (2009) 'State of loneliness', *The Guardian*, Society, 1 July 2009: 1–2.

Leadbeater, C., Bartlett, J. and Gallagher, N. (2008) 'Making it personal'. London: Demos, available at: www.demos.co.uk/publications/makingitpersonal (last accessed 28 August 2009).

Lear, J. (2006) *Radical Hope*. Cambridge, MA: Harvard University Press

Levi, P. (2000 [1961]) *If This is a Man*. London: Everyman's Library.

Levi-Faur, D. and Jordana, J. (2005) 'Preface: the making of a new regulatory order', *The Annals of the American Academy of Political and Social Science*, 598: 6–11.

Levin, D. (1989) *The Listening Self*. New York: Routledge.

Levitas, R. (2005) *The Inclusive Society?* (2nd edition). Basingstoke: Macmillan.

Lewis, A. (2004) 'Making torture legal', *New York Review of Books*, 15 July: 4–8.

Leys, C. (2001) *Market-driven Society*. London: Verso.

Lippman, W. (1925) *The Phantom Public*. New York: Harcourt Brace.

Lister, R. (2004) *Poverty*. Cambridge: Polity Press.

Littler, J. (2009) *Radical Consumption*. Milton Keynes: Open University Press.

Lucas, B. and Taylor, M. (2009) 'Start cutting from the top', *The Guardian*, 26 June.

Luce, E. (2008) 'Stuck in the middle', *Financial Times*, 29 October 2008.

Lukes, S. (1973) *Emile Durkheim*. Harmondsworth: Penguin.

Lundby, K. (ed.) (2008) *Digital Storytelling, Mediatized Stories*. New York: Peter Lang.

Lupia, A. and McCubbins, M. (1998) *The Democratic Dilemma*. Cambridge: Cambridge University Press.

Maalouf, A. (2000) *On Identity*. New York: Harvill Press.

MacIntyre, A. (1981) *After Virtue*. London: Duckworth.

Madrick, J. (2009) 'How we were ruined and what we can do', *New York Review of Books*, 12 February: 15–18.

Mainsah, H. (2009) Ethnic Minorities and Digital Technologies. PhD thesis, Faculty of Humanities, University of Oslo, Oslo.

Mansell, R. (2002) 'From digital divides to digital entitlements in knowledge societies', *Current Sociology* 50(3): 407–426.

Marquand, D. (2004) *Decline of the Public*. Cambridge: Polity.

Martuccelli, D. (2002) *Grammaires de l'Individu*. Paris: Gallimard.

Marx, K. (1959) *Economic and Philosophical Manuscripts of 1844*. London: Lawrence and Wishart.

Marx, K. (1973) *Grundrisse*. Harmondsworth: Penguin.

Massumi, B. (2002) *Parables for the Virtual*. Durham, NC: Duke University Press.

Mayhew, L. (1997) *The New Public*. Cambridge: Cambridge University Press.

Mbembe, A. (2001) *On the Postcolony*. Berkeley, CA: University of California Press.

McCarthy, A. (2004) '"Stanley Milgram, Allen Funt, and me": postwar social science and the "first wave" of reality TV', in S. Murray and L. Ouellette (eds), *Reality TV: Remaking Television Culture*. New York: New York University Press, pp. 19–39.

McCarthy, A. (2007) 'Reality television: a neoliberal theater of suffering', *Social Text* 25: 93–110.

McCurdy, P. (2009) *I Predict a Riot: A Study of Dissent!'s Media Practices and Political Contention at the 2005 Gleneagles G8 Summit*. PhD thesis, London School of Economics and Political Science, June.

McDonald, K. (1999) *Struggles for Subjectivity*. Cambridge: Cambridge University Press.

McDowell, J. (1998) *Mind World and Reality*. Cambridge, MA: Harvard University Press.

McNay, L. (2008) *Against Recognition*. Cambridge: Polity.

McRobbie, A. (1997) *Back to Reality?* Manchester: Manchester University Press.

McRobbie, A. (2005) *The Uses of Cultural Studies*. London: Sage.

McRobbie, A. (2009) *The Aftermath of Feminism*. London: Sage.

Mead, G.H. (1967 [1934]) *Mind Self and Society*. Chicago: Chicago University Press.

Melucci, A. (1996) *Challenging Codes*. Cambridge: Cambridge University Press.

Merton, R. (1938) 'Social structure and anomie', *American Sociological Review* 3: 672–682.

Meyer, T. (2002) *Media Democracy*. Cambridge: Polity.

Miller, T. (2008) *Cultural Citizenship*. Phildelphia, PA: Temple University Press.

von Mises, L. (1962) *The Ultimate Foundation of Economic Science*. Princeton, NJ: Von Norstrand.

von Mises, L. (1983) *Nation State and Economy*. New York: New York University Press.

Mitra, A. (2001) 'Marginal voices in cyberspace', *New Media & Society* 3(1): 29–48.

Mitra, A. and Watts, E. (2002) 'Theorizing cyberspace: the idea of voice applied to internet discourse', *New Media & Society* 4(4): 479–498.

Moore, H. (1986) *Space, Text and Gender*. Cambridge: Cambridge University Press.

Moore, H. (1994) *A Passion for Difference*. Cambridge: Polity.

Mouffe, C. (2000) *The Democratic Paradox*. London: Verso.

Mulgan, G. (1995) *Politics in an Anti-political Age*. Cambridge: Polity.

Mulgan, G. (2006) *Good and Bad Power*. Harmondsworth: Penguin.

Neilsen, B. and Rossiter, N. (2008) 'Precarity as a political concept, or, Fordism as exception', *Theory Culture & Society* 25(7–8): 51–72.

Nightingale, C. (1993) *On the Edge*. New York: Basic Books.

Norval, A. (2007) *Aversive Democracy*. Cambridge: Cambridge University Press.

Nussbaum, M. (1993) 'Non-relative virtues: an Aristotelian approach', in M. Nussbaum and A. Sen (eds), *The Quality of Life*. Oxford: Oxford University Press, pp. 242–269.

Nyers, P. (2008) 'No one is illegal: between city and nation', in E. Isin and G. Nielsen (eds), *Acts of Citizenship*. London: Zed Books, pp. 160–178.

Obama, B. (2007) *Dreams from My Father*. Edinburgh: Canongate.

O'Donnell, P., Lloyd, J. and Dreher, T. (2009) 'Listening, pathbuilding and continuations: a research agenda for the analysis of listening', *Continuum* 23(4): 423–439.

Olney, J. (1998) *Memory and Narrative*. Chicago: Chicago University Press.

Ong, A. (2006) *Neoliberalism as Exception*. Durham, NC: Duke University Press.

Orgad, S. (2009) 'The survivor in contemporary culture and public discourse: a genealogy', *The Communication Review* 12(2): 132–161.

Ouellette, L. and Hay, J. (2008) *Better Living through Reality TV*. Malden: Blackwell.

Palmer, G. (2002) '*Big Brother*: an experiment in governance', *Television and New Media* 3(3): 295–310.

Panitch, L. and Konings, M. (2009) 'Myths of neoliberal deregulation', *New Left Review* (ns) 57: 67–83.

Paxton, R. (2004) *The Anatomy of Fascism*. New York: Alfred Knopf.

Peet, R. (2007) *The Geography of Power*. London: Pluto Press.

Pharr, S., Putnam, R. and Dalton, R. (2000) 'Introduction: what's troubling the trilateral democracies', in S. Pharr and R. Putnam (eds), *Disaffected Democracies*. Cambridge, MA: Harvard University Press, pp. 3–30.

Phelps, E. (2009) 'The justice of a well-functioning capitalism and the reforms that will realize it, not kill it', www.columbia.edu/~esp2/Paris%27NewCapitalism%27Symp osium2009Feb26-1.pdf (last accessed 9 March 2009).

Phillips, A. (2003) 'Recognition and the struggle for political voice' in B. Hobson (ed.), *Recognition Struggles and Social Movements*. Cambridge: Cambridge University Press, 263–273.

Phillips, D. (2005) 'Transformation scenes: the television interior makeover', *International Journal of Cultural Studies* 8(2): 213–229.

Pickering, M. (1997) *History, Experience and Cultural Studies*. London: Macmillan.

Plender, J. (2009) 'How fading political will has let the banks off the hook', *Financial Times* 27–28 June.

Plummer, K. (1995) *Telling Sexual Stories*. London: Routledge.

Plummer, K. (2003) *Intimate Citizenship*. Seattle, WA: University of Washington Press.

Polanyi, K. (1975 [1944]) *The Great Transformation*. London: Octagon.

Pollock, A. (2005) *NHS plc*. London: Verso

Pollock, A. (2008) 'Operating profits', *The Guardian*, 11 June.

Posner, R. (2003) *Law, Pragmatism and Democracy*. Chicago: Chicago University Press.

Posner, R. (2006) *Not a Suicide Pact: The Constitution in a Time of National Emergency*. Oxford: Oxford University Press.

Power, M. (1997) *The Audit Society*. Oxford: Oxford University Press.

Press, A. (forthcoming) '"Feminist? That's so seventies": girls and young women discuss femininity and feminism in *America's Next Top Model*', in R. Gill and C. Scharf (eds), *New Femininities*. Basingstoke: Palgrave.

Probyn, E. (1993) *Sexing the Self*. London: Routledge.

Proctor, R. (1999) *The Nazi War on Cancer*. Princeton, NJ: Princeton University Press.

Pusey, M. (2003) *The Experience of Middle Australia*. Cambridge: Cambridge University Press.

Qiu, J. (2009) *Working Class Network Society*. Cambridge, MA: MIT Press.

Rakow, L. and Wackwitz, L. (2004) 'Voice in feminist communication theory', in L. Rakow (ed.), *Feminist Communication Theory*. Thousand Oaks, CA: Sage.

Rancière, J. (2006) *Hatred of Democracy*. London: Verso.

Relman, A. (2009) 'The health reform we need and are not getting', *New York Review of Books*, 2 July: 38–40.

Ricoeur, P. (1980) 'Narrative time', in W. Mitchell (ed.), *On Narrative*. Chicago: Chicago University Press, pp. 165–86.

Ricoeur, P. (1984a) *Time and Narrative* (volume 1). Chicago: Chicago University Press.

Ricoeur, P. (1984b) *Time and Narrative* (volume 2). Chicago: Chicago University Press.

Ricoeur, P. (1992) *Oneself as Another*. Chicago: Chicago University Press.

Ricoeur, P. (1995) 'Reflections on a new ethos for Europe', *Philosophy and Social Criticism* 21(5/6): 3–13.

Ricoeur, P. (2005) *The Course of Recognition*. Cambridge, MA: Harvard University Press.

Riley, D. (1988) *Am I that Name?* Basingstoke: Macmillan.

Ringrose, J. and Walkerdine, V. (2009) 'Regulating the abject: the TV makeover as site of neoliberal reinvention towards bourgeois femininity', *Feminist Media Studies* 8(3): 227–246.

Rizzolatti, G. and Sinigaglia, C. (2008) *Mirrors in the Brain*. Oxford: Oxford University Press.

Rodriguez, C. (forthcoming) *Disrupting Violence*. Minneapolis, MN: University of Minnesota Press.

Rosanvallon, P. (2006) *Democracy Past and Future*. New York: Columbia University Press.

Rosanvallon, P. (2008) *Counter-democracy*. Cambridge: Cambridge University Press.

Rose, N. (1990) *Governing the Soul*. London: Free Association Press.

Rose, N. (1996a) 'Governing "advanced" liberal democracies', in A. Barry, T. Osborne and N. Rose (eds), *Foucault and Political Reason*. London: UCL Press, pp. 37–64.

Rose, N. (1996b) 'The Death of the social? Reconfiguring the territory of government', *Economy and Society* 25(3): 327–356.

Rose, N. (1996c) *Inventing Our Selves*. Cambridge: Cambridge University Press.

Rose, N. (1999) *Powers of Freedom*. Cambridge: Cambridge University Press.

Ross, A. (2004) *No Collar*. Philadelphia, PA: Temple University Press.

Ross, A. (2008) 'The new geography of work: power to the precarious?', *Theory Culture, & Society* 25(7–8): 31–39.

Rothschild, E. (2001) *Economic Sentiments*. Cambridge, MA: Harvard University Press.

Rudd, K. (2009) 'The global financial crisis', *The Monthly* February. Available at: www.themonthly.com.au/monthly-essays-kevin-rudd-global-financial-crisis-1421?page=0%2C6 (last accessed 4 September 2009).

Ruggie, J. (1993) 'Territoriality and beyond: problematizing modernity in international relations', *International Organization* 47(1): 139–174.

Russell, J. (2009) 'Fear and suspicion are no way to build a good society', *The Guardian*, 4 February.

Sacks, O. (2000) *Seeing Voices*. New York: Vintage.

Sands, P. (2008) *Torture Team*. London: Allen Lane.

Sassen, S. (2006) *Territory Authority Rights*. Princeton, NJ: Princeton University Press.

Sassi, F. (2009) 'Health inequalities: a persistent problem', in J. Hills, T. Sefton and K. Stewart (eds), *Towards a More Equal Society?* Bristol: The Policy Press, pp. 135–156.

Scammell, M. (1996) *Designer Politics*. Basingstoke: Macmillan.

Schattschneider, O. (1960) *The Semisovereign People*. New York: Holt, Rinehart and Winston.

Schor, J. (1992) *The Overworked American*. New York: Basic Books.

Schudson, M. (1998) *The Good Citizen*. Cambridge, Mass.: Harvard University Press.

Schumpeter, J. (1950 [1942]) *Capitalism, Socialism and Democracy* (3rd edition). New York: Harper & Row.

Scitovsky, T. (1976) *The Joyless Economy*. New York: Oxford University Press.

Scott, J. (1992) 'Experience', in J. Butler and J. Scott (eds), *Feminists Theorize the Political*. New York: Routledge, pp. 22–40.

Sebald, W.G. (2004) *On the Natural History of Destruction*. Harmondsworth: Penguin.

Seigworth, G. (2008) 'Cultural Studies and Giles Deleuze', in G. Hall and C. Burchall (eds), *New Cultural Studies*. Edinburgh: Edinburgh University Press, pp. 107–127.

Sen, A. (1985) *Commodities and Capabilities*. Amsterdam: North Holland.

Sen, A. (1987) *On Ethics and Economics*. Oxford: Blackwell.

Sen, A. (1999) *Development as Freedom*. Oxford: Oxford University Press.

Sen, A. (2002) *Rationality and Freedom*. Cambridge, MA: Harvard University Press.

Sen, A. (2009) 'Capitalism beyond the crisis', *New York Review of Books*, 26 March: 27–30.

Sennett, R. (1977) *The Fall of Public Man*. Cambridge: Cambridge University Press.

Sennett, R. (1994) *The Conscience of the Eye*. London: Faber.

Sennett, R. (1998) *The Corrosion of Character*. New York: W.W. Norton.

Sennett, R. (2005) *The Culture of the New Capitalism*. New Haven, CT: Yale University Press.

Sennett, R. and Cobb, J. (1972) *The Hidden Injuries of Class*. New York: W.W. Norton.

Shepherd, J. (2009) 'Someone to watch over you', *The Guardian*, Education, 4 August.

Sibley, D. (1988) 'Survey 13: purification of space', *Environment and Planning D* 6(4): 409–21.

Sibley, D. (1996) *Geographies of Exclusion*. London: Routledge.

Silverstone, R. (2006) *Media and Morality*. Cambridge: Polity Press.

Simmel, G. (1978) *The Philosophy of Money*. London: Routledge and Kegan Paul.

Skeggs, B. (1997) *Formations of Class and Gender: Becoming Respectable*. London: Sage.

Skeggs, B., Thumim, N. and Wood, H. (2008) '"Oh Goodness, I am watching reality TV": how methods make class in audience research', *European Journal of Cultural Studies* 11(1): 5–24.

Skidelsky, R. (2009) 'Where do we go from here?', *Prospect*, January, 36: 40.

Sklair, L. (2001) *The Transnational Capitalist Class*. Oxford: Blackwell.

Skocpol, T. (2003) *Diminished Democracy*. Norman, OK: University of Oklahoma Press.

Smith, D. (1987) *The Everyday World as Problematic*. Boston: Northwestern Press.

Smith, J. (2008) *Social Movements for Global Democracy*. Baltimore, MD: The Johns Hopkins University Press.

Soros, G. (1996) 'The capitalist threat', *Atlantic Monthly*, September.

Soros, G. (2008) 'The financial crisis: an interview with George Soros', *New York Review of Books*, 15 May: 7–10.

Soros, G. (2009) 'The game changer', *Financial Times*, 29 January: 10.

Sparks, C. (2007) 'Reality TV: the *Big Brother* phenomenon', *International Socialism* 114. Available online at: www.isj.org.uk (last accessed 5 April 2009).

Spivak, G. (1987) *In Other Worlds*. London: Methuen.

Steedman, C. (1986) *Landscape for a Good Woman*. London: Virago.

Stewart, K. (2009) 'Poverty, inequality and child well-being in international context: still bottom of the pack?', in J. Hills, T. Sefton and K. Stewart (eds), *Towards a More Equal Society?* Bristol: The Policy Press, pp. 267–290.

Stiegler, B. (2006) *La Télécratie contre le Démocratie*. Paris: Flammarion.

Stiglitz, J. (2002) *Globalization and its Discontents*. Harmondsworth: Penguin.

Sugden, R. (2005) 'Correspondence of sentiments: an explanation of the pleasure of social interaction', in L. Bruni and P. Porta (eds), *Economics and Happiness*. Oxford: Oxford University Press, pp. 91–115.

Swindells, J. (1985) *Victorian Writing and Working Women*. Cambridge: Polity.

Tacchi, J., Watkins, J. and Keerthirathne, K. (2009) 'Participatory content creation: voice, communication, and development', *Development in Practice* 19(4–5): 573–584.

Tarrow, S. (1998) *Power in Movement* (2nd edition). Cambridge: Cambridge University Press.

Tasker, Y. and Negra, D. (eds) (2007) *Interrogating Post-Feminism*. Durham, NC: Duke University Press.

Taylor, C. (1986) 'Self-interpreting animals', in *Philosophical Papers* (volume 1). Cambridge: Cambridge University Press, pp. 45–76.

Taylor, C. (1989) *Sources of the Self*. Cambridge: Cambridge University Press.

Taylor, C. (1994) 'The politics of recognition', in A. Gutmann (ed.), *Multiculturalism*. Princeton: Princeton University Press, pp. 25–74.

Taylor, C. (2007) 'A different kind of courage', *New York Review of Books*, 26 April: 4–8.

Taylor, J., Gilligan, C. and Sullivan, A. (1995) *Between Voice and Silence*. Cambridge, MA: Harvard University Press.

Terranova, T. (2004) *Network Citizens*. London: Pluto Press.

Thaler, R. and Sunstein, C. (2008) *Nudge*. New Haven, CT: Yale University Press.

Thévenot, L. (2009) 'Committed to "performance": a critical assessment'. Paper presented to conference on Performance, Goldsmiths, University of London, 14 January.

Thompson, P. 1982) 'Introduction', in P. Thompson (ed.), *Our Common History*. London: Pluto Press, pp. 9–20.

Tilly, C. (1998) *Durable Inequality*. Berkeley, CA: University of California Press.

Tilly, C. (2006) *Regimes and Repertoires*. Chicago: Chicago University Press.

Tilly, C. (2007) *Democracy*. Cambridge: Cambridge University Press.

Touraine, A. (1988) *Return of the Actor*. Minneapolis, MN: University of Minnesota Press.

Touraine, A. (2000) *Beyond Neoliberalism*. Cambridge: Polity.

Toynbee, P. (2005) 'It is New Labour as much as the public that lacks trust', *The Guardian*, 22 November.

Toynbee, P. and Walker, D. (2008) *Unjust Rewards*. London: Granta.

Tully, J. (1995) *Strange Multiplicity*. Cambridge: Cambridge University Press.

Turner, B. (2001) 'The erosion of citizenship', *British Journal of Sociology* 52(2): 189–209.

Unger, R. (1998) *Democracy Realized*. London: Verso.

Virno, P. (2004) *A Grammar of the Multitude*. New York: Semiotext(e).

Wade, R. (2008) 'Financial regime change?', *New Left Review* (ns) 53: 5–22.

Walkerdine, V. (1997) *Daddy's Girl*. London: Macmillan.

Wernick, A. (1991) *Promotional Culture*. London: Sage.

West, C. (1992) 'Nihilism in black America', in G. Dent (ed.), *Black Popular Culture*. Seattle, WA: Bay Press, pp. 39–53.

West, C. (1993) *Keeping Faith*. New York: Routledge.

White, M. and Epston, D. (1990) *Narrative Means to Therapeutic Ends*. New York: W.W. Norton.

Wilkinson, R. and Pickett, K. (2008) *The Spirit Level*. London: Allen Lane.

Williams, B. (2005) *Descartes: the Project of Pure Enquiry*. London: Routledge.

Williams, B.A. and Delli Carpini, M.X. (2010) *After the News: Changing Media Regimes and the Future of American Democracy*. Cambridge: Cambridge University Press.

Williams, R. (1958) *Culture and Society*. Harmondsworth: Penguin.

Williams, R. (1961) *The Long Revolution*. Harmondsworth: Penguin.

Williams, R. (1979) *Politics and Letters*. London: New Left Books.

Williams, R. (1989) 'The future of Cultural Studies', in *The Politics of Modernism*. London: Verso, pp. 151–162.

Willis, P. (1990) *Common Culture*. Milton Keynes: Open University Press.

Witschge, T., Fenton, N. and Freedman, D. (2010) *Carnegie UK Inquiry into Civil Society and Media in UK and Ireland: Protecting the News: Civil Society and the Media.* http://democracy.carnegieuktrust.org.uk/civil_society/publications/protecting_the_news.pdf

Wittgenstein, L. (1958) *Philosophical Investigations.* Oxford: Blackwell.

Wolf, M. (2009) 'Credibility is key to policy success', *Financial Times*, 3 April.

Wolin, S. (2003) 'Inverted totalitarianism', *The Nation*, 19 May.

Wollheim, R. (1984) *The Thread of Life.* Cambridge: Cambridge University Press.

Wood, H. and Skeggs, B. (2008) 'Spectacular morality: "reality" television, individualization and the remaking of the working class', in D. Hesmondhalgh and J. Toynbee (eds), *The Media and Social Theory.* London: Routledge, pp. 177–193.

Young, I. Marion (2000) *Inclusion and Democracy.* Oxford: Oxford University Press.

Ytreberg, E. (2009) 'Extended liveness and eventfulness in multi-platform reality formats', *New Media & Society* 11(4): 467–485.

Zamagni, S. (2005) 'Happiness and individualism: a very difficult union', in L. Bruni and P. Porta (eds), *Economics and Happiness.* Oxford: Oxford University Press, pp. 467–485.

Index